Planning language, planning inequality

Language policy in the community

D0650744

LANGUAGE IN SOCIAL LIFE SERIES

Series Editor: Professor Christopher N. Candlin

Planning language, planning inequality

Language policy in the community

James W. Tollefson

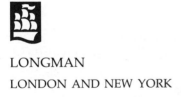

LONGMAN

LONDON AND NEW YORK

Addison Wesley Longman Limited,
Edinburgh Gate, Harlow,
Essex CM20 2JE, England
and Associated Companies throughout the world.

Published in the United States of America
by Addison Wesley Longman Inc., New York

First published 1991   -
Fifth impression 1998

British Library Cataloguing in Publication Data

Tollefson, James W.
  Planning language, planning inequality. - (Language in social life series).
  I. Language. Social aspects
  I. Title II. Series
  306.44

  ISBN 0-582-07454-1
  ISBN 0-582-04062-0 pbk

Library of Congress Cataloging-in-Publication Data

Tollefson, James W.
  Planning language, planning inequality / James W. Tollefson.
      p. cm. - (Language in social life series)
  Includes bibliographical references and index.
  ISBN 0-582-07454-1 (cased). - ISBN 0-582-04062-0 (pbk).
  1. Language policy. 2. Language planning. I. Title.
  II. Series.
  P119.3.T65   1991   90-6101
  306.4'49-dc20   CIP

Set in Palatino 10 on 12pt

Produced by Addison Wesley Longman Singapore (Pte) Ltd.
Printed in Singapore

Contents

General Editor's Preface

As the reader will have guessed, there is a deliberateness about the title of this book by James Tollefson, the latest in the new Language in Social Life Series from Longman. While the applied linguistics discipline of Language Planning is familiar to many, it has achieved at least a neutral, if not beneficial, standing among many professional scholars and teachers. This position is now beginning to be questioned in the professional literature as it has long since been the subject of controversial debate among the workers in the field, the teachers, administrators and, above all, students and their families, who are the recipients of its provisions. This incipient struggle over the key questions of what language is being planned, who is doing the planning and on behalf of whom, for what local and state purposes and with what anticipated effects, has taken its time to surface. There are systemic and particular reasons for this. Inherently, the question-ability of language planning relies on the existence, within applied linguistics, of a social theoretical basis for its principles and its activity. This itself, and indeed the awareness of the need for it, has not been in focus. There has been an absence both in the professional literature and in professional training of such an imperative, though this is beginning to change, as the new Language in Social Life Series from Longman is witness to. Immediately, issues of language planning cannot be interpreted and explained without such an historical structural and social awareness. The need for such ought to have been long ago realised if one only considers for a moment the impact of language planning on fields like educational policy and practice, migration studies, local and national participation in the political process, as well as the ethnography of personal lives. All of these, of course, require social theoretical explanations as well as demographic, sociological, sociolinguistic and applied linguistic descriptions. There needs to be a principled means of connecting macro-social structures to the micro-social decisions of the interaction order of everyday life. Norman Fairclough's book in this Series has made that case, and it is no less true for language planning as an applied linguistic discoursal practice as it is for all others we might name. How possible is it, for example, to characterise the language planning decisions in any state or institution without appeal to the historical and political identity of that system, and moreover, to the identities of the forces struggling within it? There is no sense in which language planning can be undertaken, or its effects evaluated, within some social vacuum. We need, as James Tollefson explicitly makes clear, an understanding of these as a prerequisite for explanation. Unfortunately, these governing forces of the state and the individual, power, hegemony and discrimination, have remained largely outside of debate. The ideology of language planning evokes a technical and positivistic process, untrammelled at least in the planning centre with the need for any demystification of both agenda or practice.

The time has come, however, for such debate, indeed it is long overdue. We are helped in this by major political and educational imperatives quite outside the hitherto closed applied linguistic circle. Examples currently abound internationally, the European Community and Eastern Europe, Australasia and the Pacific, Africa and, in particular, Southern Africa, and those characterised extensively in this book, Yugoslavia, The Philippines, China, Iran and the United States inter alia. Books and professional articles are beginning to appear in which the connections between language planning and decolonialisation, language planning and national, group and personal identity, and the relationships between planning itself and the necessary conditions on ownership of the plan, are being exposed. It is thus both timely and crucial that this present contribution by James Tollefson set out the issues for systematic and technically as well as socially informed debate. This must be done in a participative manner. By this I mean that writings must not themselves, paradoxically, reproduce the alienating technocracy which for many, as we have asserted, surrounds the subject-matter itself. It is for this reason that the book is constructed as it is, following a cycle of awareness through knowledge and critical discussion, to individual and social action. Chapters begin, accordingly, with exemplificatory case studies and authenticatable examples of the practice and realisation of language planning decision. Through Dr Tollefson's setting out of the issues, both local and principled, readers can engage with the discussion agendas he suggests. Ultimately, however, in applied linguistics action is required and each Chapter offers a structure for such an active program. Such a scenario has its dangers: not all questions will be relevant to all readers, not all actions either feasible or urgent. These are for the readership to rewrite and restructure. We are helped in this by the regular and consistent reconnection made between each 'case' and the theoretical and principled discussion of Chapters One and Two with their insistence on the dynamic relationship of language planning to constructs of power, state, social structure, dominance and exploitation. In short, the discursive strategy of the Series as a whole, mirrored in this book, is one which language planning itself requires.

What are the particular practical issues of language policy and use that James Tollefson identifies? They are all interconnected and reflect the challenges posed by language diversity to our everyday lives. Of course, education and language education in particular, but also economic choice or its lack, political representation and participation, social inequality and access to services, workplace and lifelong education. In short, an applied linguistic agenda in my view, and one for which this book takes on a fundamental importance not merely some special and particular role. Indeed, we could go further, and argue that the debates within language planning as set out here, are essential to *all* applied linguistics. One could not conceive, for example (or at least, one *should* not) of textbook and materials design, curriculum policy, the provision of services to the linguistically disadvantaged, the assessment of proficiency, and many other applied linguistic fields, without taking account of language planning. When as a researcher we work with data from the classroom or the court, the clinic or the telecommunication centre, when we work with text-to-speech systems or in language programming, we confront the decisions and the consequences of language planning. Indeed, we are all in some sense, language planners. Accordingly, the contents of this book have general relevance, not just some arcane and specialist concern. The Language in Social Life Series has this broad focus and this general audience in mind, and not only of applied linguistics as a guild. The concerns of language planning impinge more systematically and more thoroughly than we realise; hence the imperative that they be critiqued and evaluated.

In sum, then, the book is written to engage the readership. To do so in terms of their public practice and to ask them to reflect critically on their unexplained values and beliefs. Not, however, merely intellectually but in terms of social action and social change. We look forward to the reactions of our readers, especially if they can offer proposals for further volumes to this Series, all of which will inevitably relate to this particular contribution from James Tollefson. As he correctly identifies, the units and systems of analysis, the role of historical perspective, the criteria for evaluation of plans and policies and the role of the social scientist in general, all are foci for studies of individual and collective behaviour. In this sense, the discussion here is not even about language planning and applied linguistics narrowly conceived, but the whole discourse of social science.

Christopher N Candlin
General Editor
Macquarie University, Sydney
Australia

June 1990

Acknowledgements

This book is based upon research I have conducted over the years in the United States and elsewhere. Much of the material on Yugoslavia was made possible by two Fulbright-Hays fellowships at the University of Ljubljana in Yugoslavia, where Professor Janez Stanonik and Professor Mirko Jurak were my hosts. Sections on US policy for Indochinese refugees are based upon approximately sixteen months at refugee camps in Southeast Asia, primarily at the main US Refugee Processing Center in the Philippines, where I worked for the International Catholic Migration Commission.

I was also able to benefit from the generous assistance of government officials, university researchers, and others who provided important documents and information. In particular, I am grateful to: Norman Fairclough and Marilyn Martin-Jones of the University of Lancaster; Richard Johnson of the University of Birmingham; Celia Roberts of the Ealing College of Higher Education; Ken Young and Mrs M. Scowcroft of the British Department of Education and Science; the staff of the Linguistic Minorities Project in London; David Bradley of La Trobe University; Joseph Lo Bianco of the Australian Advisory Council on Languages and Multicultural Education; Don Plimer, Acting Director of the Languages Services Section of the Benjamin Offices of the Australian Department of Immigration, Local Government, and Ethnic Affairs; Elsa Auerbach of the University of Massachusetts; and Ron Podlaski of the Vietnam Veterans of America Foundation in Washington, D.C.

I have presented parts of this work at a number of places in recent years: the Monterey Institute of International Studies in California; the Language and Power Seminar in Comparative Studies in Ethnicity and Nationality at the University of Washington; the Southeast Asian Colloquium of the Northwest

Regional Consortium for Southeast Asian Studies; the 1989 Annual Meeting of the Washington Association for the Education of Speakers of Other Languages; and annual meetings of the Teachers of English to Speakers of Other Languages. These have provided valuable opportunity for discussion and criticism of my work.

Some of the material on US policy is based upon documents obtained from the US Department of State and the Office of Refugee Resettlement under the United States Freedom of Information Act.

Richard Dunn, Chair of the University of Washington Department of English, generously supported my work with two years of leave for research in Southeast Asia and travel funds for research in Yugoslavia.

Above all, I am grateful to Marjorie Suanda, my research assistant, who located and analysed many of the essential research materials; and Chris Candlin, General Editor of the Language in Social Life Series, whose comments and suggestions helped to shape every chapter. Of course, I alone am responsible for any errors of fact or interpretation.

The publishers are grateful to the following for permission to reproduce copyright material:

AIMAV, International Association for Cross-Cultural Communication for the *Declaration of Recife* and the *Statement of the XXIInd AIMAV Seminar*; John Benjamins Publishing Company and the author, J W Tollefson, for extracts from his article 'Language Policy in the Philippines' from *Language Problems and Language Planning* 10 (2) Summer 1986, pp. 177–85 (Pub. University of Texas Press 1986); The New York Times for the articles 'Proper English, Yes; But Educationists, No' by Theodore Levitt in *The New York Times* 18.9.89. & 'Purging 'What-Cha' and 'Ain't'' by Neil A Lewis in *The New York Times* 28.2.89; The San Francisco Examiner for the article 'Let's teach English' by Guy Wright in *The San Francisco Examiner* 23.11.86; Times Newspapers Limited for the article 'The Prince of Wales says English is taught 'bloody badly'' by David Tytler in *The Times* 29.6.89. © Times Newspapers Ltd 1989; Seattle Post-Intelligencer for a cartoon by David Horsey, published in *Seattle Post-Intelligencer* June 3, 1988.

ONE

Introduction: Language policy and language learning

Recently I had an interesting conversation with my friend Greg, a 37-year-old white monolingual speaker of standard American English, who has an M.A. degree in music education and is employed as a music teacher in an American high school. He is comfortable economically, owns a nice home in a middle-class section of town within walking distance of a beautiful lake, drives a new van, and spends summers cruising the coastal islands on his 28-foot sail boat. In our conversation, we speculated about how his life might be different if he were a native speaker of Vietnamese who had learned English as a second language in early adulthood. With that single linguistic change, what would be different about his life? First, from what we knew about Vietnamese in Washington State, we were fairly certain Greg would not be a high-school teacher. He probably would not have a master's degree, nor even a B.A. He probably would not own his own home, or if he did, it would be a much smaller home in a working-class or poor neighbourhood. He would probably have a different partner, probably a Vietnamese woman. He would not have the same friends, and would perhaps not know any of the people in his present life. As we talked, we realized that virtually everything that gave his life its character – family, friends, career, home, past experiences and future possibilities – would be radically different if he were a native speaker of Vietnamese. In fact, the more we talked, the more difficult it became to imagine Greg as a native speaker of Vietnamese at all. The individual whom we envisioned seemed to be a different person altogether.

If speaking Vietnamese would be associated with so much change in Greg's life, then we must conclude that speaking English is closely connected to his present economic circumstances and social relationships. This does not mean that speaking English is the sole explanation for his job, lifestyle, and

1

personal relationships, but clearly English is intimately associated with the experiences and qualities of life that define his identity.

Yet there are exceptions to the pattern we discussed, such as Vietnamese in the United States who have M.A. degrees, who teach music, or who own expensive homes. These exceptions suggest that there is nothing inevitable or 'natural' about the way that language influences social and economic conditions. Instead, the role of language is essentially arbitrary, meaning that human beings through their action have made language a determinant of most of our social and economic relationships.

If the role of language in human social organization is arbitrary rather than inevitable, then each generation must be taught its importance. Infants are not born with the knowledge that language will have a major impact on family, friends, occupation, home, and income. This knowledge must be learned through a process of education. This educational process is so effective that most people are unaware of how language has affected their lives. Indeed, language is built into the economic and social structure of society so deeply that its fundamental importance seems only natural. For this reason, language policies are often seen as expressions of natural, common-sense assumptions about language in society. This book explores how the mechanism of language policy arbitrarily gives importance to language in the organization of human societies.

In each chapter, I will present a case study of an individual facing important language choices. The first case is intended to expand and to clarify the ways in which language and language learning influence social and economic relationships.

CASE: XUMA AUALA

Xuma Auala is a 12-year-old black child living in Windhoek, the capital of Namibia, ruled from 1920 to 1990 by South Africa in a colonial arrangement condemned by the United Nations and most world governments (see Mazrui and Tidy 1984). Because his father is a minor official in the Namibian bureaucracy, Xuma has the chance to attend secondary school, a rare event for blacks, most of whom never attend school at all. Indeed, the most striking effect of the apartheid system of education in Namibia is the rate at which black children leave school. In the 1970s, only 58 per cent of more than 40,000 who enrolled in the first year of elementary school began the second year; and fewer than 100 individuals made it to the final class (Duggal 1981).

Like his father before him, Xuma must speak, read, and write both Afrikaans and English if he wishes to continue in school. As the Namibian lingua franca imposed by South Africa, Afrikaans is the language of most secondary instruction, though English is used in a few schools, and other languages, such as Oshiwambo, are used in the first four years of elementary school. Examinations are required in both Afrikaans and English. Xuma knows that Afrikaans, the first language of the majority of white Namibians, is the language that blacks must know if they hope to have any chance to gain one of the few good jobs available to them.

Like virtually all black Namibians, Xuma looks forward to the day that South African domination of his country ends. The South West African People's Organization (SWAPO), the popular movement to drive South Africa out of Namibia, has developed detailed plans for independence. Under United Nations supervision, an agreement was implemented in 1989 and 1990 in which South Africa gave up its direct administration of the country, though still dominating the Namibian economy. SWAPO language policy for independent Namibia declares that English, not Afrikaans, will be the official national language (Kennedy 1989). Therefore Xuma wants to speak, read, and write English so he can work for the new government. So with his father's encouragement, he studies both Afrikaans and English, preparing simultaneously to use Afrikaans to work in an economy dominated by the apartheid state of South Africa, and English for an independent Namibia.

Xuma's father has hired a man to help with the construction of a small shed near their house. Each day, the man is accompanied by his two young children, Toivo and Sam, who carry stones used in the construction. Like their father, Toivo and Sam speak Khoi-san, a non-Bantu language used by about 3 per cent of the population. They know only a few words of English and Afrikaans. Their parents cannot afford to send them to school, so they completed only two months of the first elementary grade. If they had hoped to continue in school, Toivo and Sam had to learn both Afrikaans and English, and, if they attended one of the schools that uses Oshiwambo in the first four years, they would also learn that language. Combined with their father's economic status, this formidable language learning problem makes it highly unlikely that they will ever have the language competence they need to gain access to school, to jobs in the state bureauracy, or to the political system (see Gordon 1977). For Xuma, language education is the key to the future, but for Toivo and Sam, it is a major barrier that they will probably never overcome.

Although he wants to learn English, Xuma finds it easier to speak his native Bantu language, Oshiwambo, yet he will never be able to use it in school beyond the first four elementary years, nor in government service, nor to fulfil his dream of some day attending a university.

Why will English be the language of an independent Namibia, even though it is a colonial language spoken natively by only a few whites, while Oshiwambo is spoken by a third to a half of the population? South African language and educational policies have made it difficult for Oshiwambo or any other indigenous language to serve as the national language of Namibia. The apartheid policy of 'divide and rule,' which involved the reinforcement and, in some cases, the creation of ethno-linguistic identities, has effectively limited Oshiwambo and other languages to local areas (O'Callaghan 1977). The policy of three separate educational systems for whites, 'coloureds,' and blacks, and the 'homelands' system for different ethno-linguistic groups, have isolated the local languages so that they are not used for inter-group communication.

Another possibility for a national language is Afrikaans. Although essential for the limited occupations available to blacks under South African rule, Afrikaans is not spoken outside southern Africa. Thus its use as a lingua franca, imposed by South Africa, is a means of isolating Namibians. Moreover, its association with apartheid makes it unacceptable to most Namibians.

These policies mean that Afrikaans, Oshiwambo and other indigenous languages would not be effective tools for communication in a united and independent Namibia. In response to this situation, blacks have increasingly sought to learn English, which in recent years has come to be seen as the language of liberation (Duggal 1981). Yet opportunities to learn English are severely limited. It is taught in only a few schools, and only then as a foreign language with an emphasis on grammar. Also, because whites insist that Afrikaans rather than English must be used in communication with blacks, there is little use of English in daily communication (see Carver 1986; Duggal 1981).

The disadvantage of the SWAPO policy is that only those few Namibians who speak English will be able to serve in the government and other official positions. As a result, English speakers will have significant advantages in education and employment. To prepare for independence, the United Nations Institute for Namibia in Lusaka, Zambia, offers classes in English and prepares materials for use in Namibia. With independence, the cost of providing English language education will be high, though the conflict that would result from adopting Oshiwambo or another indigenous language would probably be higher.

Given the impact of apartheid, SWAPO's decision to adopt English is probably the best policy for reducing inequality based on language. In a sense, English will equally disadvantage much of the population, unlike indigenous languages, which would grant privilege to entire groups. Even with the best effort to extend English education, this crucial policy decision will dramatically affect the educational and employment options for virtually the entire population of Namibia.

As Namibia moves toward less dependence on South Africa, English moves closer to replacing Afrikaans as the dominant language of the country. For Xuma, who already speaks English, this presents opportunities for higher education and a career in public service. For Toivo and Sam, English remains a barrier because, like many black children in Namibia, they have little chance to attend school. For them, independence will end the hated apartheid system, but it will not completely eliminate the formidable linguistic barriers to education, employment, and political participation.

THE INCREASING ROLE OF GOVERNMENT IN LANGUAGE EDUCATION

In Namibia as in much of Africa, public markets are multilingual settings filled with people speaking many languages and dialects who come to the market to buy, sell, and trade food and other goods. In order to communicate in such settings, people acquire a common language, either a simplified and specialized market pidgin or one of the languages of the surrounding area used as a lingua franca for inter-group communication. Regardless of the variety used, language acquisition results from the immediate need to communicate and from actual use of the language in the interactions of buying and selling.

Like traditional multilingual markets, the modern world economic system requires a language variety for communication among people with different mother tongues. Throughout the world, English is increasingly used for this purpose, with different dialects, registers, proficiency levels, and literacy skills required for different kinds of interactions. (Of course, within particular geographical areas, other languages may serve a similar purpose, such as Russian in parts of the Soviet Union and Serbo-Croatian in Yugoslavia.) Unlike the languages used in traditional markets, however, English is typically acquired in school (except of course in English-speaking countries). Those people who cannot afford schooling, who do not have time to attend school, who attend substandard programmes, or who otherwise do not have access to effective formal education may be unable to learn English well enough to obtain jobs and to participate in decision-making systems that use English. Because education is a major concern of the state, this fundamental shift in the manner of acquisition means that state policies play a decisive role in determining who has access to the institutions of the modern market and therefore to political power. This shift to school-based language learning is a worldwide phenomenon, and so language policy plays an important role in the structure of power and inequality in countries throughout the world.

In the past 40 years, a new industry of language education has been dedicated to meeting the linguistic needs of the millions of people who must acquire English or other languages for education, government service, political participation, and employment. The explosion in the business of language teaching in elementary and secondary schools, universities and colleges, and private institutions has led to hundreds of programmes to prepare language teachers, thousands of language textbooks and teachers' guides, new language lab technologies, a new theoretical discipline (called second language acquisition), and a rapidly growing career – the professional teacher of English as a second language.

Yet while vast resources are directed toward language teaching and bilingualism, especially involving English, more people than ever are unable to acquire the language skills they need in order to enter and succeed in school, obtain satisfactory employment, and participate politically and socially in the life of their communities. Despite the explosion in language programmes, there is widespread inability to speak the language varieties necessary for access to economic resources and political power. The great linguistic paradox of our time is that societies which dedicate enormous resources to language teaching and learning have been unable – or unwilling – to remove the powerful linguistic barriers to full participation in the major institutions of modern society.

This book investigates the reasons for the failure of millions to speak the language varieties they need to survive and prosper in the modern world. It concludes that inadequate language competence is not due to poor texts and materials, learners' low motivation, inadequate learning theories and teaching methodologies, or the other explanations that are commonly proposed. Instead, language competence remains a barrier to employment, education, and economic well being due to political forces of our own making. For while modern social and economic systems require certain kinds of language competence, they simultaneously create conditions which ensure that vast numbers of people will be unable to acquire that competence. A central mechanism by which this process occurs is language policy.

Although language policies affect a wide range of language-related issues (from the variety to be used on street signs to major constitutional questions of rights and powers), this book will focus on policies affecting language education. Language education is the key to understanding many aspects of social organization, including the structure of the labour force, ethnic and linguistic conflict, and the allocation of economic resources. Also, because education in much of the world is subject to explicit policy decisions by governmental bodies, the impact of the policy approach to solving language problems is starkly visible in language education.

There is now a large body of data demonstrating that inequalities among ethnic groups are reproduced through systematic elements of schools (see Bullivant 1987; Giroux 1983; Shannon 1989). Recognizing this fact, minorities have begun to seek some control over educational policy and curriculum. Their aim is to make educational systems serve their interests, not just those of dominant groups. Though this book is about this struggle for control of language education, it will spend little time on the topics traditionally considered central to education, such as curriculum, materials, instructional methods, motivation, and teachers. Instead, it will examine how language policy in education structures unequal social and economic relationships. Chapters will examine the relationship between language policy and access to economic resources and political institutions; the role of language in the world market and the education of the labour force; and the use of language policy to manage migration. In addition, chapters will examine language policy in a revolutionary situation, the current state of language policy theory, and the increasingly important issue of language rights.

It is one purpose of this book to examine these issues in a variety of settings around the world in order to contribute to a theory of language planning that locates the field within social theory. A second purpose is to connect language planning with the related issues of migration, political participation, and the increasingly integrated world economic system. A final purpose is to explore the impact of language policy upon people seeking to meet their essential human needs within economic and political systems offering little capacity for individual action and control.

Language policy in education

Education is closely associated with economic class. In Africa, lifetime salaries of individuals completing higher education range from seven to ten times the earnings of individuals completing elementary education (Nafziger 1988). The premium for university study over secondary education is also high, even in countries with mediocre universities and high student–teacher ratios. This is because the modern hierarchical division of labour requires a small number of technicians and managers and a large number of unskilled and semi-skilled workers. Because these groups require different skills and amounts of education, the schools serve as gatekeepers for the labour force, determining which individuals and groups will have which specific jobs. Language is one criterion for determining which people will complete different levels of education. In this way, language is a means for rationing

language as a rationing tool

access to jobs with high salaries. Whenever people must learn a new language to have access to education or to understand classroom instruction, language is a factor in creating and sustaining social and economic divisions.

Outside education, national languages serve a similar purpose by rationing access to political institutions of power. The adoption of a national language depoliticizes one variety, which is declared to be the symbol of all people (the nation). Resistance to the national language is therefore seen as opposition to national unity. Voting, service on local boards and committees, and other forms of political participation may be limited to individuals speaking the national language. In such circumstances, it may seem absurd to have a leader who does not speak the national language. Yet this means that only speakers of the national language can become leaders or otherwise participate in official political activities. In this way, national languages, which restrict access to decision making in the name of nationhood, are inherently ideological.

SOCIAL THEORY

This book is about the ideology of language policy. To examine the ideology of language policy, we need a set of concepts of a theory of social organization. These concepts are drawn from a perspective of social theory that has gained a great deal of attention in recent years due to its powerful analysis of the uses of ideology, the role of the state, and the relationship between social constraint and individual freedom. These ideas have been most developed by Jürgen Habermas (1973, 1979, 1985, 1987, 1988), Anthony Giddens (1971, 1982a, 1982b, 1984, 1985), and Michel Foucault (1970, 1972, 1979), whose work provides a useful framework for analysing the impact of language policy in society.

Power

Power refers to the ability to achieve one's goals and to control events through intentional action. Power is not a characteristic of individuals in isolation. Rather, individuals exercise power as a result of their social relationships within institutional structures that provide meaning to their actions and also constrain them (see

Fairclough 1989). Thus there is a dynamic relationship between structure and power, and power is fundamental to both individual action and social organization.

Although power implies dominance, individuals in subordinate positions in social relationships are never completely powerless, as they may carve out specific areas of control over their daily lives. Also, individuals in subordinate positions may be able to increase their power. In highly centralized bureaucratic organizations, for example, they may exercise their capacity to seriously disrupt large systems by withholding their labour. This is one reason why state bureaucracies spend a great deal of their resources attempting to control labour. Language policy is one of the key mechanisms for state control of labour.

The state

Government implies a group of individuals sharing equally in the exercise of power, whereas *state* refers to the apparatus by which dominant groups maintain their power. Also, the state is an independent source of power with an interest in retaining and expanding its dominance. Therefore I have chosen to use the term *state* rather than *government*, because the former term suggests the centrality of power. Language policy is one mechanism available to the state for maintaining its power and that of groups which control state policy. The importance of language policy is fundamentally rooted in the rise of the modern state.

Ideology

The policy of requiring everyone to learn a single dominant language is widely seen as a common-sense solution to the communication problems of multilingual societies. The appeal of this assumption is such that monolingualism is seen as a solution to linguistic inequality. If linguistic minorities learn the dominant language, so the argument goes, then they will not suffer economic and social inequality. This assumption is an example of an *ideology*, which refers to normally unconscious assumptions that come to be seen as common sense. A major theme of this book is that such assumptions justify exclusionary policies and sustain inequality.

Ideology is connected to power, because the assumptions that come to be accepted as common sense depend upon the structure of power in a society. In general, common-sense assumptions help to sustain existing power relationships. As ideology builds these assumptions into the institutions of society, it tends to freeze privilege and to grant it legitimacy as a 'natural' condition (see Gitlin 1989; Fairclough 1989). In modern societies, language policy is used to sustain existing power relationships, i.e., it is ideological. With competency in specific language varieties and literacy skills essential to the exercise of power in modern states, policies that shape language and its use inevitably affect the distribution of power.

The exercise of power depends upon coercion, including physical violence, and upon the manufacture of consent, which refers to the capacity of dominant groups to gain consent for existing power relationships from those in subordinate positions (cf. Herman and Chomsky 1988). Ideology contributes to the manufacture of consent because it leads to (ideological) assumptions about right and wrong, acceptable and unacceptable behaviour. That is, ideology shapes behaviour. Yet, because it is largely unconscious, ideology is inherently conservative. People who do not fit neatly into the dominant group (e.g., 'ethnics' in North America) must be especially cautious in those areas over which they have control (e.g., appearance and language) if they wish to be accepted by members of the dominant group. Their attention to common-sense measures of belonging is an example of ideology at work.

Language education has become increasingly ideological with the spread of English for specific purposes, curricula and methods that view English as a practical skill, a 'tool' for education and employment (see Fairclough 1989). This book will argue that requiring individuals to learn English for education and jobs often helps to sustain existing power relationships. Thus the assumption that English is a tool for getting ahead – and that teaching English is empty of ideological content – is an example of ideology. In general, the belief that learning English is unrelated to power, or that it will help people gain power, is at the centre of the ideology of language education.

Hegemony

As concepts of national identity, loyalty, and patriotism become associated with specific language varieties, ideas about language justify social divisions and social inequality. For instance, in the United States, being an 'American' is associated with speaking standard American English. By definition, those who do not speak this variety are not fully American, and therefore are denied political rights such as voting, economic opportunities, and social equality. Moreover, they suffer disadvantage in education when they are required to attend classes in which they do not understand the medium of instruction. Language is particularly effective in structuring inequality in this way because it seems 'natural' for everyone to speak one variety for intra-group communication. Thus people often feel that those who speak the preferred variety deserve to be in positions of authority and power and to control political and economic institutions.

To the extent that this feeling about the naturalness of language use becomes pervasive, the dominant group has established *hegemony*, which is the successful production and reproduction of ideology. Hegemony may be achieved in two ways: first, through the 'spontaneous consent' of the people to the direction of social life imposed by dominant groups; and second, through the apparatus of state coercive power which enforces discipline on members who do not consent to the dominant ideology (see Harman 1988). Examples of linguistic hegemony can be found in many countries, such as the USA and Britain, where linguistic minorities are denied political rights and where multilingualism is widespread but officially invisible in the major mass media, government, and most public discourse (e.g., radio talk shows and newspapers). When minority languages do not appear in these areas of public discourse, their exclusion comes to be seen as natural and inevitable. Indeed, linguists describe the use of minority languages in these domains as 'inappropriate,' which is an example of linguistic hegemony at work in the social sciences.

Structure, structural constraints, and class

Societies are not simply a random arrangement of individuals, but rather they have *structure*. I will first explain what I do not mean by structure. A common conception of social structure is that it consists of the patterns of human interactions that can be observed in a wide range of social contexts. Church attendance, for instance, may indicate the structural role of religion in society. In this view, social theory examines religious, 'racial,' ethnic, or geographical patterns of human behaviour. Structural constraints are seen as the probability that individuals belonging to these categories will engage in particular kinds of behaviour. Thus structural constraints are envisioned as external to individual actions.

A list of categories into which people may be classified is not what *structure* means in this book. Instead, structure is envisioned as both the medium and the result of human actions (cf. Giddens 1987). Institutions and societies have structural properties because of the actions of their members, and the actions of those members are given meaning by their place in social structure. Thus there is a dialectical relationship between human agency (individual action) and the social structures which action produces and which give actions their meaning.

The most important structural category is *class*, which has been analysed in greatest detail from a Marxist perspective. In non-Marxist usage, class refers to groupings of individuals according to occupation, income, or other factors. In Marxist analysis, class refers to different positions in the organization of economic production; these positions have inherently antagonistic interests that involve struggle, which is seen as the fundamental force of history.

Social groups (defined by class, ethnicity, gender, or language) must constantly be involved in struggle with others to gain or to maintain power. Struggle is not something to be ended, like warfare or violence. Rather, it is inherent to social systems in which groups have different interests, and it is the source of social change. Out of struggle arise both minor and revolutionary transformations in social systems.

Language is one arena for struggle, as social groups seek to exercise power through their control of language; and it is also a prize in this struggle, with dominant groups gaining control over language (see Fairclough 1989). This aspect of struggle is especially important in education, where dominant and subordinate groups often engage in struggle over recognition of diverse languages and cultures in the school curriculum.

Language policy can be analysed as the outcome of struggle as well as a component in it. In other words, particular policies in specific countries result from and contribute to the relationships among classes. Within this view, *structural constraint* refers to the grounding of individual action within class relationships. As class relationships are embedded in the routines of daily life (largely outside of our awareness), they define possible actions. Therefore an individual's response to a language problem or language policy is constrained by the class relationships in which that individual participates.

This notion of constraint differs from the use of *sanctions*, whereby individuals or groups deliberately seek to restrict the range of options open to others. Language policy often includes sanctions, such as loss of voting rights for those who insist on speaking their native language. But policies need not only involve sanctions. They also may play a role in constraining action by being seen as 'natural' expressions of common sense. When structural constraints block understanding of class relationships and inequality, we are in the realm of ideology.

Dominance

Choice is never totally free, but rather is always between predefined alternatives (see Harman 1988). *Dominance* refers to the capacity to expand one's range of choices. Individuals or groups are dominated (i.e., are subordinate) if their choices are constrained relative to others with whom they share social relationships. When individuals or groups within a society have different choices available to them, the major task for social scientists should be to explain the reasons for these differences. Unfortunately, most social science emphasizes the notion of choice while failing to explain the structural and historical factors that constrain choice. In general, economic disadvantage is associated with constrained linguistic choices; indeed, around the world many peasants and urban poor may have no alternative available to them to resolve their language problems. We can say that they are *dominated* by those who enjoy a wider range of alternatives.

Exploitation

The term *exploitation* refers to the use of exclusionary tactics to sustain privilege (Giddens 1982a). One example of exploitation is the use of education to control access to the labour market. In many countries, examinations in the educational system ensure that most people who enter school will fail. In Kenya, for example, the national secondary schools, which have the best teachers and materials and lead to university education, take only 5 per cent of those with a certificate in primary education (Nafziger 1988). Although national policy ostensibly provides equal opportunity for education, in fact the limitations on the number of children admitted to secondary schools and universities favour middle- and upper-class families, who can spend more money on books, private tutoring, and other methods of encouraging study. Thus large numbers of people attempt to gain the education necessary for good jobs and reasonable salaries, but in fact some groups systematically benefit more than others. In this sense, the educational system in Kenya, as in many other countries, is exploitative.

Manley (1983) correctly points out that equal opportunity to compete in an economic or educational system in which there are necessarily a large number of losers is Orwellian newspeak. It furthers inequality in the name of equality and contributes to mass acceptance of privilege for the few. In this sense, the belief that 'equal opportunity' exists is fundamentally ideological.

Exclusionary tactics of dominant groups are normally institutionalized and protected by the legal system, and therefore may be difficult to recognize as examples of exploitation. One aim of raising consciousness is to increase awareness of institutionalized forms of exploitation. A major purpose of this book is to show that language policy, as a mechanism for exclusion, is often fundamentally exploitative.

Minority

The word *minority* is commonly used to refer to groups distinguished by gender, ethnicity, religion, race, and social class. Minorities may include indigenous peoples or immigrants residing permanently or temporarily as well as established minorities, such as the Welsh in Britain, and new groups such as Ethiopians in the Sudan.

Yet size is less important than power. Although the term *minority* focuses attention on numerical size (i.e., groups that are numerically smaller than the dominant group), its more important reference is to groups with few rights or privileges. In this book, *minority* refers to groups with relatively less power, rights, and privileges than one or more dominant groups. (For a discussion of the term 'minority,' see Byram 1986).

Language policy and language planning

The commonly-accepted definition of language planning is that it refers to all conscious efforts to affect the structure or function of language varieties. These efforts may involve creation of orthographies, standardization and modernization programmes, or allocation of functions to particular languages within multilingual societies. The commonly-accepted definition of language policy is that it is language planning by governments.

The commonly-held distinction between governmental and non-governmental activities reflects an uncritical social-theory perspective that ignores the close relationship between 'public' and 'private' sectors. Moreover, the traditional definition of planning/policy expresses an implicit belief in essentially ahistorical, unconstrained action and choice. Although most people may feel that they engage in such activity most of the time, this conception provides no insight into the ideological or structural basis of language planning/policy, nor its connection with power, hegemony, and dominance, or its role in struggle and exploitation.

An alternative conception of language policy (used here to refer to both governmental and non-governmental activities) seeks to locate language policy within a general social theory. In this book *language planning-policy* means the institutionalization of language as a basis for distinctions among social groups (classes). That is, language policy is one mechanism for locating language within social structure so that language determines who has access to political power and economic resources. Language policy is one mechanism by which dominant groups establish hegemony in language use.

This conception of language policy implies that there is a

dynamic relationship between social relations and language policy. Hierarchical social systems are associated with exploitative language policies, that is, policies which give advantage to groups speaking particular language varieties. Exploitative policies are evident in educational systems that impose disadvantages on minority students, and in restrictions on bilingualism among both subordinate and dominant populations. Chapter 2 explores this alternative conception of language policy in greater detail.

USING THIS BOOK

The concepts outlined above suggest the close association between language policy, power, and privilege that is at the centre of this book. In order to better understand the relationships between language, power, and privilege, I will raise in each chapter specific, real-life language problems facing people around the world. These concrete language problems do not have simple answers. In fact, satisfactory resolution of language problems is often made more difficult by automatic, uncritical acceptance of 'common-sense' (i.e., ideological) solutions. Therefore I have sought to organize this book in a way that will encourage critical thinking and discussion and that will confront readers with the question of how different solutions to language problems may reduce or sustain injustice, inequality, and privilege.

In order to focus on practical issues of language policy and language use, each chapter deals with an important language issue in one or two specific countries. By focusing on specific countries, I do not mean to suggest that the issues are unique to particular places. Indeed, the issues in this book confront people in many countries around the world. But it is important to examine language problems in their historical context, and to discuss possibilities for individual and group action within concrete social and political systems. The study of decontextualized language ignores the inherent dynamic relationship between language diversity and human social organization.

Each chapter contains several distinct sections:

1. Preview: An overview of the major language issue to be examined.
2. Media examples: One or more items from the popular and

professional media that illustrate the subtle spread of language policy. The media examples are followed by questions to encourage critical analysis. In some instances, I will present my own answers to these questions. These answers should not be considered 'right,' but instead a source for analysis. Readers' views may differ from mine, which is interesting in itself and should provide opportunity for further discussion.

3. For discussion: Questions for group discussion at the end of each chapter. Some of these questions raise parallels between issues in the specific country discussed in the chapter and similar language problems in other settings.

4. For action: Suggestions for concrete action at the end of each chapter. For instance, readers may be asked to contact a local social service agency within an immigrant community to learn about the agency's primary aims and client groups, its main funding problems, and its most critical needs. The purpose of this section is to encourage readers to learn how individuals and groups within the local community deal with important language problems.

5. Further reading: An annotated bibliography of several key sources for further information and reading. The complete list of references cited in the text is at the end of the book.

The following is a summary of the contents of the remaining chapters.

Chapter 2, 'The ideology of language planning theory,' examines the underlying assumptions behind the dominant approach to language policy analysis, called the 'neoclassical' approach, and an alternative, called the 'historical–structural' approach. The chapter explores the differences between these approaches and argues that the historical–structural approach is essential if the relationship between language policy and social organization is to be understood and the field of language policy is to have an impact upon areas of practical social concern.

Chapter 3, 'Mother tongue maintenance and second language learning,' begins discussion of the impact of language policy upon access to employment, economic resources, and political power. With particular reference to the Swann Report in the United Kingdom, the chapter explores the mechanisms by which language policy in education fulfils a gatekeeping function for major social institutions. The analysis includes a critique of accommodation theory, especially its failure to explain constraints on the types and directions of linguistic accommodation.

Chapter 4, 'Modernization and English language teaching,' compares dramatic changes in the role of English language education in two countries that have undergone major transformations in social and economic structure: Iran and China. The aim of the chapter is to connect language teaching to the historical development of the world economic system, with particular emphasis on modernization theory and the education of the labour force.

Chapter 5, 'Language policy and migration,' examines United States language policies designed to incorporate migrants into the US labour market. The analysis calls into question the widespread view that educational programmes for immigrants seek to provide the language education necessary for economic advance, and argues instead that these programmes often restrict access to economic resources.

Chapter 6, 'Revolutionary language policy,' examines conflicts over language policy in the Philippines. By contrasting language policies of dominant and revolutionary groups, the chapter emphasizes the importance of language in the struggle over social and economic inequality.

Chapter 7, 'Education and language rights,' considers efforts to use language policy to increase access to economic resources and political power in Australia and Yugoslavia, two countries with strong commitments to language rights. The chapter explores the relationship between rights and power, particularly as evidenced by the role of language in the recent political crisis in Yugoslavia.

Chapter 8, 'Conclusion: language policy and democracy,' argues that the use of language policy to further exclusion and inequality depends upon undemocratic structures, i.e., structures in which those who make decisions are not accountable to those who are affected by the decisions. The chapter concludes that undemocratic structures lead to language policies that prevent people from using their native languages in the key activities needed to support modern life – their own education, employment, and political participation.

FOR DISCUSSION

1. Can you think of examples of language policies in your own country? Be sure to include *implicit* policies, which are unstated but nevertheless may be enforced either by explicit sanctions or social pressures.

2. In your community, how are languages acquired? Are there any second languages commonly acquired *outside of school*? How well are they acquired? How well do students *in school* learn second or foreign languages?

3. How would your life be different if you spoke a different language in your community? Would you live in a different part of town? Would you have the same friends? What kind of job would you have? What jobs would you expect to have in the future?

4. In North America, many people believe that 'socialism' and 'communism' are ideologies, while 'democracy–capitalism' is not. Ask ten people to define the word *ideology* and give an example of it. Why is it an ideological act to exclude one's own political-economic system from the realm of ideology?

FOR ACTION

1. Is there is any place in your local community, such as public markets or food stores, where two or more languages can be heard? Spend some time there observing language behaviour. What patterns can you observe? Who speaks what languages? To whom are the different languages addressed? What language(s) do the sellers speak when communicating with buyers? What language(s) do the buyers (or sellers) speak among themselves?

2. Visit an elementary or secondary school to interview a school official, such as a principal or vice-principal. Ask about programmes for people who do not speak the dominant language. Are there special classes for them? Can they take classes in their native language? How important is it for them to learn the dominant language? What is the school's responsibility towards them?

FURTHER READING

Some of the most important readings on contemporary social theory are Giddens (1971, 1987); Habermas (1979, 1983, 1985, 1987); and Foucault (1979). For analysis of the connections between language, ideology, and power, see Fairclough (1989) and Skutnabb-Kangas and Cummins (1988).

TWO

The ideology of language planning theory

PREVIEW

Chapter 2 explores the ideological foundations of research on language policy and language planning. Two approaches to research are distinguished: the neoclassical approach, which emphasizes individual linguistic decisions, and the historical–structural approach, which emphasizes constraints on individual decision making. Although the neoclassical approach dominates research, this chapter argues that the historical–structural approach offers greater opportunity for explaining language behaviour and for resolving language problems facing individuals.

Why do some people acquire languages more successfully than others? Why are some language-teaching programmes more effective than others? What policies should government agencies and educational institutions adopt to ensure that language learners are successful? The effort to answer these questions engages researchers throughout the world in the fields of second language acquisition (SLA) and language planning. In the past twenty years, their search for answers has increasingly focused on a limited set of factors called 'learner variables.'

CASE: JANE SCHRADER

Professor Jane Schrader is a American linguist and social scientist interested in understanding why some language learners are more successful than others. For nearly five years, her research has been funded by grants from the US Department of Education and the

Office of Refugee Resettlement of the US Department of Health and Human Services. In order to obtain her grants, Schrader, like researchers elsewhere, shapes her proposals to the requirements outlined in the funding materials issued by the federal agencies. These announcements emphasize that projects should investigate the role of specific factors in SLA: the motivation, attitudes, and values of learners. Schrader's research has focused on motivation: What kinds of motivation are most effective? How can low levels of motivation be increased? What kinds of language-teaching programmes are most likely to maximize learners' motivation?

Professor Schrader's research over the past several years has shown that learners who wish to assimilate – who value or identify with members of the target-language community – are generally more successful than learners who are concerned about retaining their original cultural identity. They are also more successful than learners who merely wish to increase their salary or employment options. Schrader's findings support programmes for immigrants to the United States that are designed to encourage learners to 'become American' – to adopt certain values and attitudes considered appropriate for immigrants and to shift allegiance from their native culture to the dominant American culture.

Yet Schrader has recently become concerned about two persistent problems. First, some learners remain unsuccessful, regardless of the amount of effort expended in assimilation programmes. Have these unsuccessful learners, in effect, refused to acquire English? Are they responsible for their own failure, by being unwilling to 'become American?' Second, some learners who seem anxious to assimilate are nevertheless unsuccessful. In other words, even individuals who seem perfectly suited to language programmes emphasizing acculturation may fail to achieve an acceptable level of proficiency. Does this mean that factors other than motivation determine their degree of success in SLA? If so, what are those factors? And do they have an effect upon motivational levels?

These questions have immediate practical importance for thousands of language learners. In federally funded refugee programmes based on Schrader's research, refugees are given only twelve months to learn English before they are required to leave school for employment. During those twelve months, they are taught 'American' values and they practise the behaviours to demonstrate that they understand those values. They learn to change their style of dress and their food, to limit the number of children in their families, to change traditional male and female family roles, to stress the importance of time (to be on time, to remember that 'time is money,' and to not 'waste time'), and to undergo many other shifts in the basic cultural principles which organize and give meaning to their lives. Throughout these ESL programmes, it is assumed that these changes in culture lead to language learning and to improved prospects for employment.

Problems persist, however, for those who do not assimilate. For them, the programme ends in failure, in a cutoff of additional educational aid, and in minimum-wage jobs providing little opportunity to learn English. Though Schrader's research on motivation leads her to believe that their failure is due to low motivation, she has come to know some of her subjects personally, and is beginning to wonder whether that explanation is too simple. She questions whether their failure is truly their own fault, or whether other factors, beyond their control, ensure that they do not learn English.

Yet Schrader is unsure how to investigate these issues. Though she wants to study factors that seem to exist outside the individual learner, she is unsure what those external factors might be. And if she wants to have her funding renewed, her proposal must emphasize internal psychological variables. '

RESEARCH ON LANGUAGE LEARNING AND LANGUAGE POLICY

Professor Schrader's dilemma raises important questions about our understanding of how people acquire languages. Why are virtually all individuals within some communities multilingual, while individuals in other communities seem unable to learn second languages, despite years of study in school? Is it because people in some communities are more motivated to learn? Why are immigrants in some countries bilingual? Is it because these immigrants are highly motivated? In societies with great differences in wealth, why are multilingual individuals often poor rather than rich? Is it because the poor have greater motivation to learn? Also, why is it important for poor immigrants to speak the 'standard' language? Why are some languages studied in school as academic subjects for college-bound students, while other languages are associated with 'compensatory' or 'remedial' programmes? And, in such circumstances, why are some languages acquired more effectively than others? Is it because students studying some languages are more motivated than others?

MEDIA EXAMPLE 2.1

In late 1985, the US National Institute of Education reported major research findings of a federally-funded study to measure 'the extent to which factors such as instructional approach and student characteristics affect the English language and general academic development [of limited-English-proficient students]' (Garcia 1985, p. 2). The study concluded that instructional variables, particularly quality of instruction and opportunities to practise English, 'were found to interact in complex ways with two types of learner variables: (1) the initial English language proficiency of the . . . student and (2) the *characteristics of the student's ethnic group* [emphasis added]' (p. 2).

In early 1988, the Director of the US Office of Bilingual Education and Minority Languages Affairs announced the research agenda for federally-funded programmes for the new fiscal year. This research agenda focused on instructional variables, including classroom methodology and teacher preparedness, as well as characteristics of students and the outcomes they achieve. The announcement stated that funded studies must be 'designed to improve the accuracy and quality of information available about the numbers, background characteristics, and educational experience of limited-English-proficient, language minority children' (Coro 1988, p. 2).

The three funded projects included a study designed to assess various tests of English proficiency; a study linking language proficiency with educational experience and grades; and a study to follow the educational progress of a nationally representative sample of students from the eighth grade through high school in order to gather data on the relationship between language and school performance.

These research projects fit well with major SLA theories that emphasize learner variables to explain second language acquisition. For instance, one of the most popular attempts to develop a theory of SLA is the Monitor Model of Stephen Krashen. This model claims that comprehensible input is necessary for acquisition. What is comprehensible is determined by the learner's affective filter. That is, the learner must be 'open' to input, which depends on low anxiety, high self-confidence, and positive feelings about speakers of the target language (see Krashen 1981). Like other models of SLA, Krashen's emphasizes learners' personality and character as the key to successful second language acquisition.

Questions

1. Make a list of all the factors you think will affect someone's ability to learn a second language. Which of these factors do you think a learner can easily change? Age, for instance, cannot be changed at will. What about time available for study? Personality? Attitudes towards the target language? Can these be changed in a way that will improve someone's ability to learn a language?

2. How does an emphasis on learner variables help or hinder the teacher's ability to understand a student's difficulties in learning a new language?

3. For most adults, learning a language fluently takes many hundreds, even thousands of hours, of study and practice. How many hours do you have available during the next three years to devote to learning a new language? What does your answer suggest about the difficulty of the task of second language learning?

Neoclassical approach to language-planning research

In order to understand why second language acquisition and language policy are dominated by a concern with learner variables such as motivation, we must look at the recent history of these fields of study. Since SLA and language policy began to take shape as distinct disciplines in the 1960s, the amount of published materials has grown so quickly that there are now introductory textbooks, several journals (e.g, *Language Problems and Language Planning*, *Studies in Second Language Acquisition*), newsletters, dozens of theoretical essays, and hundreds of case studies.

Yet attempts to synthesize language planning and language acquisition research into a comprehensive theoretical framework have proved inadequate. The difficulties facing this research include the lack of comparable methodologies of empirical studies, the trivial or *ad hoc* nature of many generalizations, the irrelevance of much research to the policy-making process, the failure to relate language planning and policy to broader sociopolitical changes, and the prevalence of what are essentially ideologies and political values passing for theoretical frameworks.

Research on learner variables is not monolithic, as important differences characterize research and affect the quality of generalizations. Yet research on learner variables across disciplines is united by certain assumptions which it shares with a wide range of work on language learning and language policy. In second language acquisition, for instance, researchers seeking to develop a theory of SLA often propose lists of variables which they believe must be incorporated in a theory; these lists are dominated by characteristics of learners, such as age, language aptitude, attitudes towards the target language, time spent in the target culture, educational level, sensitivity to criticism, and motivation (e.g., Schumann 1978). Many studies seek to link these characteristics with language learning ability. For instance, positive attitudes towards the target culture have been found to correlate with successful performance in second language classes (Krashen 1980). Ego permeability, or the ability to put oneself in another's shoes, has been proposed as a major causal variable aiding acquisition (Guiora et al. 1975). Such research assumes that learners' talent, personality, and experience are the keys to successful language learning, even though the mechanisms linking these characteristics to language acquisition have not been specified.

This work on learner variables forms the basis for a great deal of language planning research. Perhaps the best known are Canadian studies on the effectiveness of deliberate efforts to increase motivation in order to bring about improved language learning (Gardner and Lambert 1972). Similarly, educational programmes for recent immigrants to the United States assume that learners' characteristics – specifically, their attitudes and values – determine their success in acquiring English. Therefore these American programmes seek to change immigrants' attitudes and values in order to bring about language learning, cultural adaptation, and employment (Tollefson 1986b). Other language-teaching projects emphasize individuals' openness to innovation, their adaptability, and similar characteristics of individual learners as the keys to successful language learning.

In all of these cases, including research on motivation, the primary causal variables are located *within the individual*. This research may be termed the 'neoclassical' approach. Within the neoclassical approach, the rational calculus of individuals is considered to be the proper focus of research. Factors affecting language learning and language use are presumed to be those that vary from individual to individual.

Neoclassical research extends throughout the social sciences, and is characterized by certain primary assumptions: that the key to understanding social systems is the individual; that differences between sociopolitical systems are the result of the cumulative effect of individual decisions; that individual decisions are predictable but free; and that the proper focus of social research is analysis of individual decisions. Examples of the neoclassical approach in social science research include such disparate work as Schrader's research on motivation and the 'equilibrium model' of economics that is expressed most explicitly in supply-side theory (see Bach and Schraml 1982).

The premises of the neoclassical approach are, of course, articles of faith, comprising an ideology that is not subject to empirical verification. Nevertheless the premises profoundly affect the relationship of language-planning researchers to the object of their inquiry. Most importantly, they insulate language planners from any evaluation which is 'external' to the planning process. The researcher is seen as an observer who is not part of the historical context and whose primary responsibility is to analyse the planning process without 'interfering' in it. This is one reason for the enormous concern with research methodology. The researcher's only criterion for evaluating language policies is whether stated goals are achieved. As a result, the field of language planning generally does not ask what might be *appropriate* policies. Researchers do not judge the equity or fairness of policies; indeed, the neoclassical model presents a theoretical obstacle to such involvement in the planning process.

The premises of the neoclassical model have seriously limited the ability of the field of language planning to respond to the disillusionment with social planning that has characterized the social sciences generally since the early 1970s. Neoclassical analysis of 'ineffective' planning is theoretically limited to critiques of individual decisions. It does not include analysis of the forces that lead to the adoption of the planning approach, the historical and structural factors that determine the evaluative criteria by which plans are judged to be ineffective, or the political and economic interests that benefit from the perceived failure of planning. In response to criticisms resulting from the perceived failure of social planning in the 1960s and 1970s, advocates of the planning approach can argue only that future decisions must be made on the basis of more accurate information. Finally, the neoclassical approach is ill equipped to explain how the perceived failure of planning in the 1960s may protect and preserve dominant economic interests.

The neoclassical model is particularly unsuited to confront three crucial linguistic issues:

1. How do language communities form and how do they come to invest their language(s) with varying degrees of value? This question focuses on the social issue of language acquisition: when do groups acquire a common language variety? Neo-classical theory derives typologies of language communities based on structural characteristics of language varieties, degrees of multilingualism, and range of functional variation (Kelman 1971; Fishman 1968; Kloss 1968), but it has been unable to develop a theory to account for the formation and development of language communities and their range of linguistic variability.

2. Why do some groups learn languages easily, perhaps losing their native language altogether, while other groups cling tenaciously to their mother tongue despite enormous pressure to change? Neoclassical theory is unable to explain why some communities are willing to go to war over language issues, while others easily accept language loss, and most exhibit a flexible attachment to language patterned by forces that are outside the concerns of neoclassical theory.

3. What are the mechanisms by which changes in language structure and language use take place, and how does the language-planning process affect those mechanisms? The neoclassical approach is limited to correlating planning decisions with changes in language structure and use, but it is unable to explain how, and under what conditions, planning decisions bring about linguistic change. Instead, it posits the meaningless notion of 'natural' language change (cf. Williams 1986).

Due to the dominance of the neoclassical approach, these issues are widely believed to be outside the scope of the field of language planning. The formation and development of language communities is seen as a central concern of anthropologists, while political scientists are assumed to be interested in the relationship between language communities and political structure (e.g., Das Gupta 1970), and historical linguists, psycholinguists, and microsociolinguists are expected to examine language change. The field of language planning has generally tried to use the results of research in these fields as the basis for analysis of case studies. In this sense, language planning as it is conducted within the neoclassical approach is appropriately considered an area of applied studies.

Professor Schrader's research on motivation is a key example of the neoclassical approach. Following Kelman (1971), most motivation research examines two broad types of attachments to language communities: instrumental and sentimental. Individuals who are instrumentally attached to a community feel that their economic needs are being met by the community. Adequate food, housing, and employment are the key instrumental factors. Individuals who are sentimentally attached to a community feel that their personal identity is tied to the group, and that their sense of connection to history and to humanity depends upon the group. These different attachments seem related to different forms of motivation, termed *instrumental* and *integrative* motivation. Examples of instrumental motivation for language learning include learning a language in order to pass a degree requirement or to gain a better job. Integrative motivation involves a feeling of personal identity tied to the target-language community. For the integratively motivated individual, language acquisition is a means to gain membership in the new community. Like other neoclassical research, this distinction fails to explain the reasons why particular groups are required to learn new languages, the historical development of instrumental or integrative motivation within specific groups, or the impact of historical and structural factors upon individual language learning.

Neoclassical researchers like Professor Schrader view both types of motivation as existing within the individual. This view explains motivation as follows. Imagine two people who react quite differently to the requirement that they learn a language in order to graduate: one student may study hard and do well, while the other may fail to learn the new language. Neoclassical research views the former student as highly motivated, the latter as lacking in motivation. Thus, neoclassical researchers such as Schrader must ultimately argue that the dropout is responsible for his or her own failure to learn the language.

Why is that conclusion unsatisfactory? The reason is that the probability of success or failure in language learning is not equal for every individual student. Some students – members of particular economic and ethnic groups – are far more likely to 'fail' to learn a language than other students. Does this mean that they, as a group, lack motivation? Or does it mean that there are factors other than motivation that determine their language learning success? Most importantly, to what extent are they able to exercise control over those additional factors?

Historical–structural approach to language-planning research

In order to answer these questions, SLA theory and language-planning theory must go beyond a limited concern with learner variables. Fortunately, a counter-tendency in language policy studies has developed alongside the neoclassical approach. This counter-tendency rejects the neoclassical assumption that the rational calculus of individuals is the proper focus of research, and instead seeks the origins of constraints on planning, the sources of the costs and benefits of individuals' choices, and the social, political, and economic factors which constrain or impel changes in language structure and language use. This approach to language planning may be termed the *historical structural approach* (cf. Bach and Schraml 1982; Wood 1982).

The differences between the neoclassical approach and the historical–structural approach involve:

1. the unit of analysis each employs;
2. the role of historical perspective;
3. criteria for evaluating plans and policies;
4. the role of the social scientist.

These conceptual differences reflect more fundamental differences between the two frameworks, particularly:

1. the underlying ideological orientations of the proponents of the two approaches;
2. their different views of the relative importance of individual choice and collective behaviour in social science research.

The differences between the neoclassical approach and the historical–structural approach are especially striking with respect to the unit of analysis. While the neoclassical approach emphasizes the rational decisions of individuals, the historical–structural approach emphasizes the origins of the costs and benefits confronting individuals and groups. For example, an individual faced with learning a new language must expend certain costs (hours of study, tuition fees) in order to achieve certain benefits (a degree, a better job). Within the neoclassical approach, the individual's 'decision' whether to learn the language is seen as the result of this sort of cost–benefit analysis. Within the historical–structural approach, the focus is on the sources of the costs and benefits involved in the choice. Why must that individual expend those particular costs? Why are those particular benefits rather than others available to that individual? What are the costs and benefits for other people in the community? What language choices do they confront?

Within the historical–structural approach, language policy is viewed as one mechanism by which the interests of dominant sociopolitical groups are maintained and the seeds of transformation are developed. The major goal of policy research is to examine the historical basis of policies and to make explicit the mechanisms by which policy decisions serve or undermine particular political and economic interests. Language-planning institutions are seen as inseparable from the political economy, and are no different from other class-based structures. Though this approach permits a wide range of viewpoints, its primary insights are derived from critical theory (e.g., Forester 1985).

The difficulties that have afflicted attempts to develop a theory of language planning can be traced to the dominance of the neoclassical emphasis on the individual. Therefore we must consider whether the historical–structural emphasis on collective behaviour can advance a theory of language planning, and whether it can help to relate language policy to broader issues of economic development and sociopolitical change.

In contrast to the neoclassical model, the historical–structural model assumes that the primary goal of research and analysis is to discover the historical and structural pressures that lead to particular policies and plans and that constrain individual choice. Structural factors influence language-planning decisions through their impact on the composition of planning bodies and on the economic interests that are expressed by the sociopolitical goals to which those bodies are committed. Thus language planning is considered a macro-social rather than a micro-social process (Tollefson 1981a). Moreover, language planning is conceptualized as an historical process inseparable from structural considerations. The unit of analysis is thus the historical process as opposed to the neoclassical approach that treats language planning as the sum of individual choices.

Explanations for planning and policy decisions may refer to a wide range of historical and structural considerations. These include: the country's role in the international division of labour (Tollefson 1986b); the country's level of socioeconomic development; the political organization of decision making (Tollefson 1981a); and the role of language in broader social policy (Forester 1985).

The neoclassical assumption that planners formulate plans and policies in response to their perception of the language situation constitutes a theoretical separation of the planning process from history. This 'freezing' of history precludes analysis of the historical causes for the adoption of the planning approach or for specific decisions. Moreover, the neoclassical assumption that planners' decisions are based upon their analysis of costs and benefits ignores issues of political organization that might explain the composition of planning bodies, their interests, and their goals. Critics of the neoclassical approach point out that costs and benefits are never equally distributed throughout affected populations, and that costs and benefits are determined by existing political and economic structures, of which language-planning bodies are usually only a small part. The historical–structural approach assumes that variables identified by the neoclassical approach (such as motivation and attitudes) have some underlying explanation.

When applied to the issue of motivation, the historical–structural approach seeks the reasons for different degrees and types of motivation and their effects on acquisition. It is not assumed that motivation is a 'learner' variable, but rather that motivation is determined by broader sociopolitical factors, such as economic interests associated with different language varieties, ideological support for language learning, and access to quality education. In short, the historical–structural approach views motivation as a result of historical and structural factors rather than as a primary cause of language acquisition.

If planning bodies reflect the interests of dominant political groups (and this is one of the main claims of the historical–structural approach), then the neoclassical model provides the theoretical basis for preserving those dominant interests. That is, the model provides no basis for a social-scientific critique of the goals and aims of plans and policies in such areas as language rights or the distribution of economic wealth and political power. That the neoclassical model is both ahistorical and amoral in its evaluation of plans and policies can be seen in the case of Germany's attempt to eliminate the Serbo-Croatian and Slovenian languages from certain areas of southern Austria during the 1930s and 1940s. Within the neoclassical model, that policy must be analysed as having been successfully implemented because its goals were achieved (by means of violence and other forms of coercion). The costs associated with failure to comply were so great that virtually everyone complied. Stated simply, the policy ensured that the population would be sufficiently motivated. In this case, as in others, the neoclassical approach presumes that language choices are predictable (according to cost/benefit analysis) but 'free.' That is, the model assumes that populations affected by policies analyse the costs and benefits of alternatives and then make a 'free' choice on the basis of this analysis. In Austria, potential learners of German weighed costs and benefits, and acted rationally by acquiring the language to a necessary proficiency level.

Yet this analysis fails to recognize that there may be no real alternative. Within the neoclassical approach, there is no theoretical difference between the acquisition of German among Slavs in Austria and the acquisition of French by a highly motivated group of English college students living in Paris. To attribute the Slavic community's acquisition of German and loss of Serbo-Croatian and Slovenian to a cost–benefit analysis utterly fails to capture the historical context of this language shift.

The failure of the neoclassical model to adequately accommodate coercion is part of a larger issue. The model explains decisions by planners and policymakers as well as decisions by individuals affected by plans and policies in the same manner: costs and benefits of alternatives are weighed. Yet others argue (e.g., Giesbers, 1985) that 'decisions' by policymakers or by an affected population are in fact manifestations of the historical and structural factors that determine which alternatives are available as well as their relative costs. In this view, the alternative to learn a language (or not to learn one), and its costs and benefits are the result of historical and structural variables which the neoclassical model holds constant, and thus ignores.

Thus the primary aim of the historical–structural approach is to locate individual actions within the larger political–economic system, primarily with reference to class, the central macro-structural unit of analysis of the historical–structural model. Yet this aim leads to its primary difficulty, namely, that there is no necessary link between structural categories (such as class, mode of production, or historical process) and the actions of specific planners or groups. The approach assumes that if we know the position of policymakers in the historical–structural situation, then we can predict the policies they will support. The problem with this assumption is that not all policymakers act according to the interests of their group (class). For instance, some individual members of a planning agency may enthusiastically formulate a policy, some may reluctantly support it, and others may actively undermine and subvert the policy. There may be no way within the historical–structural approach to explain these different actions, nor why a successful struggle within a population affected by policies does not necessarily lead to changes in policy. The resilience of policies which persist long after planners have concluded that they are not in their interests is well known, as is the capacity of the politico-administrative system to alter or subvert plans as they are implemented. At times, the historical–structural approach seems to view individuals strictly as victims or beneficiaries of historical and structural factors. One critic of the approach, Abu-Lughod (1975, p. 201), charges that it views human beings like iron filings, controlled by forces that leave them no room for creativity, innovation, and choice. With such a view of human decision making, the historical–structural model cannot explain individuality in planning.

Yet the emphasis on collective behaviour means that the historical–structural approach, in contrast to the neoclassical approach, encourages a broad range of evaluation. The historical–structural model presumes that plans that are successfully implemented will serve dominant class interests, and thus assessing whether plans are successfully implemented is relatively unimportant. Of far greater importance is evaluation of the effects of plans and policies on the distribution of economic resources and political power. A central concern of evaluation is to determine the degree to which plans and policies may (ultimately) undermine existing class structure. Concern for language rights is an associated issue, in that the exercise of language rights reflects the varying economic resources and power of different language groups, and the issue of language rights may be the focus for struggle between competing groups.

A central tenet of the historical–structural approach is the basic sociological premise that the action of groups is fundamentally different from the sum of the individual actions of its members. Thus the actions of planning bodies as well as of the populations they affect are viewed as products of history and the social relationships which organize groups. The primary task for researchers is to develop a theory of language planning that makes explicit the mechanisms by which planning processes interact with other historical–structural forces that form language communities and determine patterns of language structure and use. Emphasis on individual decisions by planners and policy-makers cannot fulfil this need.

A central difficulty with the neoclassical model is the assumption that language is a resource like other resources, with economic value for which costs are expended. This assumption is the basis for viewing language learning and language change as resulting from the sum of individual cost/benefit analyses. Within the historical–structural approach, however, language is unlike most other resources (though it is like labour; cf. Bach and Schraml 1982) because of the social relationships that give it form in language communities. The essential point is that language involves both the code and its use – the person's language and the person. Unlike most other resources, all language change involves real people living in history and organized into groups according to symbols, roles, and ideologies that may not correspond to the economic logic of cost/benefit analysis. That is, the possibilities for decisions and for action are fundamentally located in the social organization of language groups, rather than in individual cost/benefit analyses. The task for research is to explain the link between the organization of society, changes in its language structure and use, and the policy-making and planning process.

One aspect of this task is to understand the interaction between the structural organization of society and the language policies that flow from the political system. It is essential to recognize that social organization may be compatible or in conflict with language-planning bodies and processes. People may not acquire a language or they may refuse to alter the structure of their language because the social relationships in which they are embedded constrain such action. A plan that aims to achieve such goals must transform existing social relationships. As a result, analysis of language planning cannot be analytically separated from historical processes of structural transformation.

In its concern with structural transformation, the historical–structural model rejects the neoclassical separation between the researcher and the language-planning process. The approach assumes that the shifts in theoretical perspectives that characterize scientific analysis have a historical basis, and that all theories are embedded in sociopolitical structure. A central task of the approach is analysis of the ideological basis of social science theory. This central concern for the underlying ideology of social theory has not been widely applied in the field of language planning (though see Giesbers 1985).

The primary theoretical task which currently faces historical–structural analysis is to specify the role of language in the processes which structure societies, and the ways in which planning can affect these processes. At present, we can roughly outline the direction which this inquiry is likely to take: historical–structural factors are responsible for delimiting a society. The society may develop language varieties which it perceives to be its own without regard to the 'facts' of linguistics (e.g., most Serbs and Croats consider Serbian and Croatian to be quite distinct, though structurally they are quite close). The development of these varieties follows historical processes that operate for other characteristics of societies (geography, religion, ethnicity, etc.). Planning affects language change to the extent permitted by historical–structural factors, while planning itself is subject to the same historical–structural forces that shape language.

This sketch suggests directions for research:

1. Under what (historical and structural) conditions will language come to be an identifying characteristic of a group?
2. What (historical and structural) conditions permit language to lose its identifying power?
3. How do language groups perceive the role of planning bodies, and what factors account for varying perceptions?

4. Under what conditions will distinct linguistic groups be transformed into a unified group?
5. What are the constraints of the ideology of language upon planned attempts to change language structure?

These and other research questions are a part of the difficult effort to develop a theory of language planning. Ultimately, a theory of language planning and a theory of language must be integrated: language change is central to both. Until that broad synthesis is achieved, the field of language planning would benefit from a sustained effort to examine: (a) the historical and structural context of the planning approach, planning institutions and decision-making processes; and (b) the causes and effects of planning within the sociopolitical communities in which it takes place.

JANE SCHRADER'S CHOICES

Within the historical–structural approach, how might Professor Schrader re-examine and modify her plan to conduct research on motivation? One way is to seek to understand the social and economic forces that determine the varying motivations of individuals. Yet Schrader faces the constraints imposed by funding agencies: her research must deal with the impact of learner variables upon second language learning. Also, major SLA theories emphasize learner variables; without theoretical justification for investigating motivation as a result rather than a cause, Professor Schrader could not gain funding for her proposals.

A new direction in research will depend upon researchers being willing to connect learner variables to social science theory in fields other than SLA. One such connection is with sociology and social theory, in which language is seen as a social phenomenon rather than an individual one. Researchers like Schrader must seek to understand how social forces affect both learners' motivation and instructional variables, including quality of teaching, and theory must locate the language learner within a social context. Although second language acquisition research has begun to examine 'context,' it has limited the term to a narrow, neoclassical meaning, primarily verbal action patterned by 'strategies' of individual speakers within the 'context' of conversation. Researchers in pragmatics and sociolinguistics have been unwilling to extend the context of conversation to larger social institutions and societies (for a critique of the neoclassical approach to context, see Fairclough 1989).

One way to begin to broaden the study of context is to extend the range of people whose language-learning experience is studied. Like other researchers, Schrader studies college students, because they are accessible as subjects. But what about multilingual individuals in preliterate societies? How do they acquire language without schooling? What about the hundreds of millions of people throughout history who were multilingual, without the benefit of schools, teachers, and textbooks? Perhaps if she begins to expand her vision and the scope of her subjects, Professor Schrader can begin to study the forces affecting the life-determining 'choices' confronting language learners.

USING THE CONTRAST BETWEEN NEOCLASSICAL AND HISTORICAL–STRUCTURAL APPROACHES

In the rest of this book, I will present cases of individuals in different countries who face important language decisions about such matters as learning a new language, supporting mother-tongue teaching, or claiming language rights in education. Within the neoclassical framework, each choice is seen as an individual event with consequences for the individual and the immediate family. The neoclassical analysis of each choice is fairly straight-forward, any uncertainty a result of difficulty in weighing the costs and benefits of alternatives and in predicting the long-term consequences of alternatives. In contrast to the neoclassical perspective, I will examine the historical and structural context of each case, in particular the social, economic, and political forces that impose the specific alternatives available in the individual cases. I will try to show, in each case, that discussion of solutions to the language problems facing individuals must begin with a deep appreciation for the powerful historical and structural forces that pattern individual language behaviour.

Chapter 3 will examine one of the most controversial language issues: the use of pupils' mother tongues for instruction. The case will focus on immigrants in Britain.

FOR DISCUSSION

1. A widely used introductory language planning textbook states: 'Modernization and preservation efforts are seemingly happening everywhere, to provide all people with access to the modern world through technologically sophisticated languages and also to lend a sense of identity through encouraged use of their first languages (mother tongues)' (Eastman, 1983, p. 31). What do you think the author might mean by a 'technologically sophisticated language'? Why are 'technology' and 'modernity' associated with specific languages such as English, whereas 'identity' is associated with 'mother tongues'?

2. At a meeting of English teachers in the late 1970s, a well known researcher stated that the 'why' of second or foreign language learning is largely a matter of 'fate', a result of the accidents of one's job, parents' language, school curriculum, and so on (see Tollefson, 1981a). In this view, classroom variables such as quality of instruction can be manipulated to improve learning, but most other factors are not within the control of educational planners. Do you agree that parents' language, job, and school curriculum are matters of 'fate' or of historical factors? What are some of the historical factors that determined your native language(s), your second language(s), and the chance that you will acquire additional languages?

3. Think of some skill or area of knowledge in which you feel you are successful, such as music, athletics, public speaking, etc. How would you describe your motivation to spend the time needed to be successful in this area? Is your success due to motivation? To innate 'talent'? Or to other factors? Do you know why you are successful?

FOR ACTION

1. Sit in on a language class. Notice that some students are more attentive and more interested than others, despite the fact that all students have the same teacher. Why might some students seem more 'motivated' than others? What factors in their lives might explain their different levels of motivation?

2. Interview five experienced ESL instructors. Describe to them hypothetical students with identical language proficiency from

five different native language groups: Vietnamese, Japanese, Arabic, Mexican Spanish, and Russian. Ask them to decide which student they feel would be most likely to excel in a speaking class; a grammar class; a reading class; a writing class; and a listening comprehension class. Then ask them to decide which of the five students would be most effective in the following roles in a group discussion: organizer and leader; major participant; minor participant; notetaker; disruptive participant. Finally, ask the teachers whether they have ever had students from the backgrounds you describe. Do the teachers agree in their answers to your questions? If they agree, why do they? What do their answers suggest about the generalizations teachers may make about students from different backgrounds?

3. Contact an ESL programme that serves immigrants in your local community. (If possible, find a programme serving pre-literate students.) Find out what factors in the students' lives limit their ability to attend class, to study, and to practise their English with native speakers. Ask the programme director or instructors whether motivation is a problem for the students. If it is, find out what the programme does to increase their motivation. If it is not, find out how programme officials explain lack of progress among some students.

4. Cost–benefit analysis assumes that human beings will acquire a language when the benefits outweigh the costs. This analysis can be applied to any situation. For instance, students in a high-school foreign language class may fail to learn the language because the costs required to do so are not outweighed by any benefit for learning the language. A similar analysis can be applied to the instance mentioned in this chapter – Slavic regions in southern Austria during the 1940s, when Nazi policy required speakers of Serbo-Croatian and Slovenian to avoid using their native languages and instead to speak German. In this case, the policy was effective, as the population decided the benefits (avoiding imprisonment) outweighed the costs of learning German. Proponents of cost–benefit analysis claim that its applicability to such a broad range of situations is one of its strengths, while critics point out that it fails to consider the impact of coercion and the morality of policies imposed by force. What do you think?

5. Two of the most influential models of second language acquisition are the monitor model, developed by Stephen

Krashen, and the acculturation model, developed by John Schumann. Read either Krashen (1978) or Schumann (1977). What is the role of 'learner variables' in the model you read? Are historical and structural factors included? If not, could the model be adapted to include historical and structural factors?

FURTHER READING

Krashen (1981) is an excellent example of a major theory of second language acquisition that does not include historical and structural factors. Rubin (1975), like Krashen's model, does not include historical and structural factors. Giesbers (1985) is one example of an effort to show that ideology inevitably underlies sociolinguistic theory.

THREE

Mother-tongue maintenance and second language learning

PREVIEW

Chapter 3 examines the controversy over using languages other than the dominant one for school instruction. Focusing on the debate over mother-tongue education in Britain, the chapter explores the ideological bias implicit in the Swann and Kingman reports, two British government reports that include important language-policy statements. The chapter also shows that contemporary social psychological theories of language behaviour, in particular accommodation theory, contain an implicit 'monolingual ideology' which helps to preserve the dominance of standard language varieties in education.

In every country, schools adopt one or more languages of instruction. Pupils who do not speak the language of instruction may be at a disadvantage if required to compete with native speakers. This is true for pupils who speak nonstandard varieties of the dominant language, as well as those who speak different languages. Therefore many countries provide special language classes to help pupils acquire the school language. Some schools offer classes in pupils' mother tongues. Because education plays such an important role in employment and in gaining access to political power, mother-tongue education – or its denial – is one of the most important issues in language policy and language education.

CASE: HARIB PAL

Harib Pal is a 14-year-old boy in the East End of London, whose parents came to England from Bangladesh in 1972 (cf. Orzechowska 1984). Harib was born three years later, but returned to Bangladesh with his mother from 1980 to 1983 when she was unable to find work during the recession of the early 1980s. While in Bangladesh, Harib attended school for about one year, and so he acquired only rudimentary literacy skills in Bengali. When Harib returned to England in late 1983, he attended school full time at a special language unit, a separate school for linguistic minority children that emphasized English as a second language. After two years in the unit, Harib transferred to an ordinary school where he was placed in remedial classes, but he continued to attend English classes at the special unit for three hours a week for another year.

Like his parents, Harib speaks Bengali and Sylheti, a regional language in Bangladesh. His mother understands some English, though she is embarrassed when she tries to speak it, and so she has little contact with English speakers in London. She works as a maid at a small hotel run by a local family of Bangladeshi origin, and speaks Bengali at work, though she cannot read or write Bengali. Harib's father knows enough English to do his job on the production line at a local factory. He has little contact with English-speaking co-workers, and eats his lunch with other workers from Bangladesh. He has good reading and writing skills in Bengali and can also read the Koran in Arabic. He cannot read or write English, though he has learned to recognize and understand important signs and notices. He does most of the family's shopping at stores operated by families of Bangladeshi origin in the neighbourhood where the family lives.

Harib speaks and understands English quite well when he is with other children. In the playground, he participates enthusiastically in games with English-speaking children and children of Bangladeshi origin. Occasionally, he says something in Sylheti or Bengali. When only other children of Bangladeshi origin are nearby, this presents no problem, but some English-speaking children resent it, and may insist that he stop speaking what they call 'Paki.' Like other children from Bangladeshi families, Harib tries not to speak Sylheti or Bengali when playing with English-speaking children, but it is sometimes difficult to avoid doing so, especially when he is excited and having fun.

In class, Harib has much more difficulty with English, particularly with understanding some of the vocabulary used in his school subjects. Even in the remedial classes which he attends, where many children speak English as a second language, he finds it difficult to keep up because he reads and writes very slowly in English. Often, when he tries to speak in class, he cannot remember English equivalents for Bengali or Sylheti vocabulary. Because his teacher does not understand Bengali or Sylheti and other students make fun of him if he uses a Bengali or Sylheti word, he is reluctant to speak at all. Although Harib works hard at his studies, he continues to fall behind in school and is beginning to look forward to quitting school to find a job to help out his family. But his parents firmly oppose such a move, and will insist as long as they can that he remain in school. Also, they have enrolled him in Bengali classes organized by local Bangladeshi families. Along with 40 other children divided into two classes, Harib studies Bengali literacy and culture for three hours each weekend (see Linguistic Minorities Project 1984). Although this is not enough to make rapid progress, he is gradually learning to read simple texts and to write letters to relatives in Bangladesh.

Yet, at the same time, Harib has not acquired a large Bengali vocabulary, and so when he speaks Bengali at home or with other speakers of Bengali in London, he uses some English words and phrases. Harib is also responsible for interpreting for his parents when they communicate with government officials or other monolingual speakers of English, such as his mother's doctor. At the doctor's office, Harib struggles to understand English in unfamiliar subjects that make him uncomfortable.

Harib's linguistic life is very complex. Nearly every day, he must communicate in three languages, using a range of formal and informal varieties of each, including reading and writing. Often, speakers of Bengali/Sylheti and English are present, such as in school, on the playground, in the stores, and on the streets. He constantly must select which language variety to use in each circumstance. Which variety should he use in class or in the playground? In class, for example, when he cannot think of the English vocabulary, should he use Bengali or Sylheti and rely upon other students to translate it into English for the teacher? If he does this, he incurs the disapproval of other students and the teacher. Yet this may be the most effective way to communicate what he knows and to have the chance to learn the English equivalents. On the playground, should he relax and have fun, even though this means that sometimes he will use a Bengali or Sylheti word or phrase that English-speaking students may criticize? When he speaks to another child of Bangladeshi origin in the presence of English-speaking children, should he use English? What is more important – communicating easily and quickly in Bengali or Sylheti, or conforming to the demands of English speakers? On what basis should he make these decisions?

These questions suggest that Harib faces numerous language *choices* that have consequences for the effectiveness of communication and for his relationships with friends, family, teachers, and the school system. Indeed, because the consequences of his linguistic choices determine his grades and school performance generally, as well as how he feels about being in school and about studying, these choices affect his commitment and his enthusiasm for school, as well as his future job prospects.

But is it accurate to say that Harib has 'choices' about which language variety he uses? 'Choice' suggests freedom to select from alternatives without coercion. Is Harib 'free' to decide between alternative language varieties for use in the playground and in classes? Or do external forces determine which language variety he will use in any particular circumstance? These are important and complex questions that focus on the relative roles of individual choice and collective behaviour. Because these questions involve assumptions and beliefs about what are appropriate social practices, they must be examined with respect to ideology, as well as the social system within which individual actions are given meaning. In order to better understand Harib's language 'choices' at school, we must examine the role of English and minority 'mother tongues' in British education.

MOTHER-TONGUE EDUCATION IN ENGLAND

The term 'mother tongue' is normally used in Britain to refer to the first language acquired by children. Although the term could refer to all native languages, in fact it typically refers to languages other than English. More recently, the term 'community language' has gained acceptance as a broader category that includes lingua francas and languages of literacy. Yet this term too carries the connotation of minority languages, as distinct from standard English and 'modern languages' that may be taught as school subjects (see Martin-Jones 1984).

Mother-tongue education – the use of minority students' native languages as means of instruction – is widely considered to be valuable *for some purposes* for particular students. The issue that divides educators and policymakers is the question: in what circumstances and for what purposes should mother-tongue education be encouraged by official policy?

Four major answers to this question may be distinguished. One group supports mother-tongue education for the purpose of maintaining and supporting languages other than English. This group views use of the native language as a right that government must protect, and individual bilingualism as a societal resource which should be fostered by policies that encourage it for all citizens.

A second group supports mother-tongue education as a transition to English-only classes. This groups worries that children who do not speak English may be seriously dis-advantaged by having to compete in English-medium classes. Therefore the principle of equality requires the government to provide mother-tongue classes until students are able to parti-cipate equitably in English-medium classes.

A third group supports mother-tongue literacy for business and commerce. Because bilingualism is seen as aiding inter-national business and Britain's ability to compete in the world market, classes that develop literacy in minority languages are supported, but the *right* to use the mother tongue is denied, as well as its use in ensuring equality in education. This group views languages other than English as useful for society generally, but divisive when they gain official status and are used in ways that overlap with English.

A fourth group opposes any public support for minority languages except in traditional modern-language classes, arguing that minority languages are inherently divisive and therefore the responsibility of specific ethnic groups, who may organize weekend and after-school classes for their children, but who should not be given public funds for any purpose.

Of course, the boundaries between these groups are often unclear. Some policymakers and educators, for instance, oppose the official use of languages other than English, but are uncertain how to best ensure students' rapid transition to English – whether through transitional mother-tongue classes, immersion in English, or some combination of English immersion and mother-tongue literacy. The major public policy issue is whether public funds should be used, and for what purposes.

There is now a growing literature on British mother-tongue education, along with related issues such as the organization of ESL programmes, the use of bilingual staff, local versus central control of schools, and testing and evaluation. Several reports by government agencies and private research organizations address specific policy issues. One of the most important of these is *A Language for Life*, the report of the Committee of Inquiry into the teaching of English, known as the Bullock Report after its chair, Alan Bullock (Bullock 1975). The Bullock Committee was charged with responsibility for examining all aspects of the teaching of English, including teacher training, assessment of students' progress, and steps for improving the current system. The 600-page report covered a great range of issues, including attitudes towards English, national literacy standards, the relationship between home language learning and school instruction, the teaching of reading and effective teaching methods, the relationship between language and literature, the use of drama to teach language, the relationship between speaking/listening and reading/writing, handwriting and spelling, the organization of schools and their impact on language instruction, children with special reading difficulties, adult illiteracy, libraries and language-teaching technologies, and teacher training. The Bullock Report was the first document to give primacy to a pluralist view of language education. Despite its scope, however, the report was soon overcome by the movement toward reducing the role of local school authorities and increasing that of the national government. In this movement, the pressure increased rapidly for a unified national policy on language and mother-tongue education.

In addition to the Bullock Report, the 1977 European Communities Directive on the Education of Children of Migrant Workers (European Communities 1977) also intensified the debate over mother-tongue education. The EC Directive supported policies to improve the education of linguistic minorities. At the urging of the British and German governments, however, the EC report had not included a statement supporting the right to mother-tongue education. Moreover, the report was seen by many in Britain as a form of interference in the operation of the relatively decentralized British school system, and therefore it may have exacerbated tensions rather than aided the movement to support mother-tongue education (see Linguistic Minorities Project 1985). Nevertheless, within the debate over mother-tongue education in Britain, the EC document provided strong arguments for those who favour mother-tongue classes in state schools.

One of the most visible responses the British government made to the EC Directive was the Linguistic Minorities Project (LMP) at the University of London Institute of Education. The Department of Education and Science funded the LMP in 1979 in order to measure the extent of bilingualism among the school population and the scope of mother-tongue teaching. Subsequently, the Project staff argued successfully that language in education could only be properly understood within the broader context of language in society, including how languages are acquired, their role outside school, parental attitudes, and economic differences among language groups. Thus the LMP expanded its scope to gather valuable information relevant to a broad range of language policy issues. This information was organized into four important surveys conducted during 1979–83: the Schools Language Survey, the Secondary Pupils Survey, the Mother Tongue Teaching Directory Survey, and the Adult Language Use Survey (Linguistic Minorities Project 1983, 1985). (The Mother Tongue Teaching Directory Survey gathered data on the scope and resources available to classes such as Harib's Bengali class.) Although the Project reports are not official government policy statements, their data and conclusions have become part of the policy debate, and the Project Director, Verity Saifullah Khan, has actively participated in this debate.

Without doubt the most important government document on the education of ethnic minority children in Britain is *Education for All*, known as the Swann Report after its chair, Michael Swann (Swann 1985). In addition to a final report, the Committee commmissioned studies which reviewed research on pupils of South Asian origin (Taylor 1985), Chinese origin (Taylor 1987b), and Vietnamese, Cypriot, Italian, and Ukrainian origin, as well as Romanies and Liverpool Blacks (Taylor 1987a). The Swann Report elicited a great deal of debate and comment, and is the central document guiding government policy at the present time. Therefore this report will be examined in detail below.

Two closely related reports are the interim report of the Swann Committee when it was headed by its first chair, Anthony Rampton (Rampton 1981), and a review of research into the education of Afro-Caribbean pupils (Taylor 1981), which was commissioned by the Rampton Committee. Recognizing that Afro-Caribbean children are widely subject to stereotyping treatment by educators, the Rampton Report emphasized the wide gulf in trust between schools and Afro-Caribbean families, and blamed teacher-training institutions for the failure to prepare teachers for multicultural classes. Split between committee members who wanted to examine further the impact of racism upon the education of Afro-Caribbean children and members who favoured focusing on revisions to curricula and teacher training, the Rampton Report did not fully explore the implications of its criticism of existing educational institutions. Nevertheless, its suggestion that racism is the cause of poor school performance by Afro-Caribbean children created a storm of controversy, and may have been a factor in the decision by the Conservative Minister who received the report to replace Rampton as chair. In any case, the interim Rampton Report was soon supplanted by the final Swann Committee Report issued in 1985.

Another important publication was *Education for Some*, a report on research directed by John Eggleston, funded by the government Department of Education and Science, and known as the Eggleston Report (Eggleston 1986). Carried out in 1981–82, the project examined the educational and vocational experiences of 15–18-year-old ethnic minority students. Based on survey questions, the project showed that these students had a greater tendency to persevere in school than their white peers in hopes of obtaining desirable jobs. The study concluded that racism in school and in the job market counteracted the efforts made by these young people. The title of the report was an implicit criticism of the Swann Report, and conveyed Eggleston's conclusion that major social forces, beyond factors solely within the educational system or minority families, must be considered when accounting for the differences between school performance of ethnic minorities and middle- and upper-class whites in Britain. Though its recommendations did not include proposals for significant changes in educational policy, the report was an important analysis of the impact of racism on black children in British schools.

A final key government document is the *Report of the Committee of Inquiry into the Teaching of English Language*, known as the Kingman Report after its chair, John Kingman (Kingman 1988). Focusing on the role of English in British education, the Kingman Report was issued at the height of increased concern in Britain about standards of English and the importance of English in the school system. The Kingman Report and the Swann Report, taken together, form the basis for current policies affecting mother-tongue teaching and language education in Britain. Therefore I will examine each report in turn, along with the major criticisms that have been directed against them.

THE SWANN REPORT

Summary of the Swann Report

A key goal of the Swann Report was to explain and to make policy recommendations regarding the research which has shown since the 1960s that Afro-Caribbean and other minority children consistently score lower than white children on tests of ability (e.g., IQ tests), on standardized tests of achievement, and on classroom measures such as grades. In the 1960s, the most common explanation was that an impoverished home background and culture created disadvantages which the children brought with them to the schools. Although later research raised serious questions about this explanation, it persists in most discussions of the issue. For instance, in one of the surveys of research commissioned by the Rampton Committee, the child-rearing practices of Afro-Caribbean parents were blamed for their children's school performance (Taylor 1981, pp. 42–3):

> Many writers have suggested that although West Indian [Afro-Caribbean] parents are evidently concerned about their children's development they often do seem to lack understanding of the developmental importance of play, toys, communication, and parent–child interaction in the early years. . . For example, . . . the West Indian parent does not seem to regard the importance of stimulation by conversation or use of toys as part of the function of

the baby minder. . . Since the demonstrated importance of
mother–child interaction . . . has been known for some while . . . ,
this may indicate a serious deprivation.

During the 1970s, such explanations were seriously questioned on
the grounds that they are purely speculative and reflect an
ethnocentric rather than scientific analysis. In their place, the
1970s saw a rise in explanations based upon the role of adverse
economic conditions at home and teachers' expectations and
attitudes at school. By the early 1980s, this view had evolved into
the conclusion of the Rampton Report, which explicitly blamed
societal racism for educational difficulties of minority children.
Even the Swann Report, which did not support mother-tongue
education, cited racism as one basis for the educational problems
of minority children.

Yet the growing recognition of racism in education did not lead
the Swann Committee to recommend changes in institutional
organization and power. Instead, the Committee's recommendations emphasized changing the content of educational programmes and working to improve teachers' attitudes toward
linguistic minorities and linguistic diversity. That is, it relied upon
improved educational content to resolve the negative consequences of societal racism. This proposal was based upon the
Committee's belief that racism is based on ignorance. Thus it
defined racism and prejudice as 'any mistaken impressions or
inaccurate, hearsay evidence' (Swann 1985, p. 13).

The Swann Committee argued that there must be a balance
between commonly-accepted values, practices, and procedures on
the one hand, and diverse cultures and lifestyles on the other.
Because the report blamed racism on ignorance of cultural
minorities by the majority group, it argued that racism will
disappear as members of the majority group gain accurate
information about minorities. Thus the function of education,
according to the Committee, is to counter prejudice and racism,
primarily through revised teacher training and school curricula
that are 'more responsive to the needs of ethnic minority pupils
and genuinely multicultural in character' (p. xxiii). Like other
'common-sense solutions' to complex social problems, this
proposal assumed that the schools are 'outside society' and not
characterized by racism and prejudice. Thus the Committee
defined the educational task as creating 'an overall unity of

purpose which will encompass the concept that to be British you do not have to have a white skin nor to have family origins only in this country' (p. 36). Yet, as we shall see, the Committee implied that, to be British, you do have to speak English.

The Committee's analysis of the causes of 'underachievement' placed the major blame on teachers and parents of minority children. The report blamed teachers' attitudes and expectations on what the Committee considered to be unintentional racism (p. xxii). Based on this analysis, the Swann Committee proposed 'education for all' as the educational solution to racism and the problems of minority children. 'Education for all' entails recognizing that the schools have a responsibility to properly educate all children, not merely those having difficulties. In other words, the Committee's recognition that some children suffer special disadvantage due to racism led it to the conclusion that educational programmes should not be designed solely for these children. Its main argument was that special programmes reflect and further social divisions based on racist attitudes. Thus the Committee rejected separate language programmes for linguistic and ethnic minorities and ESL students.

The Committee's proposed strategy for implementing the principle of 'education for all' involved fostering a pluralist perspective among school staff; adopting pluralism throughout the curriculum; ensuring that texts, other materials, and examinations reflect cultural diversity; holding conferences to consider the implications of education for all; and developing pilot projects to be used as examples of successful educational initiatives. This approach to the educational problems of minorities is similar to 'mainstreaming' proposals in the United States in its refusal to confront the structural basis of inequality within the school system. Chapter 5 will examine the consequences of this approach as it is applied to Southeast Asian refugees and immigrants in the USA.

In chapter 7 of the Swann Report, a number of specific recommendations were made for language education. The most important was that ESL should not be taught in separate language centres such as Harib attended, nor in separate units within schools. Instead, the Committee recommended that ESL be offered within mainstream classes as part of a comprehensive programme of language education for all children (p. 392). The basis for this recommendation was stated as follows:

We recognize that in the case of pupils of secondary school age arriving in this country with no English some form of withdrawal may at first be necessary. Nevertheless, we believe that this should take place within the mainstream school. We have already emphasised our fundamental opposition to the principle of any form of 'separate provision' which seeks to cater only for the needs of ethnic minority children since we believe that such provision merely serves to establish and confirm social and racial barriers between groups. (Swann 1985, p. 392)

A second key recommendation was that mother-tongue education should not be supported, except when minority languages are taught as school subjects within the modern-language curriculum. The Committee argued that mother-tongue classes do not help ethnic minority students, that they increase social barriers between groups, and that equality of opportunity is afforded only through ensuring that all students have a good command of English. Although the Committee recommended that bilingual approaches may be appropriate in the early years of school and that community languages may be taught in the exam years of secondary school, it recommended no provisions for mother-tongue classes in the crucial middle years of school. The Committee concluded that mother-tongue classes should only be taught in weekend, lunchtime, and after-school classes organized and funded by ethnic communities without public funds. Indeed, the Committee essentially argued that community languages other than English have no problems of survival:

> If a language is truly the mother tongue of a community and is the language needed for parent/child interaction . . . or for access to the religious and cultural heritage of the community, then we believe it will survive and flourish regardless of the provision made for its teaching and/or usage within mainstream schools. (p. 408)

The Committee did suggest, however, that school classrooms should be made available free of charge for community-based language classes.

Finally, the recommendation which the Committee believed would have the greatest impact involved teacher-training programmes. The Committee recommended that these programmes revise their curricula to foster appreciation of ethnic and linguistic diversity, and that institutions should encourage more individuals from ethnic minorities to become teachers. The Committee rejected, however, ethnic quota systems for the hiring of teaching staff.

Critique: Ideology in the Swann Report

Because of its role in recommending policy, the work of the Swann Committee has undergone extensive analysis, with detailed criticisms coming from the Director of the Linguistic Minorities Project (Khan 1985), the National Council for Mother Tongue Teaching (National Council for Mother Tongue Teaching 1985), and specialists in race relations and multicultural education (Burchell 1984; Devall 1987; M. Jones 1987; Mullard 1984). Criticisms focus on two main areas. The first is that the Report, despite references to pluralism, accepts a monolingual ideology, defining problems in such a way that minorities are shouldered with the major blame for their circumstances. A second area of criticism is that the Report ignores the relationship between language and power, and thus is inconsistent in applying its declared pluralist principles. Both criticisms draw attention to the failure of the Swann Report to consider historical and structural factors involved in issues of power, domination, and hegemony in language education.

The critique of the Swann Report prepared by the National Council for Mother Tongue Teaching (NCMTT) outlines the Committee's monolingual ideology. The NCMTT pointed out that occasional references to pluralist principles are outweighed by the assumption in the Swann Report that minority languages should be restricted to the home and to narrow community interests. For instance, the Report rejects efforts by the schools to integrate child development with native language learning: 'The role of education cannot be, and cannot be expected to be, to reinforce the values, beliefs, and cultural identity which each child brings to school' (p. 321). Instead, the Report calls merely for language-awareness classes emphasizing appreciation of language and culture.

The Swann Report further denies pluralist principles when it equates being British with speaking standard English. The Report declares, for instance, that the English language is a central unifying factor in 'being British', despite the fact that many citizens speak other languages (p. 404). By implication, other languages are divisive, and the speakers are less than British.

Furthermore, the identification of a particular language variety with national identity contradicts the fundamental principle of pluralism that there is no necessary link between one's native language and citizenship or national identity.

The Committee's identification of language and national identity depends upon an analysis which ignores the connections between language and social structure. Specifically, the Swann Report ignores evidence that standard English (SE) is associated with economic class, and instead claims that only SE is above structural categories, while varieties other than SE are associated with particularism. Moreover, Swann's faith that language loss will not happen to languages which are truly the mother tongues of living communities denies the historical connections between language, power, and domination. In the Committee's view, communities which have lost their languages are responsible for language loss, not the social, economic, and political forces which pressure those communities into English monolingualism. The Committee's proposal for mother tongue classes at lunchtime and immediately after school (p. 409) suggests that it is insensitive to the consequences of marginalization.

Swann's ahistorical and astructural analysis of language and society led the Committee to inconsistent analyses of school achievement that contradict its stated respect for language education for all. For instance, the Report acknowledges that Asian school leavers perform as well as all leavers generally, except in English language; the Report does not, however, acknowledge that these children outperform all leavers generally in Asian languages. In other words, Asian children's 'failure' to speak English as fluently as native speakers of English is seen as a serious deficit, but the accomplishment of speaking Asian languages is not acknowledged. Instead, the Report ignores the positive links between first and second language, dismisses first language literacy, and fails to consider research suggesting that children should reach a level of literacy and education in the first language before beginning work in a second language (NCMTT 1985). The result is that the Report rejects most bilingual schooling, emphasizing instead the importance of gaining fluency in English as quickly as possible (cf. Cummins and Swain 1986).

Ideology can be seen also in the Committee's analysis of the problem of 'underachievement.' The Committee accepts data showing that minority children perform more poorly than white middle-class children across a broad range of measures, including standardized test scores, graduation rates, and occupation after schooling is completed. One could define the problem, therefore, as follows (cf. Burchell 1984): what is it about schools that makes them fail to educate minority children? What is it about schools that makes the fact that children speak a language other than standard English a problem for them? Such questions define the problem as the underperformance of the schools, and places responsibility for the solution on the schools. The Swann Report does not define the problem in this way, however, but instead accepts the premise that explanations for the 'underachievement' of minority children are to be located in family structure and values, individual self-esteem, and other 'characteristics' of minority populations (see Carby 1982). Referring to Afro-Caribbean pupils, for instance, the Swann Report claimed that 'racism . . . cannot be said alone to account for the under-achievement of West Indian children. . . Evidence points to the cycle of West Indian underachievement having its roots in the pre-school years' (p. xix). Thus the Swann Report removes the problem from the institutional structure of education and places it in the minority home, family, and culture. In this way, the Report expresses neoclassical assumptions, much like the motivation research discussed in Chapter 2.

The ideological nature of this analysis can be seen clearly if we imagine a situation in which, year after year, similar proportions of white children score poorly on standardized tests, do not learn basic skills such as reading and mathematics, fail to graduate in large numbers, and end up in low-paying jobs in the peripheral economy. Middle- and upper-class white parents would demand, and school officials would enact changes in the schools to deal with these problems. Of course, this imaginary situation would never be permitted to happen, because authorities ensure that the schools do whatever is necessary to adequately educate these children. Yet precisely this situation exists for minority children in Britain as well as in the United States and other countries. Year after year officials and researchers try to determine what is wrong with the minority population that makes them perform so poorly in school, while failing to examine their own and the schools' responsibility for this pattern of inequality. (Of course, the issues are not simply language and race, but instead differences in education along class lines generally.)

experiences and prior knowledge

Thus, in its recommendations the Swann Report fails to address institutional biases. Although the Report acknowledges that the schools have failed to adequately educate minority children, it suggests that the solution to this problem is more education for teachers. But if racism in institutions is the problem, then there is no reason to expect those same institutions to develop teacher-training curricula to counter racism.

Despite these criticisms, the Swann Report remains the most influential policy statement about language education in Britain. It is the basis for ongoing debates about language curricula, about progammes for linguistic minorities, and about the causes and consequences of bilingualism. Its influence can be seen in the continuing effort of local education authorities to respond to its recommendations.

A more recent government policy statement, the Kingman Report, is a conservative attack against the principle of pluralism. Although it does not focus explicitly on the education of minority children, the Kingman Report has important implications for educational approaches to the economic and social problems of linguistic minorities.

THE KINGMAN REPORT

Summary of the Kingman Report

The *Report of the Committee of Inquiry into the Teaching of English Language*, known as the Kingman Report (Kingman 1988), was part of the state's effort to reassert the dominance of standard English. Kenneth Baker, the Secretary of State for Education and Science at the time, was a forceful proponent of a national curriculum with explicit norms and assessment standards. In order to build support for a national curriculum and assessment programme, he raised concern that standard English was being 'crowded out of the school curriculum' (Kingman 1988, p. 1), with a resulting drop in the prestige and knowledge of standard English (SE). Thus he appointed the Kingman Committee to prepare: (a) a model of English that would serve as the basis for teacher training and all aspects of English teaching; (b) recommendations for principles by which schools should teach English; and (c) recommendations for what pupils need to know about English at the ages of 7, 11, and 16. In its report, the Committee forcefully rejected what it called three 'distractions' in schooling, namely, the argument that it may be valuable for children to be exposed to varieties of English without an imposed standard; that conscious knowledge of grammar is unnecessary, often boring, and potentially harmful; and that upholding a standard variety entails supporting a social hierarchy in which speakers of SE gain advantage.

MEDIA EXAMPLE 3.1

The Kingman Model of the English Language (Source: adapted from Kingman (1988))

Part 1: The forms of the English language
1. Speech
2. Writing
3. Word forms
4. Phrase structure and sentence structure
5. Discourse structure

Part 2(i): Communication
1. Context: place/time; topic; type of discourse; what has already been said.
2. Speaker–Listener

Part 2(ii): Comprehension – some processes of understanding
1. Interpreting speech sounds
2. Working out what the speaker refers to in the world or in previous discourse
3. Working out what the speaker presupposes
4. Inferring what the speaker means

Part 3: Acquisition and development
1. Children gradually acquire the forms of Part 1.
2. Acquisition continues throughout life.

Part 4: Historical and geographical variation
1. Language changes over time.
2. Regional changes develop from population movements. The dialect used for writing may emerge as the standard language; it will share many characteristics with other related dialects.

Questions

1. The model presents a summary of what teachers are expected to know about language and language use. Do you consider the model

complete? How might teachers use the model? What else do you think teachers should know if they are to make informed decisions about pupils' language acquisition and language use?

2. In his dissenting opinion, Kingman Committee member Henry Widdowson criticized the Committee for failing to show a relationship between the model and any explicit educational objectives. What do you think should be the objectives of English language education? Does the Kingman model provide a mechanism for achieving those objectives?

The Kingman Report strongly supported the primacy of SE. In the Committee's view, SE conveys the best of the national heritage; it is the language 'we' have in common (p. 14); it is the only variety not associated with a particular geographical region (see Cameron and Bourne 1989); and it is inherently better suited for literature, literacy, and the transmission of culture.

The Kingman Committee's analysis of language variation is the key to understanding this view of SE in English society. The only source of variation acknowledged by the Committee is geographical. The standard language is seen as the variety used for writing, which 'will, of course, share many characteristics with the other related dialects' (Kingman 1988, figure 5). In the Committee's view, SE is not the variety spoken by a particular class or other structural group, but rather an overarching variety available to the entire nation. Indeed, the Committee metaphorically describes SE as a great resource *equally* available to all: SE is 'like a great social bank on which we draw and to which we all contribute' (p. 14). The Report does not consider whether the language of some groups may be more closely tied to the 'bank' of SE than others, or whether some groups may profit more than others from the dominance of SE. Rather than viewing judgements of quality (e.g., beauty, explicitness) as the arbitrary result of the hegemony of speakers of the standard, the Report implicitly argues that SE is in fact of a higher quality than nonstandard varieties, and particularly suited to its position as the standard.

The Committee's recommendations reflect its emphasis on SE. All primary and secondary schools should designate a language consultant to coordinate the teaching of SE. A national committee should draw up attainment targets for different grade levels, and national tests should be developed to assess pupils' achievement in them. All teacher-training institutions should develop pre-service and in-service courses using the Committee's model of English. Additional government funds should be earmarked for upgrading the teaching of SE and a National Language Project should implement and develop the Committee's recommendations further. The first steps to implement these recommendations took place in late 1989 (Department of Education and Science 1989).

The imposition of attainment targets means that language variation must be ignored or suppressed. This is because linguistic variation is not easily tested. Clearly the intent of these recommendations is to reassert the dominance of SE throughout the educational system and to resist the movement towards mother-tongue education in primary and secondary schools. Thus the Kingman Report seeks to implement the monolingual ideology implicit in the Swann Report, while rejecting the pluralist principles to which the Swann Report paid lip service.

Critique: Ideology in the Kingman Report

Through its attempt to associate SE with the nation and to deny its association with class and other structural categories, the Kingman Report implicitly rejects a historical–structural analysis of SE which associates standard varieties with hegemonic domination of society by groups having control of economic resources and political power. It does this by emphasizing SE grammar (called 'knowledge about language' in the Report) as a mechanism for national unity. The Report argues that only SE is a truly 'national' language representative of all citizens, while minority languages and nonstandard varieties of English are representative of specific groups. Indeed, the Committee implies that citizenship entails an implicit duty to learn SE, and that participation in society is dependent upon knowledge of the standard. Language education policies recommended by the Kingman Report follow this logic. Mother-tongue teaching is rejected. English is assumed to be the first language and the medium of instruction for all pupils, and varieties other than SE are alien, the temporary result of the accidents of history rather than essential features of twentieth century migration of labour (Cameron and Bourne 1989).

The identification of SE with the nation and with English citizenship assumes that the standard variety is *normal*. That is, by accepting the view that SE is the best that has been written in English, the Kingman Report denies that the standard is essentially the arbitrary result of domination by its speakers. Instead, the Report implies that SE is the standard because it is better than other varieties. By viewing SE as a 'national heritage,' the Report advocates SE as the centre of a uniform national curriculum designed to produce a common culture. Although Kingman, like Swann, uses some of the rhetoric of pluralism, its assumptions and recommendations inevitably push nonstandard varieties and minority languages to secondary status and associate them with the home and narrow 'community' interests.

In his dissenting report, Committee member Henry Widdowson pointed out that the Report failed to examine adequately the complexities of adult language use, and therefore it could not provide a rationale for its proposals for preparing pupils for the language demands of adulthood. He criticized the Committee for failing to provide a rationale for its recommendations, noting that this is particularly important in the area of language education, where 'prejudice and unfounded assertion' are so common.

Thus by accepting the 'normal', 'common-sense' policy of making SE the language of all instruction, the Kingman report represents a deliberate move away from the pluralist philosophy voiced in the Bullock Report and reiterated occasionally in parts of the Swann Report. That this policy inevitably grants advantage to children whose home language is SE – and disadvantages immigrants and native speakers of nonstandard varieties of English – is never acknowledged. In this way, the policy is a clear example of ideology, and its impact is to preserve and protect the hegemonic domination of the educational system by SE speakers.

MEDIA EXAMPLE 3.2

Prince of Wales says English is taught 'bloody badly'
'The people in my office can't write properly
. . . I have to correct all the letters myself'
BY DAVID TYTLER
EDUCATION EDITOR

The Prince of Wales said yesterday that English was taught 'so bloody badly' that even his own office staff could not speak or write the language properly.

The Prince said: 'All the people in my office can't speak properly, can't write properly and can't punctuate. I have to correct all the letters myself. English is taught so bloody badly.

'I do not believe English is being taught properly. You cannot educate people properly unless you do it on a basic framework and drilling system.'

The Prince, educated at Gordonstoun, Geelong Grammar School, Australia, and Trinity College, Cambridge (where he read History), gave his views on the country's schools – and his staff of 20 – to a group of senior businessmen and chief education officers at the launch in London of the Foundation for Education Business Partnerships, which is aimed at developing closer links between schools and industry.

The Prince, who gained two A levels – a B in history and a C in French – said: 'It is a fundamental problem. We have got to produce people who can write proper English if we want to produce people who can write good plays and good literature for the future. It cannot be done by the present system . . . and the nonsense academics come up with.'

The Prince received some support from Mr Kenneth Baker, Secretary of State for Education and Science, who said: 'Prince Charles echoes the concerns of many parents. That is why we are introducing a national curriculum with English as a core subject.

'We have already set out standards for seven year olds which focus on reading, writing, speaking, grammar, spelling and punctuation. High standards have to start in primary schools.'

Mr Baker has fought a running battle with educationists on the teaching of English grammar.

Last week the National Curriculum Council published English guidelines for five to 16-year-olds which do not recommend a return to traditional grammar teaching. The working party, chaired by Professor Brian Cox of Manchester University, agreed that all children should have a knowledge of grammar and know how to speak and write standard English, although phrases such as 'we was' were acceptable at home and between friends.

Mr Doug McAvoy, deputy general secretary of the National Union of Teachers, the largest teachers' union, said: 'Prince Charles should stick to the things he knows about from first hand. It certainly is not teaching and he has not received the benefits of a state education.

'To motivate children, you have to make lessons exciting and interesting, and you do not do that by teaching grammar by rote.'

Mr Nigel de Gruchy, deputy general secretary of the National Association of Schoolmasters and Union of Women Teachers, said: 'I did not realize the Royal Prerogative meant you could ignore all the evidence. More children pass more examinations than ever before. He probably does not pay enough to attract the right quality of people to type his letters.'

Mr de Gruchy added: 'If he has to swear, he is proving that the public schools are as bad as the state ones. It is a case of the pot calling the kettle black.'

Mr Walter Ievers, President of the National Association of Headteachers, said: 'The fact is that the vast majority of schools are doing a very good job. There is no evidence that in the past years people could write and spell correctly to a greater extent than they do at the moment.'

The Prince told the conference that as Chancellor of the University of Wales he had tried to persuade academics to seek help from business-men, but added: 'There is a ghastly hiatus and nobody seems to do any-thing. People do need shaking up.

'Civil Servants do not always know what is going on and Government is more likely to respond to ideas from business. The point is not to expect that business will do everything for the Government by putting in money and resources, but by generating new ways and new ideas of looking at these problems which will make the Govern-ment think "Thank God someone has done the thinking for us," and get to work on these ideas.'

Expressing his concern for the underprivileged, Prince Charles said: 'There is this overriding social problem in which people find themselves when they are out of school. There is no encouragement from parents which disadvantages the children through all their life. How do you get over that lack of encouragement?'

The 12 or so members of the Prince's staff working at St James's Palace yesterday refused to take his criticisms personally. One said: 'It does not appear as an attack on us but rather a way of drawing attention to a general problem in which the Prince drew on his own personal experience.'

Secretaries said they tried hard to get the letters from the Prince's office absolutely right, but added, 'We are human.'

The Prince's office is headed by Sir John Riddell, his Private Secretary, who was recruited from international banking. His deputy, Mr David Wright, is on secondment from the Foreign Office. There are two assistant private secretaries, Commander Richard Aylard, who also acts as the comptroller of the Prince and Princess's household, and Mr Guy Salter, a businessman on secondment from Business in the Community.

The office is completed by Mr Richard Arbiter, recruited from Independent Radio News to be press secretary to the Prince and Princess of Wales and assistant press secretary to the Queen; former Scottish newspaper executive Mr Philip Mackie, the Prince's media advisor; and Commander Alistair Watson, his equerry.

Posts are advertised and staff are recruited from secretarial colleges, agencies or by personal recommenda-tion after a shorthand and typing test and full interview.

● Plea to landowners: The Prince of Wales, in his capacity as Duke of Cornwall, and other great institutional landowners, such as the Church of England and Oxford and Cambridge universities, should be encouraged to improve their properties or release more land for development, it was said yesterday. The Government Property Services Agency should also be com-pelled to release large tracts of publicly owned land and property or be disbanded, according to Mr John Redwood, Tory MP for Wokingham, in a Conservative Political Centre pamphlet, *Rebuilding Britain*.

Mr Redwood, who as head of the Prime Minister's Policy Unit at No 10 did some of the Government's earlier thinking on urban regeneration before he became an MP, said that a too rigid green-belt policy had put too much pressure on the South-east.

Source: *The Times* of London, 29 June 1989

Questions

1. According to Prince Charles, the reason for teaching everyone to 'write proper English' is that only this will ensure that the schools will 'produce people who can write good plays and good literature'. Is there any evidence that the teaching of standard English improves the quality of literature? Is this a good reason for requiring everyone to study standard English?
2. Prince Charles blames parents for pupils' problems when he says 'there is no encouragement from parents which disadvantages the children through all their life'. How is this an example of neoclassical assumptions about language learning?

MEDIA EXAMPLE 3.3

Proper English, Yes; But Educationists, No

BY THEODORE LEVITT
CAMBRIDGE, MASS.

I grew up in a small farm town in Germany where all of us spoke an ungrammatical version of Plattdeutsch (low German). In our two-room schoolhouse, we were taught, with the discipline of a stick, to speak and write Hochdeutsch (or high German) – the German version of the 'Queen's English.'

When I was 10 years old, my family, none of us knowing any English, came to Dayton, Ohio, and lived in what would now be called a slum neighbourhood. I learned English on the streets – the crude language of poorly educated migrants from Appalachia. 'Briarhoppers,' they were called contemptuously. But in elementary school, we all learned to speak and write standard English, with regular rigorous drills in grammar. There were no exceptions for my brother and me.

Not long ago, Prince Charles attacked a British Government committee report that recommended against the 'too early' teaching of standard English to schoolchildren. The committee advocated toleration of the children's own 'equally valid' irregular forms of English, such as 'he aint' and 'done good.'

This echoed a longstanding debate in America. Most recently, the chairman of the National Association for the Teaching of English argued in favor of a 'contextualized' approach to teaching – for example, accepting the use of 'black English' in the classroom to help black children learn their lessons more readily than via an imposed standard English. The rationale is that they'd be more comfortable learning in the dialect of their families and their streets.

In my family, in Dayton, we spoke a jumbled stew of Plattdeutsch, Hochdeutsch, briarhopper English,

---

Theodore Levitt, professor of business administration at Harvard, is editor of the Harvard Business Review.

standard English, occasional pieces of Hebrew, and, when relatives visited, fractured Yiddish. We children were often confused as to which was which and what was right.

A remarkable number of my colleagues at Harvard grew up in homes where they, too, spoke 'contextually' – Yiddish, German, Italian and God-knows-what in the streets. Today, they are accomplished standard English-speakers, with Nobel, literary and other honorific recognitions. Many are members of the American Academy of Arts and Sciences.

The same God saved us all from being permanently disabled by the stupid good intentions of unctuous educationists – who, one supposes, were never young in the streets or experienced the exhilaration and rewards of getting corrected in standard public schools.

Source: *New York Times*, 18 September 1989

Questions

1. Professor Levitt's opinion is that nonstandard varieties of English should not be tolerated in schools. What reasons does he offer for his opinion?

2. What does the article mean by 'contextualized' language use? What is wrong with it, according to the article?

3. According to his description, what were the roles of standard and nonstandard varieties in Professor Levitt's childhood? Does his description suggest that tolerating nonstandard varieties in school will cause damage to today's children?

4. Professor Levitt and his distinguished friends spoke a multitude of varieties in childhood and were 'often confused as to which was which and what was right', yet they won Nobel prizes and became members of the American Academy of Arts and Sciences. Why would today's children be 'confused' by policies that permit additional varieties in schools?

5. Both media examples criticize 'academics' and 'educationists'. These appeals to 'common people' in contrast to elite educators are

made in an effort to gain popular support for standard English. How is this an example of hegemony through the 'manufacture of consent'?

Beyond Swann and Kingman

In 1989, the principles and policies outlined in the Swann and Kingman reports were gradually being implemented. The Home Office continued to provide some funds under the Local Government Act to local authorities to staff progammes for ethnic minorities, though the scope and quality of these programmes varied considerably. These funds did not restrict the focus or level of English classes, and there was no tie between social security benefits and enrolment, except that students were permitted to attend only 12 hours per week. In reality, most ESL classes were at basic levels.

Similar limits on language education occur in employment training programmes funded by the government's Training Agency. In the past, such progams were full-time courses (36 hours per week) specifically designed for ESL students, but those programmes have been eliminated. In their place, supplementary funds were made available to employment training programmes enrolling a significant number of ESL trainees. This has meant a general deterioration in both vocational and language programmes, which is likely to have the effect of making it more difficult for people who do not speak English to obtain jobs.

In mid-1989, the National Curriculum Council followed the lead of the Kingman Report by issuing standards for the teaching of English that called for more rigorous attention to the grammar of standard English and renewed emphasis on Wordsworth, Dickens, and Shakespeare (Department of Education and Science 1989). The original draft of the report was criticized by the Secretary of State for Education and Science for being too lax in its attention to standard English. Thus the final report was an unequivocal declaration of the primacy of standard English in the British school system.

MOTHER TONGUES AND THEORIES OF LANGUAGE USE

A central ideological underpinning of the Swann and Kingman reports is the assumption that there is a natural process of language change which leads to *appropriate* patterns of language use. The clearest example is the statement in the Swann Report that languages which are truly the mother tongues of living communities will be maintained without official intervention. This assumption rests upon the notion that individuals 'choose' to speak the language variety which they believe is appropriate for the situation. If an individual 'decides' to stop using his or her mother tongue in certain settings, it is because that language is no longer seen as being appropriate. In the case of Harib, this panglossian faith in individual choice interprets his 'decision' to speak English in school as the result of his successful acquisition of the sociolinguistic rules of language use. Although he has the alternative of choosing to speak Bengali or Sylheti, he does not exercise this choice because he understands that it would be inappropriate.

Such an interpretation of language behaviour relies upon an implicit notion of natural law, that is, that 'free' human interaction 'naturally' structures society. Of course, any theory based upon a human conception of natural law is inevitably ideological, as it provides a powerful argument that current social practices reflect natural principles and that groups which propose change are disruptive of the natural system. Examples of theories which depend upon an implicit notion of natural law include language change theory, which asserts that 'natural' language change, as distinct from 'planned' change, evolves from 'natural' human interaction (see Rubin and Jernudd 1971); language planning theory, which assumes that successful plans are those which follow the 'natural course' of social change (see Haugen 1966; Jernudd and Das Gupta 1971; Tauli 1968); and micro-sociolinguistics, which interprets the apparent agreement among individuals to use particular language varieties in particular settings as the result of the acquisition of appropriateness rules (see Fishman 1972b; Ervin-Tripp 1971). In such research, the role of power and domination is ignored.

But perhaps nowhere is the ideological faith in natural law more central to a popular and powerful theory than in accommodation theory, identified primarily with the work of Howard Giles and his colleagues. Because accommodation theory was developed primarily in Britain, it is appropriate in this chapter to examine the ideology of accommodation theory, particularly as it relies upon notions of 'choice' to explain the structure of interactions taking place between Harib, his teachers, and other speakers of English – individuals with different positions in the hierarchy of power and domination.

ACCOMMODATION THEORY

The principles of accommodation theory

One of the most important areas of language research is face-to-face interaction between individuals from different ethnolinguistic groups. What happens when individuals interact who are members of groups in an unequal power relationship, such as Harib and his teachers? Accommodation theory seeks to explain the structure of such interactions by examining the adjustments individuals make to their speech.

The scope of accommodation theory can be seen by a brief list of some of the research topics examined within the theory. Accommodation theory has been used in the conceptualization of social identity (Bourhis and Giles 1977), language attitudes, (Giles, Hewstone, and Ball 1983; Ryan and Giles 1982), and inter-ethnic relations (Giles and Saint-Jacques 1979). Giles and Byrne (1982) have developed an approach to second language acquisition based upon accommodation theory, while Giles and Hewstone (1982) have sought to integrate social-psychological and cognitive variables within the theory. Beebe and Zuengler (1983) have used accommodation theory to explain style shifting in second language dialects. The relationship between values, language, and cultural differentiation has been examined in the Welsh–English context (Johnson and Giles 1982). Price, Fluck and Giles (1983) have examined the effects of the language of testing upon pre-adolescents' attitudes toward Welsh and varieties of English. Giles, Rosenthal, and Young (1985) have explored how Anglos and Greeks in Australia interpret the social forces affecting language. Also in Australia, Ozolins (1988) has used key concepts of the theory to explain patterns of language maintenance and loss. Saint-Blancat (1985) has examined the socio-psychological strategies of Valdotans in Italy. More recently, Giles and his colleagues have examined overaccommodation and underaccommodation in interaction between the young and elderly, particularly their role in expressing stereotypes and in interpreting behaviour (Giles 1989; Coupland, Coupland, Giles, and Henwood 1988).

Accommodation theory includes a set of descriptive terms used to analyse the adjustments speakers make in interactions. The key terms are as follows:

1. *Convergence* refers to speakers' adjustments that make their speech more similar to that of an interlocutor. These adjustments may involve lexical, morphological, syntactic, or phonological changes.
2. *Divergence* refers to speakers' adjustments that make their speech less similar to that of an interlocutor.
3. *Speech maintenance* refers to no change in an individual's speech. Accommodation theorists interpret this as a refusal to converge, and therefore as one particular type of divergence.
4. *Psychological convergence* refers to a situation in which the speaker intends to converge, but may in fact diverge linguistically. This often happens when the individual converges toward a stereotype of the speech of the interlocutor (e.g., as in hypercorrection).

These terms are further refined to describe adjustments of individuals having unequal status:

1. *Upward convergence* occurs when the individual of lower status adjusts toward the individual with higher status.
2. *Downward convergence* occurs when the individual of higher status adjusts toward the individual with lower status.
3. *Upward divergence* occurs when the individual of higher status emphasizes those features of his or her speech that mark higher status.
4. *Downward divergence* occurs when the individual of lower status emphasizes features that mark lower status.

Although these terms were initially proposed to describe face-to-face interaction, they have been extended to the process of second language acquisition and language loss. For instance, Trudgill (1981) proposes two types of accommodation: short-term accommodation, which occurs when individuals adjust their speech in face-to-face interaction, and long-term accommodation, which refers to shifts in language over time. That is, accommodation theory views language learning and language loss as two types of long-term accommodation.

Accommodation theory seeks to explain language learning and language loss with reference to the *ethnolinguistic vitality* of groups. Ethnolinguistic vitality is measured with reference to three sets of structural variables: status, demographics, and institutional support (Husband and Khan 1982). Status variables refer to a group's economic resources, its social status, and the prestige of its language. Demographic variables include the number of speakers of a language, their distribution relative to speakers of other languages, and population trends measured primarily by birth rates and migration. Institutional support refers to the representation of speakers of a language within formal and informal institutions. According to accommodation theory, language groups have greater ethnolinguistic vitality if their languages have higher status, favourable demographic variables such as rising birth rates, and significant institutional support.

The predictive power of the theory consists of its capacity for using measures of status, demographics, and institutional support to predict language acquisition, language loss, and changes in patterns of bilingualism and language use. For our purposes, the key prediction is that mother tongues of communities with high ethnolinguistic vitality will be retained, while those with low ethnolinguistic vitality will tend to be replaced by the dominant language. This is essentially the same prediction as that made by the Swann Committee when it claimed that 'true' mother tongues will survive without official intervention.

Beebe (1988), a supporter of accommodation theory, claims that it has powerful predictive capacity because it combines four social psychological theories into a unified theory of human linguistic behaviour. The first of these subsumed theories, *similarity attraction theory*, claims that people are attracted to those whom they perceive as having similar beliefs, values, and attitudes. This is the basis for linguistic convergence, as well as the argument behind assimilation programmes, such as the one for Southeast Asians in the United States (see Chapter 5), that seek to change immigrants' values, attitudes and beliefs so that they more closely resemble those of the dominant group. *Social exchange theory* argues that the decision to converge or diverge is based upon cost–benefit analysis. For instance, children have the choice of incurring the cost of teachers' disapproval of their own non-standard variety, and in return they can obtain the benefit of peer approval. According to accommodation theory, this cost–benefit analysis explains choices such as Harib's. *Causal attribution theory* assumes that individuals seek to attribute motive to convergence and divergence. In some circumstances, for example, convergence may be interpreted as an expression of solidarity, while in others it may be seen as a manipulative attempt to get something. Finally, *ingroup distinctiveness theory* seeks to explain linguistic and cultural variation by claiming that groups look for ways to increase their distinctiveness in a way that seems favourable to them. Thus the tendency towards accommodation is continually offset by the tendency to preserve differences.

Accommodation theory describes Harib's use of English at school as upward accommodation to his teacher and his classmates. When he inadvertently uses Bengali or Sylheti with his peers, he is psychologically converging by expressing his sense of friendship with them, though linguistically his utterances are not convergent to English speakers. His 'decision' to use English at school is explained as a result of his cost–benefit analysis of the social value of English for gaining the approval of his peers and his teacher, as well as his desire to get good grades. His difficulty learning English is seen as resulting from the relatively high ethnolinguistic vitality of the Bangladeshi community, as indicated by the large number of Sylheti and Bengali speakers in Harib's neighbourhood, the prevalence of community stores and other institutions, and the popularity of the Bengali community school which Harib attends.

Critique: The ideology of accommodation theory

As the analysis of Harib's linguistic situation suggests, accommodation theory locates the explanation for individual language behaviour in the individual, and the explanation for language acquisition and loss in characteristics of the minority group. As a result, the theory ignores key historical and structural variables that explain the range of 'choices' available and the constraints operating upon individuals that determine the meaning of their 'choices'.

Husband and Khan (1982) point out that the failure to consider historical and structural factors means that accommodation theory relies upon variables that are not clearly distinguished or motivated by an underlying social theory. For instance, 'social status' and 'economic wealth' are analysed as distinct, independent variables affecting ethnolinguistic vitality, despite the fact that social status is based, at least in part, upon economic factors and upon the hierarchical (class) structure of society. Because these variables are not independent, any measure of ethnolinguistic vitality based upon the sum of social status, economic wealth, and other variables is necessarily confounded. The lack of any social theory to generate a list of distinct variables leads to endless debates aimed at achieving a consensus about the best list, but not a theoretically based one. In their response to this criticism, Johnson, Giles and Bourhis (1983) admit that these variables are often confounded, but argue that the relationship between them remains a matter for further empirical study.

A second difficulty with an ahistorical and astructural analysis also involves measuring ethnolinguistic vitality. One measure of vitality is the socio-historical status of a language – its rich history that symbolizes a group's collective struggle (cf. Fishman 1972a). Accommodation theory assumes that each group has an objective history, and therefore that some groups have a richer history with greater socio-historical status than other groups. (Giles and his colleagues acknowledge that dominant groups may manipulate perceptions of history – Johnson, Giles and Bourhis 1983). A historical–structural perspective, however, emphasizes that history itself is shaped by relationships of power and domination. Groups that control the writing and dissemination of history are able to elaborate a rich linguistic heritage, shaping it into a prestigious story of achievement, while the history of subordinate languages may be ignored or denigrated. Thus colonial languages are typically described as having a rich literary heritage, elaborate stylistic variation, and powerful artistic achievements worthy of respect, preservation, and transmission through the ages. In contrast, the languages of colonized peoples are typically described as subordinate and traditional, and lacking higher literary forms. These assessments of value must be understood as reflections of relationships of power and domination rather than 'objective' linguistic or historical 'facts'. By ignoring such issues, accommodation theory provides theoretical support for existing relationships of power and domination. In this sense, accommodation theory is fundamentally ideological.

Accommodation theory is also astructural in its reliance on the imprecise category 'ethnolinguistic group' and its failure to consider class, gender, age, and other structural divisions (Husband and Khan 1982). In addition, the conceptualization of 'vitality' assumes that it is a characteristic of minority groups rather than a reflection of the dynamic relationship between groups. Thus accommodation theory does not capture the impact on individuals of the competition over control of economic resources and power. Let us take the example of the child whose persistent use of a nonstandard variety in school elicits the teacher's disapproval. Accommodation theory analyses this action as a refusal to converge upward, resulting from the child's preference for the benefits of peer approval rather than the teacher's approval. Moreover, the child is seen as being willing to incur the costs of the teacher's disapproval, such as low grades. This analysis fails to focus attention on the key fact that the teachers' disapproval is a result of his or her membership in the dominant group, while the child's action is interpreted as 'refusal to converge' only because the use of the mother tongue in school is defined as inappropriate within the hegemonic system. Within a historical–structural perspective, what is interesting about the teacher–child interaction is not that the child 'refuses' to converge, but rather that the position of the mother tongue in the social system is such that its use is interpreted as 'refusal', as 'failure' to cooperate, or as 'opposition' to the teacher's authority. The relationship between the dominant and subordinate groups – a relationship that fundamentally involves power and inequality – must be seen as the ground for ascribing meaning to language behaviour. By ignoring issues of power and domination, accommodation theory cannot adequately ground its analysis of language behaviour.

The failure to consider issues of power and domination has another implication. Accommodation theory does not provide an analysis of the sources of the costs and benefits of the choices available to individuals. Why does Harib have to decide between approval of teachers or peers? It is because Sylheti and Bengali, which are not accorded official status, are subordinate to SE. Speakers of the dominant variety do not face such a choice. In face-to-face interaction, the consequences of converging or diverging are not determined by the individuals involved. Rather, the range of available choices and their consequences are a result of the historical–structural relationship between languages and the groups which speak them. In a job interview, for example, the subordinate individual seeking the job must decide how and to what extent convergence will help or hinder getting the job: the wrong decision can mean unemployment. The interviewer, on the other hand, while also facing decisions about whether to converge or diverge, does not face consequences involving equivalent economic hardship. Moreover, the linguistic repertoires of the participants are determined by their class and associated educational level. The point is that, in job interviews and school playgrounds, the choices available to individuals about the kinds of accommodation they may make are constrained by the historical and structural relationship between their languages and the groups to which they belong. By ignoring the factors that constrain speech adjustments, accommodation theory fails to acknowledge that adjustment to speech (accommodation) is a dependent variable. Moreover, the fact that language behaviour is linked to these consequences at all – that the failure to converge properly will mean that the subordinate individual is labelled as 'uneducated', 'stupid', or 'unemployable' – is a reflection of the domination of one group by another. In its analysis of such unequal interactions, accommodation theory does not address the source of the consequences of individual choice, or the reasons for the linkage between language and power that the consequences of individual choice imply. As a result, the theory cannot adequately explain language loss.

Like neoclassical theory generally (see Chapter 2), accommodation theory also cannot deal with coercion. The theory explains language loss and language shift as due to low ethnolinguistic vitality. When applied to cases involving extreme coercion, the failure of the theory becomes obvious. To assert that the shift to German among Slavs in Austria under Nazism reflects low ethnolinguistic vitality utterly fails to capture the key role that power and coercion played in their lives. Although less extreme, the forms of coercion facing Harib exert a parallel influence over his language behaviour. The survival of minority languages is not simply a function of the *internal* vitality of minority groups, but rather the strength of the dominant group and the historical consequences of hegemony.

A final problem with accommodation theory involves its perspective toward second language acquisition. One of the uses of the theory has been to predict which minority groups will become fluent in dominant languages. For example, Giles and Byrne (1982) propose general characteristics of linguistic minorities that will facilitate or impede second language learning. They argue that a strong link between the mother tongue and ethnic identity, as well as high ethnolinguistic vitality and clearcut group boundaries, make it likely that subordinate group members will not become fluent in a dominant language. Under such circumstances, the group may adopt 'non-assimilation' as a conscious programme to maintain cultural distinctiveness, and the group may favour policies that support its mother tongue. Giles and Byrne also argue that a weak link between the mother tongue and identity, as well as low vitality and open group boundaries, will facilitate second language learning.

A major difficulty with this explanation for second language learning is that it is without empirical support. It assumes that individuals who identify with their mother tongue cannot also be fully bilingual, and that bilingualism depends upon losing one's identification with a non-dominant group. In these assumptions, accommodation theory accepts the hegemonic ideology that links language and national identity and that views bilingualism as a characteristic of marginal people (cf. Husband and Khan 1982). Most strikingly, it denies the obvious fact that many people who strongly identify with a minority group also speak dominant languages. Thus it provides a theoretical justification for language education programmes that seek to weaken learners' ties to their mother tongue and their community.

CONCLUSION: MOTHER-TONGUE EDUCATION AND HARIB'S LANGUAGE CHOICES

The debate over mother-tongue education in Britain has continued with a great intensity since the late 1960s. After two decades, the government has clearly allied itself with the view that mother tongues are appropriate as school subjects only, and should not be supported as part of a commitment to a genuinely pluralist society in which linguistic diversity is maintained.

Indeed, the terms of the debate over mother-tongue education reflect the dominant monolingual ideology. Calling minority education 'mother-tongue' education implies that the dominant group has no mother tongue, no ethnicity, and no group boundaries. Thus the Kingman Report claims that the 'bank' of standard English is equally available to everyone, and that everyone can acquire it (draw from it) or contribute to it through the influence of their language upon it. There is, of course, considerable evidence that this is not an accurate reflection of the language situation in Britain (Hewitt 1986; Trudgill 1984). Yet this view is adopted even by members of linguistic minorities. For instance, an applicant to an American graduate programme who was born in India sought to demonstrate her commitment to English by giving assurance that she no longer 'jabbered away in Hindi' as she had when she was young. The hegemony of the dominant monolingual ideology is evidenced in such 'consent' by minorities.

It is also significant that there is no official discussion of programmes for the majority operated by the minority (cf. Pattanayak 1987). This is because the majority has been de-ethnized, its language de-nationalized, and its educational system defined as 'education for all'. As a result, there is little official recognition that the problems of minority pupils are fundamentally not due to their choices, but rather are located in the institutions which have failed to educate them.

The work of experts must also be seen as contributing to linguistic inequality. By studying minority groups rather than the educational system which fails them, researchers locate the problem within the minority population. By viewing the standard language as a solution to inequality rather than a cause, researchers imply that the mother tongue is the source of problems and that multilingualism is the aberrant exception. By adopting ahistorical and astructural theories such as accommodation theory, experts support current patterns of inequality.

It is within this framework that Harib's language 'choices' at school must be reconsidered. It is significant that neoclassical analyses of Harib's language 'choices' ignore those of his teachers, his friends, school officials, and others who benefit from rules for 'appropriate' linguistic practices. His teacher 'chooses' not to learn Bengali or Sylheti, despite having many pupils of Bangladeshi origin. School officials 'choose' to define Harib's use of his mother tongue as lack of cooperation or resistance, rather than the most effective means to express himself. Because teachers and school officials are more powerful than Harib, their 'choices' preclude Harib's 'choice' of speaking Bengali or Sylheti at school. Thus Harib must speak English in class if he wants to be a 'good' student, and he must try to avoid Bengali and Sylheti in the playground if he wants to have English-speaking friends. The alternative that might be best for Harib – for his teachers and friends to learn Bengali or Sylheti – is not considered. In this sense, Harib's use of English, Bengali and Sylheti does not involve 'choice' at all, if choice means the freedom to select from alternatives without coercion. Instead, his language behaviour involves the dynamic interaction between his linguistic repertoire and the system of social and economic inequality in which he lives.

FOR DISCUSSION

1. In health care, as in schools, immigrants face the problem of speaking a language in which they may not be fluent in situations having important consequences to communicative action. The two most common ways immigrants and doctors communicate are through translators (often immigrant children such as Harib) and through the immigrants' use of simplified English medical vocabulary. Rarely, if ever, do the doctors learn the language of their immigrant patients. Yet it might be easier for a few doctors to learn medical vocabulary in a minority language than for hundreds or thousands of minority patients to learn English medical vocabulary. Why is it so rare for doctors to learn the patients' language, despite the fact that it may be simpler and more efficient than the current system? Consider also a similar solution to the educational problems of children who speak minority languages. What would be required for their teachers to learn the language of their pupils? Why is this not done in England, the United States, and elsewhere?

2. Consider your own language. What nonstandard dialects are there? Do you know anyone who speaks a nonstandard dialect? What variety do they use in school? In class? In the playground? What would happen to them if they consistently spoke their nonstandard native dialect in class?

FOR ACTION

1. Visit a class in a bilingual education programme. What kind of programme is it? Who is enrolled in the programme? What are their native languages? What is the purpose of the programme? Observe how the languages are used in class. Are both languages used in a single class? Do pupils ask questions in their native language(s)? What language is used by the teacher?

2. An interesting group project would be to document the language behaviour of a bilingual individual who uses two or more languages each day. Try to obtain permission to accompany a bilingual person for an entire day. Keep notes about the circumstances in which each language variety is used. Who are the interlocutors? What is the setting? What is the topic of conversation? After you have had time to review your notes, ask the person to explain why particular languages were used in particular circumstances. Find out what it would mean to use a different language in particular circumstances.

FURTHER READING

The two most useful reports of the Linguistic Minorities Project are Linguistic Minorities Project (1983, 1985). A good description of the complex linguistic life of children such as Harib is Orzechowska (1984). A useful summary of accommodation theory is Beebe (1988), while the most important critique of the theory is Husband and Khan (1982).

FOUR

Modernization and English language teaching

PREVIEW

Chapter 4 examines two aspects of the role of ESL in 'modernization' theory: (1) ideological assumptions underlying the view of English as a practical tool for modernization; (2) the relationship between modern ESL teaching methods and issues of power. The chapter focuses on two countries in which ESL has played an important role in modernization efforts: Iran and China.

One of the major justifications for requiring immigrants in Britain and elsewhere to learn English is that it will benefit them economically by helping them find work. This argument is also used to justify the spread of English to countries in which it is not spoken as a mother tongue. In Third World countries in Asia and Africa, English is seen as an essential tool for importing Western technologies and building economic ties with Europe and North America. As countries around the world seek to 'modernize', English teaching and learning play a key role.

CASE: PAULA MARTINSON

Paula Martinson is an English teacher from London with 21 years of experience. During the early 1970s, she taught for the British Council in Africa and at a university in Eastern Europe. Then she got a job in Iran, and was teaching ESL there until just before the fall of the Shah in 1979. With less than one week's notice, she left Iran just after the triumphant return from France of the Ayatollah Khomeini. Finding herself suddenly without a job, she spent nearly three months looking for work before she found a low-paying and unexciting position at a local English-language academy just outside London.

In late 1989, Martinson decided to accept a job training ESL teachers in China. Like Iran before the revolution, China is hiring teachers and trainers as part of its modernization drive. The job pays well, and, like others in her profession, Martinson is attracted by the sense of adventure China offers and is intrigued by the dramatic changes that seem to be underway there. But she worries about the uncertainty of working in China, particularly since the student demonstrations in mid-1989 and the government's military response. In Iran, she learned that political changes can have a major impact on the demand for ESL. Her work in China will depend in part upon the likelihood that China will continue on its path of modernization.

Trainers in China are hired as 'foreign experts' to prepare Chinese specialists to modernize the nation's English teaching programme. Martinson sees her job as bringing modern ESL practices to China. To do this, she must decide which textbooks and materials she should bring with her, and which teaching methods would be most appropriate. She wants to use methods and materials that will not make her students dependent on her. After she is finished with her work, they must be able to fill positions of authority in the state's effort to expand English language learning across China.

ESL AND MODERNIZATION THEORY

Martinson's role in the modernization of China is part of a global process. The primary reason for the spread of English in China is that English is the major language of international communication. It is the most important language of business and commerce, of governments and international agencies, of science and technology, and of tourism, film, and music.

Numbers alone cannot account for the phenomenal expansion of English in recent decades. Indeed, varieties of Chinese, taken together, easily qualify as the world's largest language. In Asia, Europe, and North America, Chinese is a language of the family, home, and personal identity, due to the fact that it expanded its geographical range as a direct result of the migration of people (Kaplan 1987). In contrast, the spread of English has not resulted from migration, but instead from processes much more complex and important than mere demographics. The penetration of English into major political and economic institutions on every continent of the globe is a result of the economic and military power of English-speaking countries and the expansion of the integrated global economic market which they have dominated. The processes that bring about the spread of English have come to be known as 'modernization'.

The central idea of modernization theory is that 'underdeveloped' societies must break free of 'traditional' institutional structures that limit economic development and prosperity. Modernization sometimes is seen as identical to 'Westernization', a view that presumes that 'developed' industrial societies have basically similar institutional structures (Giddens 1982b). More generally, modernization theory asserts that 'underdevelopment' can best be overcome by the adoption of institutions and patterns of behaviour like those found in industrial societies.

Modernization theory is linked to the conflict between capitalism and socialism. It supports the alternative of private capital in its assumption that state-protected, privately held industrialization is essentially a progressive, liberalizing force that leads to particular kinds of 'democratic' state structures as well as economic prosperity. Stated simply, modernization theory claims that Western societies provide the most effective model for 'underdeveloped' societies attempting to reproduce the achievements of 'industrialization'.

The spread of English – and of ESL teaching – is linked to modernization theory in two ways. First, English is seen as a tool for the process of modernization. Second, monolingualism (preferably in English) is seen as a practical advantage for modern social organization, while multilingualism is seen as a characteristic of 'unmodernized', 'traditional' societies.

Grabe and Kaplan (1986) summarize this view. They argue that modern information systems require a single dominant language for three reasons. First, scientific information, upon which modern technological development depends, is cumulative. In order to be up to date, scientists and others involved in research and development must have access to research conducted around the world. For this reason, a common language of research is useful; increasingly, that language is English. Second, as research and development become ever more expensive, they depend upon government support for technical innovation and application. Although in different countries the mix of government and private industry involvement varies, everywhere the market-driven demand on research and development places a premium on the latest information. Thus the entire process of research, development, and application requires access to the latest research worldwide. Again, English is seen as the most effective tool for this access. Third, the growth of information is exponential, requiring sophisticated systems of retrieval and access. Approximately 7,000 scientific articles are published every day, while other resources are available in government publications, conference proceedings, reports of private industry, and computer networks. The Fédération Internationale de Documentation, a branch of UNESCO dealing with scientific information, notes that approximately 85 per cent of all information stored or abstracted worldwide is in English (Grabe and Kaplan 1986, pp. 49–50). The capacity to access and manage such a complex array of information requires vast linguistic skills at the national level. For every country, this means a large cadre of people fluent in English.

Critique of modernization theory

Although the belief that English is a useful tool to facilitate 'modernization' is widely accepted, it is incomplete in that it fails to connect the spread of English to inequality and exploitation. That is, the spread of English – and the 'tool' metaphor which justifies it – is ideological.

Modernization theory has come under serious criticism centred on its key ideological assumption, namely, that all societies are involved in a linear historical process, with Western industrial societies further along because they have expanded private ownership of capital and 'democratic' state institutions, while 'underdeveloped' societies lag behind because they have failed to undertake needed reforms. Critics of modernization theory argue instead that 'underdevelopment' in some societies is a *result* of 'development' in others. That is, all societies exist in the same historical period, with differences in development due to their relationships of inequality and exploitation. The metaphor of

English as a tool for modernization is subject to two similar criticisms: (1) that the spread of English supports unequal relationships between 'developed' and 'developing' societies; and (2) that English is associated with the institutionalization of inequality in 'developing' societies.

The dominance of English contributes to unequal relations between 'developed' and 'developing' countries because access to information does not depend solely upon language fluency. It also depends upon institutional structures and relationships. Countries with small or nonexistent computer networks, for instance, may not be able to retrieve and use information stored in computers. Governments or businesses may be denied access to information for political reasons, or they may find that procedures for gaining access are cumbersome and time-consuming. Therefore, in order to gain full access to English-language resources, nations must develop the necessary institutions, such as research and development offices, 'think tanks', research universities, and corporations, as well as ties to institutions that control scientific and technological information. But the small countries of the world may be unable to carry out these steps on their own, and so must turn to the world's major powers for assistance. From the perspective of 'modernizing' countries, the process of modernization entails opening their institutions to direct influence and control by countries that dominate scientific and technical information. Because this process is not reciprocal, the result is an unequal relationship between 'developed' and 'developing' societies.

The spread of English is also associated with inequality within 'developing' societies. Most colonial and post-colonial societies are characterized by a dual system, i.e., two sets of institutions, separate from one another, but linked in important ways. These two sets of institutions include a 'developed' ('Westernized', 'industrialized') sector, and an 'underdeveloped' ('pre-industrial', 'traditional') sector. Because these sectors differ widely in their wealth and income, migration occurs from rural 'underdeveloped' areas to urban 'developed' areas. Migration does not diminish the effects of dualism, however, as much of the urban population may live in slums geographically separated from 'modern', 'Western' 'centres'.

This economic and geographical separation between 'modern' and 'traditional' is often accompanied by linguistic separation as well, brought about in part by the fact that the spread of English is not universal or consistent across both sectors. Individuals and groups in the 'Western' sector are much more likely to speak English; indeed, speaking English may be a criterion for membership in this sector. (A similar situation exists in post-colonial Francophone countries.) In contrast, residents of the 'traditional' sector often do not speak English and may have no opportunity to learn it. Of course, inequality in the spread of English is not responsible for the existence of this unequal distribution of wealth, but it helps to institutionalize the gap between sectors and to establish a significant practical barrier to anyone seeking to move from one to the other.

Chapters 1 and 5–7 explore more fully the range of issues involving the impact of English upon inequality and exploitation. The key point in this chapter is that arguments favouring the spread of English for 'modernization' are inherently ideological in their insistence that English is merely a practical tool for development rather than a mechanism for establishing and institutionalizing unequal social relationships.

Like all mechanisms for inequality in the distribution of economic resources and political power, the spread of English engenders resistance and struggle within 'developing' societies. In order to understand more fully the role of English in 'modernization' and the reasons for resistance to the spread of English, it is useful to examine two cases involving struggle between forces which favour English and which oppose it. These two cases are Iran and China.

ENGLISH IN IRAN

Before the Iranian revolution of 1978–79 expelled the secular Pahlavi dynasty ruled by Mohammad Reza Shah, replacing it with a Shi'ite Islamic republic under the leadership of Ayatollah Ruhollah Khomeini, English was widely taught and studied as part of the country's push for rapid modernization. Hundreds of foreign ESL instructors worked throughout the Iranian educational system, while thousands of Iranians studied in English-speaking universities in England, the United States, India, and the Philippines. Between the mid-1950s and late 1978, English steadily expanded as the most common second language in Iran, and became the major technical language of business, the military, higher education, and the media.

Despite the penetration of English into vast areas of Iranian life, its use decreased dramatically after the revolution of 1979. One reason was its close association with the United States, which was the primary external opponent of the revolution. But a more important reason was the abandonment of the modernization programme in which English played a key role, and which had become identified with increasing domination of Iran by a Westernized elite and by Western institutions which they supported.

English under the Shah

In Iran, as in other countries, the relationship between English and modernization must be understood within the context of recent history. Although the history leading up to the Iranian revolution is beyond the scope of this book, it is impossible to explain the fate of English after 1978–79 without a basic understanding of its role in Iran under the Shah. Under the Pahlavi regime, Iran was increasingly integrated into the Western military and economic structure, with English as its primary language. Though this process of integration began in the 1950s, it dramatically accelerated in the 1970s due to two main factors: the rise in oil prices beginning in 1973, and the close military alliance between the Shah and the United States.

The OPEC oil price increases initiated in 1973 stimulated an incredible surge in Iranian GNP, 34 per cent in 1973 and 43 per cent in 1974, adjusted for inflation (Vakil 1977; Beeman 1986, p. 202). From less than a tenth of the total GNP in 1959, oil came to represent nearly half of Iranian GNP by 1974. As a result of this spectacular growth, Iran was awash in oil-based monetary wealth. With a long history of Western involvement in Iranian business and politics, Americans and Europeans aggressively sought to exploit this wealth. Business investors by the thousands came to Tehran seeking government-subsidized contracts and entrance into the oil-rich Iranian market. Hundreds of companies established offices in Tehran, while dozens built company towns and complexes that included housing, recreational facilities, supermarkets, and other services. More than 200 American educational institutions arranged cooperative ventures with

Iranian universities, often as a way to bankroll American colleges hit with rapidly rising costs and shrinking enrolments during the 1970s (Beeman 1983).

At the same time, the Shah undertook a major expansion and modernization of the Iranian military, spending billions on new weapons and military technology. Virtually all high military officers went to the USA for training, including ESL classes. Thousands more military personnel enrolled in ESL classes in Iran to prepare themselves to work with American advisors, to service aircraft and other equipment purchased from the United States, and to train with US military forces. In 1973, an estimated 3,600 US technical specialists were working on military projects alone, while thousands of what some critics called 'white collar mercenaries' were employed in other sectors of the economy (Klare 1980, p. 51).

Among this group were large numbers of ESL instructors and teacher trainers, who found their skills in great demand under the Shah's modernization programme. Private employers sought instructors for programmes run by multinational corporations and the military (for instance, to teach helicopter repair crews how to read English-language repair manuals). Universities in the USA hired instructors for exchange programmes in Iran. Iranian universities sought full-time ESL instructors and teacher trainers for regular faculty positions. Schools enrolling children of foreign business and military families hired English-speaking instructors for all subjects. At the same time, hundreds of thousands of Iranian students went abroad to study English. So many Iranians entered American universities that professional publications in ESL printed articles focusing exclusively on the language problems of Iranians in the United States (e.g., Monshi-Tousi, Hosseine-Fatem, and Oller 1980).

The Shah sought to link English and modernization by using English for many of his speeches and his most important writings. In his major statement of his vision of Iran's future, *The White Revolution*, the Shah quoted Washington, Lincoln, Emerson, Shakespeare, Wellington, and Disraeli (Pahlavi, no date). He called Western countries 'progressive' and praised Iranian students studying abroad. He instituted changes in vocational education that prepared Iranians to work for international and Western agencies, and he praised Iran's close ties with the West.

At the same time, the Shah sought to establish new educational institutions based on Western models. Teacher training colleges, a network of private high schools, and new programmes at existing institutions were established. Although justified in the name of 'modernization', these steps were also designed to weaken the influence upon education of the Islamic clergy, the Shah's principal domestic opponents (see Bakhash 1984). For this reason, the educational system would be a particular focus for change after the revolution.

English in the Islamic revolution

The Islamic revolution of 1978–79 was partly a revolution shaped by rhetoric, in particular the Friday sermons by Moslem clergy that effectively defined issues and shaped public opinion. Moreover, the close association of English with the Shah's modernization programme ensured that the revolution would have linguistic consequences.

As Beeman (1986) has shown, the key cultural issues in the revolution were the tension between the 'internal' and the 'external', and the rights and responsibilities of leadership. The debate over what is internal and external involved the question of what constitutes 'pure' Iranian culture. Beeman's analysis identifies three aspects of Iranian (internal) culture in revolutionary rhetoric. The *moral* dimension required that the self must be pure in thought and action. The *national* dimension proclaimed that core Iranian identity is pure, and that the political and economic corruption which had infected the country was due to external foreign forces. The *historical* dimension emphasized the frequent invasions by corrupting foreign forces, from Alexander and the Greeks, to the Arabs, the Mongols, and the British. The central responsibility of leadership, according to revolutionary rhetoric, was to resist the external forces of corruption. The brilliance of Khomeini's rhetoric was his ability to identify the Shah's regime with corrupt external forces, and the Islamic clergy with protecting Iranian purity.

In contrast to the Shah's support for English, Khomeini associated English with Western subjugation of the Iranian people (1980, p. 206). He urged his followers not to buy or read books in which foreigners were quoted and he complained about the use of English in the names of stores, streets, clothing, and other common objects (1980, pp. 205, 209). He linked English to opponents of the revolution, charging that the enemies of Islam were corrupted by agents of colonialism who communicated secretly in a foreign tongue (1979, p. 63). In his writings, Khomeini condemned Western schools (1979, pp. 4–5) while stressing that liberation and justice were possible only through prayer, which was one aspect of Iranian life not penetrated by English (cf. Bakhash 1984). Khomeini's call to revolution was expressed as a demand for an end to corrupting external influences (1979, p. 14). When the Shah was identified with corruption, his downfall was implied.

In his analysis of the qualities of leadership appropriate to a purified Iran, Khomeini emphasized the ability to read, interpret, and teach the Koran; thus facility in Farsi was central to the ruler's legitimacy (1979, p. 27). Leadership in the Iranian hierarchy, according to Khomeini, should depend not upon foreign education, but instead upon religious purity. These principles were applied after the revolution.

English after the 1978–79 revolution

With the success of the revolution, the Islamic clergy did not need to invoke English as a symbol of the foreign domination of Iran. Instead, the revolution sought to nationalize the use of English. The end of the modernization programme begun by the Shah meant that English was no longer the dominant language of business, government, the military, and industry. Thus English was gradually restricted to limited areas in which it would be beneficial to newly defined Iranian interests (e.g., diplomacy and other contacts with foreign countries; access to scientific literature).

A reduced role for English also helped to restrict the power of the Western educated elite. Purges of Westernized elements were particularly extensive in the Ministry of Education, which was seen as crucial for the development and spread of revolutionary ideology; only in the military were purges more widespread. In the school system, non-Islamic teachers and students were purged during 1980 and 1981; it is estimated that 20,000 teachers were fired (Arjomand 1988, p. 144; Bakhash 1984, p. 112). Textbooks and curricula were revised throughout the school system, with the primary goal of eliminating Western influences that had spread under the Shah. As the revolution sought to consolidate itself in early 1980, Khomeini delivered an especially harsh attack against the university system, declaring: 'We are not afraid of economic sanctions or military intervention. What we are afraid of is Western universities and the training of our youth in the interests of West or East' (Bakhash 1984, p. 122). This speech led to an attack against Tehran Teachers' Training College, Shiraz University, and other institutions. Finally, the government closed the universities in order to undertake Islamization of the institutions. They did not reopen until 1984.

These actions meant that Iranians who were most closely connected to American institutions and who spoke English lost their communicative advantages. While proficiency in English had been essential before the revolution for many activities in government, the military, and business, after the revolution students were subject to political and religious tests. Applicants to teacher-training schools were required to be practising Muslims and to declare loyalty to the Islamic Republic and the revolution. Non-Muslims were allowed to enter as students only in accounting and in foreign language study (Bakhash 1984, p. 226). In the military, the technical language of the army was no longer English; the officers who had been trained in the USA were gone (Ashraf 1989). As the new revolutionary institutions began to take shape, they relied primarily upon Farsi. Moreover, a mass literacy campaign extended to large numbers of Iranians the opportunity for higher education in Farsi and involvement in politics and government (see Halliday 1989).

Thus the end of English domination was associated with the changing structure of power in Iranian society. By breaking economic, military, and industrial ties with the United States, post-revolutionary Iran dramatically reduced the need for English teachers. It nationalized its own cultural symbols and rhetoric, defined for itself what is 'Iranian' and what is 'foreign', and eliminated many mechanisms for the spread of Western culture and language. One symbol of the nationalization of English was its use on television. In 1988, nearly ten years after the revolution, fifteen minutes of English-language news was read each day on the state-run television by a woman wearing a chador (Simpson 1988).

As Iran sought increased ties to Western European nations in the late 1980s, some political leaders proposed foreign investment and aid for reconstruction after the war with Iraq. Once again, foreign delegations came to Tehran, hoping to secure contracts. By 1989, discussion of the appropriate foreign role in reconstruction had become central to Iranian political debate. After Khomeini's death, the prevailing view seemed to be that foreign debt should be avoided because it entails foreign domination, but expertise may once again be welcome (Hooglund 1989). This policy may lead to expanded English language education, but it is unlikely that English will become the major technical language as it was under the Shah. As long as Khomeini's followers dominate Iranian political leadership, the role of English is likely to remain limited.

ENGLISH IN CHINA

Like Iran under the Shah, China in the 1970s sought to 'modernize' its institutions. In this process, China also adopted the metaphor of English as a tool for development. By the late 1980s, however, China's leaders began to question some aspects of modernization, including the spread of English. Although by late 1989, China had not restricted English as much as Iran, its leaders were increasingly concerned about the political consequences of the spread of English.

English before the 1970s

The spread of English for modernization in China must be seen within a long historical context in which language use and language education have been closely tied to economic and political policy. In the late seventeenth century, the British gained a foothold in Canton. During the eighteenth century, the East India Company established trade. With British control of Hong Kong beginning in 1841, merchants, missionaries, and government officials began to arrive in China in large numbers. As Britain asserted its control along the coast and to some inland areas, English spread as well. Yet English did not expand as far as in Africa and South Asia, because the British colonized only limited areas such as Guangzhou (Canton), Shanghai, and Fuzhou (Foochow). In addition, the Chinese considered the British to be culturally inferior, and English was seen as an evil language (Cheng 1982; Pride and Ru-Shan 1988). Thus, English was restricted to a very small elite, primarily merchants and religious leaders, while some pidgin varieties evolved for use with servants and low-level staff in businesses (see Hall 1944).

With the victory of Mao's forces in 1949, English began a steady decline, due to changes in the ruling elite, the association of English with colonialism, and China's reduced contacts with Western governments and businesses. In an effort to rid China of impure influences and any remnants of capitalism, the Cultural Revolution, which lasted from 1966 until the Ninth Party Congress in April 1969, further reduced English language training and use. Universities and secondary schools were major targets for reform, many closing for up to four years. When they reopened, most work in the humanities and social sciences had been changed or eliminated, including linguistics, anthropology, sociology and psychology. Research institutions, publishing houses, and trading companies that relied upon contacts with other countries, or that employed non-Han minorities in key positions, were closed. In some parts of the country, languages other than Chinese were vilified as backward and useless, or as tools of feudalism and capitalism (Light 1978; Yin 1985). Foreign books and periodicals were burned and people punished if they were caught reading English. Language teachers were forced to change professions, often becoming farmers on rural cooperatives. In regions where language education continued, programme quality and continuity suffered as secondary schools and higher education no longer coordinated the content and levels of their programmes.

Although the Cultural Revolution officially ended in 1969, its effects persisted into the mid-1970s in a series of intense ideological campaigns. Finally, after Mao's death and the overthrow of the Gang of Four in 1976, China's new leaders shifted to a policy of fostering scientific and technological modernization. This policy required a reduction in hostilities with countries that controlled access to science and technology – primarily the United States and other capitalist countries.

Modernization in China

The goal of 'modernization' initially meant access to Western science and technology, which led in the late 1970s to new priorities for China's system of foreign language instruction, namely: (1) educating students in the national languages of countries having diplomatic relations with China; (2) training a sufficient number of interpreters and translators; (3) teaching reading skills in at least one foreign language to all educated Chinese (Light 1978). In order to meet these needs, China began to develop exchange programmes and to hire language teachers from other countries. Thus the increasing numbers of foreign government officials, scientists, and technical advisors who began to arrive in China in the late 1970s were followed by English teachers and teacher trainers from Britain, the United States, Canada, Australia, and New Zealand.

China's commitment to teaching English in order to improve access to science and technology was soon supplanted, however, by an even greater impetus to English language instruction: the policy of encouraging direct foreign investment and privately owned enterprise in China. Gradually adopted from 1984 to 1987, this policy was widely described in North America and Europe as a movement away from the fundamental tenets of communism. Special economic zones were created to encourage investment from Hong Kong and other capitalist countries. Managers were given greater control over industry, while the authority of central planners was curtailed. Collective farming was largely abolished. Farm land, though technically owned by the state, gained *de facto* private status as families obtained long-term government leases, which they bought and sold like deeds. Private shops selling a growing range of consumer goods opened in cities across China.

Visitors to China increased greatly during this period. From less than a quarter million foreign visitors and 1.5 million overseas Chinese in 1978, China had 1.5 million foreign visitors and more than 20 million overseas Chinese by 1986 (Schell 1988, p. 55). Western investors flocked to Beijing, much as they had to Tehran two decades before. From $900 million in 1974, total China–US trade reached more than $15 billion by 1988 (Schell 1988, p. 52).

As more and more foreign investors, scholars, and government officials arrived, staff were needed to interpret during business meetings, to translate exchange agreements and investment documents, to translate and summarize academic journals and other sources of information, and to work with computers, lasers, and other technologies purchased from the West. Universities from English-speaking countries sent teachers and other academic specialists to China, while thousands of Chinese scholars and teachers enrolled in universities abroad. By 1987, there were 20,000–25,000 Chinese students in the USA alone.

Under the new economic policy, English became the most commonly studied language across China. By 1988, nearly all middle-school students selected English to fulfil their foreign language requirement (see Pride and Ru-Shan 1988). In addition, over 1.5 million college and university students studied English as a required subject, far outnumbering those who selected Japanese, French, or German. Up to 100,000 graduate students also studied English. To serve such a huge population of English students, more than 320,000 Chinese English teachers were supplemented by radio and television classes that reached millions of listeners. All of this exposure to English, along with the new economic policy, meant the spread of Western cultural symbols such as Coca Cola, discos, beauty contests, rock concerts, and golf (Schell 1984, 1988).

As the importance of English increased, the government undertook efforts to upgrade the quality of textbooks, examinations, and teaching. New college English syllabuses were published in 1980 and 1985, followed by subject-area texts designed for reading and listening classes (Der-min 1988). A new testing system raised standards of proficiency, while modernized teacher-training programmes emphasized alternatives to grammar translation. The desire to adopt new teaching practices was one of the main reasons behind the decision to hire foreign ESL experts such as Paula Martinson.

Unlike the first educational exchanges in the late 1970s, the new programmes were not limited to improving China's access to science and technology. They were designed also to transform the Chinese economy through greater integration with Western economies. Thus learners began to give new reasons for studying English. In the early 1970s, the most common explanation was 'To serve the revolution,' an answer which reflected English lessons that focused on topics such as 'a barefoot doctor', 'visiting a working family', 'serving the people', 'carrying the struggle to criticize Lin Piao and Confucius through to the end', and 'recounting the family's revolutionary history' (Lehmann 1975, pp. 76–7). In the late 1970s, learners stated that they studied English in order to facilitate access to modern science and technology (Cowan, Light, Matthews, and Tucker 1979, p. 466).

By the mid-1980s, learners had begun to associate the study of English with economic and political reforms, as well as with foreign cultural influences.

Despite the emphasis on study abroad and English language instruction at home, however, China has been unable to meet its English language instruction needs. Perhaps as many as 90 per cent of the university population studies natural and social sciences, in which English is crucial, but they lack language materials specialized in their fields of study (Cowan, Light, Matthews, and Tucker 1979). Many teachers throughout the country have inadequate proficiency in English, particularly in rural areas, where 80 per cent of the population resides (Yin 1985; also see Barnes 1983). Teachers who do not speak English well must rely on rote memorization as the primary teaching method in their courses (Grabe and Mahon 1981). The need for translators and interpreters is so great that university graduates are immediately placed into demanding jobs (Light 1978).

Resistance to the spread of English, 1987–89

The drive to 'modernize' China and the resulting increased importance of ESL was offset in the late 1980s by growing concern over the impact of economic reforms and foreign influence on Chinese life, culture, and politics. When English was associated only with science and technology, its political significance was limited; as it became associated with the new economic policy, it became a symbol of the shift to private ownership of capital, openness to Western culture, and political liberalization. This was particularly true among the growing number of Chinese studying abroad, many of whom decided to remain permanently outside China. Some Chinese leaders began to worry that the new policies would lead to class differences and other forms of structural inequality. For instance, one early effect of the movement towards capitalism was increased regional variation in wealth and income. Wages in the province of Guangdong, the location of the Canton experimental zone of foreign investment, rose more quickly than in surrounding provinces, which led in a few weeks in early 1989 to an estimated 2.5 million people flooding to Canton looking for work (Kristof 1989b).

Student demonstrations in 1987 and 1989 led to vigorous debates within the Chinese leadership about the new economic policy. As a result, authorities tried to manage political debate while maintaining the movement towards economic reform (Kristof 1989a). Restrictions were placed on the number of Chinese scholars permitted to study abroad. Some educational exchanges and programmes to bring foreign teachers to China were cancelled or cut back. After the violence of mid-1989, China's leaders showed a continuing commitment to trade and investment with the West, but serious concern about its political consequences.

Concern about the political consequences of the new economic policy means that continuing debate is likely about the scope of English language study and its proper role in Chinese society. Should China decide to end the policy of experimental capitalism and direct foreign investment, the demand for foreign ESL instructors could drop significantly, as it did in Iran after the revolution. Despite recent retrenchment and caution, however, Chinese leaders seem committed to economic policies that will require the continued spread of English.

Like ESL professionals in Iran before the revolution, Paula Martinson will prepare Chinese students to work for multi-national corporations, international investment firms, and foreign and domestic educational institutions that provide personnel, research, and other forms of support. As long as the policies of importing Western technology, creating special economic zones, and developing greater trade with Western countries continue, there will be a need for English teachers and English speakers in China. The risk in Martinson's decision to teach in China is that fluctuations in economic policy could jeopardize her job, just as the Iranian revolution suddenly ended her career in Iran.

ESL AND MODERNIZATION

Events in Iran and China since the late 1970s demonstrate the close relationship between the spread of English and the 'modernization' of non-English-speaking countries. In Iran, English was identified with a despised regime that became a symbol of foreign domination. When the Shah was overthrown, his supporters, who had enjoyed economic and political advantage in part because of their ability to use English, found themselves confronted with a revolutionary ideology that emphasized Iranian purity rather than 'modernization'. In China after the Cultural Revolution, English rapidly expanded first as a means of increasing access to science and technology and then as a tool for increasing foreign investment.

In addition to the link between ESL and broad transformations in economic and social policy in Iran and China, both countries also sought to modernize English language teaching. That is, they have sought to benefit from the modernization movement within the field of ESL. Indeed, one of the primary justifications given for hiring foreign ESL specialists is that they bring up-to-date theory and teaching practices with them. Therefore in order to fully explore the connections between English language teaching and modernization, we must examine modernization within English language teaching.

Modernization theory in ESL teaching

In modernization theory, Western 'experts', including ESL specialists like Martinson, are viewed as repositories of knowledge and skills who pass them on to elites who will run 'modernized' institutions. This means that experts are a source of power for a new elite. Critics of modernization theory point out, however, that foreign experts' knowledge and skills are not distributed equally throughout the 'developing' societies, and therefore they may facilitate the development of inequality through dualism. Moreover, the transfer of power may be illusory, with experts claiming to give up power while in fact maintaining it by playing an ongoing role in 'modernized' institutions. Thus experts often have an ideological function, reproducing institutional structures that engender inequality and exploitation.

These criticisms apply specifically to ESL specialists. Rarely, if ever, is ESL available equally to all individuals and groups in a 'developing' society. Instead, it is usually available only to groups who already enjoy other economic and political advantages. Moreover, ESL experts are often hired as consultants to dispense 'solutions' to complex educational problems in countries about which they know very little (see Clarke 1982, 1984). Faith in them is based upon the belief that their theory and methodology are 'modern'; this belief expresses the common assumption that whatever comes from 'modernized' countries is, by definition, 'modern', and therefore better that 'traditional' practices.

But the ideological nature of ESL is not limited to the role of experts in modernization. It extends as well to the 'content' of what ESL experts pass on. The key issue here is the role of power in contemporary ESL teaching practices. The role of power in ESL methodology is central to recent changes in ESL teaching practices. Since the 1970s, 'traditional' ESL instruction has been criticized for hierarchically organized classes in which students sit at attention while teachers direct them in choral practice of memorized English sentences. In the 1970s and 1980s, many classes shifted to 'modern' methods in which students were expected to take more responsibility for their own learning. Like modernization theory, which claims that 'foreign experts' turn over power to citizens of developing societies in the name of economic development and political democracy, 'student centred' teaching methods claim that ESL instructors turn over power to students in the name of effective learning and classroom democracy.

MEDIA EXAMPLE 4.1

'Giving Away the Power' by Joan Klyhn
TESOL Newsletter, October 1987.

How do I run a course [in advanced ESL] that is going to challenge every participant? How can each one go as far as possible toward his or her goals? The answer, I believe, is for students to assume responsibility for their learning in the course. They need to determine what to go for and how, and when to go for it. I need to set up a supportive environment with the tools and information that will best assist them. And the first thing I need to do is to hand over the power.

The challenge is to provide a scenario that avoids high teacher/low student initiative. Much of the planning, decision making, choice and running of activities, and above all, most of the talking, including feedback, should be done by the students. . .

As the group bonds, I fade into the background; I'm there, guiding people to work in pairs, and small groups, and getting them all together from time to time for group reports. I'm also there to tell them the possibilities of the course; what activities, what materials, what hardware and software are available. . .

At times during the days that follow, it is hard to take a back seat, especially when things are not going as well as they could and it looks as if I could set things [straight] so easily. It is also hard to stay out of a lively debate when my role is to observe and make language notes for a feedback session. . . Instead of leading, I follow students who progress more on their own than with my lead. . .

Letting go [of power] can be scary at first, but the rewards will come: motivated, high-achieving students, and a deeper, more personally involving experience for students and teachers.

Questions

1. Does Klyhn assume a *universal* definition of successful classrooms? Do you think it applies to all countries, such as China and Iran?
2. Does the teacher in the classroom described by Klyhn give up all 'power', or only some of it? In what ways does the teacher maintain power? Consider decisions about the content of curricular materials, the organization of the course, and the evaluation of students' performance.
3. What is 'power' in a classroom? Is it undesirable for the teacher to exercise power?

Most contemporary ESL methods and materials claim to empower students. The Silent Way (Gattegno 1972), Total Physical Response (Asher 1977), the Natural Approach (Krashen and Terrell 1983), Counseling–Learning (Curran 1976), and other methods claim to increase students' control over the learning process and over what happens in the ESL classroom. An ad for Total Physical Response, for example, asserts that student-centred classes increase students' motivation by transforming work into play. Proponents of the Silent Way argue that the students gain great power because the teacher rarely speaks. Such claims are based upon a popular, though implicit, view of what classroom education should be. This view is summarized by Rounds (1987, p. 666) in her analysis of classroom communicative competence: 'Successful classroom discourse can be characterized as what emerges from the teacher's ability to develop an atmosphere of cooperative interaction and consensus – a sense of working together to achieve a common goal.'

Despite widespread belief that modern methods and materials empower students, these methods reinforce unequal power relationships in two ways: (1) the paradoxical situations in which students and teachers are placed; and (2) the distortions implicit in their depiction of students' lives.

Clarke and Silberstein (1988) explore the rise of *pragmatic paradox* in modern ESL teaching. Pragmatic paradox occurs when three conditions are present: individuals in a significant relationship have unequal power; an injunction is issued that cannot be ignored, obeyed, or violated; and the situation cannot be resolved through discussion. When these conditions hold, individuals are in 'double binds' in which it is impossible to act, although action is required. When students are told to 'take control of the classroom', for instance, they are placed in a double bind. They know that the teacher is in charge, and therefore they do not have the power to truly take control of the classroom. Yet, because the teacher is in charge, the students must obey the command to take control.

Many teaching practices place students in such paradoxical circumstances on a regular basis. For example, methodologies claim that the best class is one which most resembles 'real life', and so instructors require students to discuss intensely personal topics (abortion, extramarital sex), even though the students may feel that the classroom is an inappropriate place for such discussion. Because the teacher has the power, however, the students are not free to refuse to participate, as they would be in a 'real' discussion outside of class.

Pragmatic paradox is not only a condition of students in modern ESL classes: it is also pervasive in the daily work of teachers, who are expected to resolve major social problems even though their power within society is marginal compared with other professionals such as doctors and attorneys. The emphasis on communicative and humanistic teaching methods creates the illusion that there are simple solutions to educational questions, and that education can resolve major social problems rooted in economic inequality. Thus teachers work within institutions in which they have little power, while they seek 'solutions' for problems over which they have little control. This perspective is implicit in the recommendation of the Swann Report that education can resolve racist attitudes and societal inequality.

The second aspect of the ideological nature of ESL classrooms is the depiction of reality implicit in classroom practices and in textbooks and other materials. In surveys of the 'hidden curriculum' of 'survival' ESL, Auerbach and Burgess (1985) and

Auerbach (1986) found that most texts ignore the economic, political, and social problems that underlie students' educational needs. For instance, lessons on housing emphasize the tenant's (i.e., the student's) responsibility to pay rent, but ignore the landlord's responsibility to maintain health and safety standards. Lessons on finances offer simplistic dialogues in which individuals easily obtain mortgage loans, even though many ESL students cannot qualify for them. Overall, Auerbach and Burgess found that many texts ignore students' real-life problems and do not encourage discussion of alternative solutions to them. Instead, they offer simplistic solutions in dialogues that are of little value in hierarchically structured societies. More generally, many ESL classes assume that personal discussions in ESL classes can sufficiently empower students that they will be able to resolve their major economic and social problems. This optimism is grounded in the neoclassical assumption that problems and solutions are located in individual students rather than in historical and structural forces largely beyond their control.

The effect of both pragmatic paradox and unrealistic lessons in survival English is that many ESL classes do not offer a tool for overcoming the inequalities which many learners suffer in 'modern' and 'modernizing' countries. Students and teachers try to conform their classrooms to mandated teaching practices that educational theorists claim will lead to effective language learning, higher education, better jobs, and fewer social and psychological problems (Clarke and Silberstein 1988, p. 692). The result is that ESL classes, like 'modernization' processes generally, operate with an illusion of progress that may help to sustain unequal social relationships.

CONCLUSION: PAULA MARTINSON'S CHOICES

Paula Martinson's decision about whether to teach in China is essentially an ideological one. If she goes to China, she will become a minor actor in a massive effort to provide China with an essential 'tool' for modernization that may contribute to economic and social inequality. Yet it is misleading to claim that ESL is merely a non-ideologized tool for development. Instead, it is closely connected to 'modernization' processes that reproduce unequal relationships between 'developed' and 'developing' societies, and between 'Western' and 'traditional' sectors within 'developing' societies. Similarly, modern ESL teaching practices must be examined for their impact upon the relationship between students and teachers, and for their ideological assumptions about the roles of teachers and students in society. The faith that educational institutions can resolve economic and social inequality rooted in the organization of society places teachers and students in an impossible role, and ultimately serves to sustain inequality.

FOR DISCUSSION

1. On a 1988 edition of the popular late-night American television news programme 'Nightline', Ted Koppel interviewed an official of the Iranian revolutionary government who had graduated from the University of California at Berkeley, and had been involved in the taking of US hostages in Tehran many years earlier. Although the official acknowledged that he could speak English well, he spoke Farsi on the broadcast, using an interpreter for the English translation. Impatient with the time required for translation, Koppel repeatedly insisted that the official speak English. After several minutes of such pressure, the official reluctantly spoke English, but then shifted back to Farsi, insisting that he was under no obligation to speak English.

What reasons might the official have had for insisting on speaking Farsi? Do you think Ted Koppel would accept his reasons as legitimate?

2. Both Iran and China present excellent examples of the power of propaganda to mobilize citizens for mass action. In Iran, clerical leaders adopted revolutionary rhetoric in their sermons, while in China during the Cultural Revolution the Red Guards dispatched special cadres to the regions to conduct the struggle, reportedly disseminating nearly 3 billion copies of Mao's works in the process (Liu 1971). In both countries, language became an issue that divided people into opposing camps.

What other examples do you know of effective political rhetoric in which language plays a key role? What individuals, such as religious leaders, politicians, community activists, or others, have been able to mobilize large numbers of people for direct action by referring to language issues? Locate texts, including speeches, pamphlets, videos, or other media, and examine their use of language, both in terms of specialized rhetoric and explicit statements about language.

FOR ACTION

Contact the foreign student office at a college or university to find out the major fields of study of students from China, Iran, or other countries from Asia, Africa, or Latin America undergoing modernization programmes. If possible, contact several of these students and ask about their future role in modernization and development plans. Inquire about English language education in the students' home country. How did they learn English? What are the most common major fields of study of these students? What do they expect to do after graduation?

FURTHER READING

Kachru (1982) is a collection of articles that surveys English in countries in which it is not a native language. Essays examine language structure, standardization, policy alternatives, and stylistic and rhetorical variation. Keddie (1983), a collection of articles from a 1980 conference at the Berlin Institute for Comparative Social Resarch, examines the religious foundation for Iranian politics. Of particular interest to language specialists is the article by Beeman on language in the Iranian revolution. Beeman (1986) analyses language and social structure in Iran, with particular emphasis upon meaning as a negotiated social process. Examining stylistic variation in Farsi, Beeman shows the close interaction between linguistic structure and social organiza-tion. Schell (1988), a popular book written for a general audience, traces the struggle over economic and political reform in China during 1986–88. Schell is particularly interested in the cultural impact of capitalism within Chinese society. Although dated, Liu (1971) is a fascinating analysis of mass persuasion under Mao. Focusing on the Cultural Revolution, Liu explores the use of propaganda in broad areas of Chinese life, including book publishing, film, and radio and television.

FIVE

Language policy and migration

PREVIEW

Chapter 5 explores the relationship between migration and language policies in education. As the worldwide phenomenon of the migration of labour increases, ever greater numbers of people must learn a new language in order to find work in their new countries. Special educational programmes are often established for them, as in the case of Southeast Asian refugees in the United States. Yet these programmes may be subordinate to labour policy, so that language education is designed to channel learners into particular kinds of jobs. The chapter argues that migrant language education, widely considered to be intended to benefit the migrants, often is part of a broad policy to channel migrants into marginal jobs in the peripheral economy that offer little security and no opportunity to gain additional language or job skills.

The spread of English as a tool for modernization takes place within already 'modernized' societies such as the United States, Britain, and Australia. In these societies, English is seen as a tool for immigrants to improve their economic standing. In the United States, ESL programmes are central to state efforts to prepare Southeast Asian refugees and immigrants for employment. The continuing difficulties of those who have successfully completed the ESL programme suggests that ESL is not as directly related to economic advancement as the tool metaphor suggests. Moreover, special educational assistance for immigrants has been met with resistance from groups opposed to languages other than English.

CASE: BINH NGUYEN

In Vietnam, Binh Nguyen worked as a diesel mechanic in Ho Chi Minh City, formerly called Saigon. He was 25 years old, a soldier in the South Vietnamese army, when the North Vietnamese tanks rolled through the streets of Saigon. Unlike some of his age, he had never learned English, except for a few words he and his friends used with American soldiers on the streets of his city. After the war, Binh and his wife supplemented his income by doing laundry from two small hotels in the city. With two children, eight and thirteen years old, they left Vietnam by boat in late 1985 along with 73 other refugees, finally arriving in Malaysia where they were placed in the Pulau Bidong refugee camp. Binh was fortunate to have a sponsor, an uncle who had worked for an American company during the war and fled to the United States in the first wave of refugees in 1975. After being accepted for resettlement in the United States, Binh's family was transferred to a processing centre in the Philippines to study English, cultural orientation, and pre-employment skills for six months.

In the United States, Binh enrolled in special refugee ESL classes. Using materials prepared by the Office of Refugee Resettlement and the Center for Applied Linguistics, these classes emphasize competencies for jobs considered appropriate for refugees. For instance, several lessons emphasize the importance of apologizing appropriately. 'What do you say to your supervisor when you make a mistake?' the teacher asks. 'I am sorry. I won't do it again,' the class practises over and over. Students also punch a time clock as they enter class and follow 'company rules' posted on the bulletin board, such as 'No horseplay. Work quickly and accurately – don't waste time and materials. If you don't understand, ask. Your mistakes are expensive and cause delays in work.' (see Limpanboon 1987; Schumacher, undated). So that students practise appropriate workplace behaviour, the classroom is periodically transformed into an assembly line where students put together a simple lamp, or a fast-food restaurant selling hotdogs and hamburgers to other students on Friday afternoons. The teacher acts as the supervisor, issuing orders, checking for accuracy, and timing the students to ensure that they work quickly. She especially emphasizes safety, telling students to 'Check your tools before you begin work and report any problems to your supervisor.' She also encourages students to work quickly, reminding them that 'time is money'. The students often work in silence, demonstrating that they can follow directions while working efficiently.

In the United States, Binh was anxious to become fluent in English so he could find a job as a mechanic. Yet the federal refugee programme only supported 180 hours of class time. Federal policy assumes that this is sufficient for refugees to move into the labour market. Therefore, after attending class every day, studying every night, listening to the radio, and trying to read everything he could to improve his English, Binh still does not speak English well enough to find a good job.

So Binh faces a difficult choice. His resettlement case worker at the welfare office tells him that he must apply for a job immediately after completing the ESL programme or he will lose his right to public assistance and federally subsidized health insurance. With two children, he is especially concerned about health care: one day in the hospital could cost several hundred dollars. Although welfare will continue while he seeks work, he is required to accept the first job he is offered, even if it pays the minimum wage and offers no health insurance coverage. Binh knows his English is not sufficient for a mechanic's job, and that most work for which he might be hired will pay less than $5.00 per hour, or a maximum of $800 per month if he is fortunate enough to find a full-time job. His rent is about $475 per month. If he works at two jobs for 16 hours a day like many other refugees, he will barely earn enough for his family's essential needs. He knows that most refugees on minimum-wage jobs do not speak English at work, and they have no time to take additional English classes. So Binh worries that he will be stuck in an insecure, poorly paid job, with little probability that he will ever be hired as a mechanic. Therefore his oldest son has offered to delay going to school in order to help support the family while Binh works one job during the day and attends ESL classes at night at the local community college. Perhaps in a year or two, Binh will be able to speak English well enough to find a job as a mechanic, and then his son could return to high school. But Binh is not sure that two years is enough, and he worries that his son might never return to school.

MIGRATION THEORY

Why do people like Binh leave their homes at great sacrifice and peril? Migration theory normally distinguishes two sets of factors causing migration. One set, called 'push' factors, are those conditions in the home country that encourage migration. These include scarcity of resources such as food and housing, lack of adequate employment, war, and natural disasters. 'Pull' factors are those in the receiving country that encourage migrants to move towards that country, including labour shortages, high wages relative to surrounding nations, relative peace, and a low cost of living. Push and pull factors work together in an interactive manner, with the impact of any particular factor dependent upon the strength of others. For instance, a slight improvement in wages in a receiving country may be insufficient to 'pull' immigrants in and of itself; but if combined with food shortages, natural disaster, or the threat of war in the source country, then massive migration may take place. In any event, individuals who migrate seldom have any control over either push or pull factors, and thus have little choice in whether they stay at home or seek asylum elsewhere.

Countries that resettle Indochinese refugees have long argued that the availability of resettlement is a pull factor that increases the number of people who leave Vietnam, Cambodia, and Laos. In an attempt to minimize its impact, the United States has encouraged Thailand to interview refugees arriving at the border in order to determine whether they are 'economic' migrants motivated by pull factors, or 'political' refugees pushed out of their homes by the fear of persecution (Loescher and Scanlan 1986). Those who are judged to be economic migrants are imprisoned until they can be repatriated to their home country. Some have been forcibly repatriated, resulting in many deaths (US Committee for Refugees 1986).

In Southeast Asia, the distinction between push and pull factors is difficult to make. Conditions in Vietnam – inflation, high unemployment, food shortages, and inadequate infrastructure – are the result of decades of war and the policy by Western governments of strangling the Vietnamese economy. The United States also encourages refugees to leave Vietnam in order to embarrass the communist government of that country.

Despite reduced refugee admissions in the late 1980s, the US economy benefits from admitting some refugees, who fill jobs in low-paying service industries and light manufacturing, such as electronics assembly. Thus both push and pull factors have been maintained in part by the United States and other pull countries.

It is misleading to suggest that conditions in Vietnam are unrelated to the policies of resettlement countries, or that push and pull factors are completely distinct.

Refugees who are judged to be eligible for resettlement are permitted to apply to one of the resettlement countries. Most apply to the United States, where since 1975 approximately 900,000 people from Vietnam, Cambodia, and Laos have been resettled. In early 1989, appoximately 3,000 Indochinese per month continued to arrive from processing centres in Thailand and the Philippines, while 400,000 others remained in camps in the region.

The function of language policy for refugees arriving in the United States is to regulate the role of the educational system in integrating them into the social, political, and economic life of their new country. As Binh's class indicates, language policy for Indochinese is designed to channel them into jobs in the peripheral economy, primarily at or near minimum wage. This means that refugees are educated for work as janitors, waiters in restaurants, assemblers in electronics plants, and other low-paying jobs offering little opportunity for advancement, regard-less of whether the refugees have skills, as Binh does, suitable for higher-paying jobs. Thus refugee ESL classes emphasize language competencies considered appropriate for minimum-wage work: following orders, asking questions, confirming understanding, and apologizing for mistakes (Auerbach and Burgess 1985; Tollefson 1986a).

Problems among Indochinese refugees in the United States

Binh's difficult decision is typical of the kinds of problems facing most resettled refugees. Federal policies emphasizing short-term ESL followed by minimum-wage employment do not address the critical social, psychological, and economic problems of employed and unemployed Indochinese in the United States.

Communication problems are among the most serious diffi-culties facing Southeast Asians in the USA. Well-intentioned sponsors may buy them hotdogs at baseball games rather than take them to the local Asian food store where they can purchase familiar food. Refugees often see resettlement agencies as hostile bureaucracies, and so their behaviour may be aggressive and, from the perspective of the agencies, inappropriate (Taylor and

Nathan 1980). Interactions with health and other service agencies cannot be easily managed; even the widespread use of translators and interpreters does not resolve problems of communication rooted in cultural differences.

The impact of resettlement on families often leads to a general collapse of traditional social structure. Most refugees lack the extended families that provided support and security in Indochina, yet they often live in areas with other refugees who exert pressure in the form of gossip and community censure. Young and old come into increasing conflict, as older refugees seek to reinstitute traditional family and religious practice (Menard-Warwick 1987). Particularly serious are pressures resulting from changes in the relationships between men and women. In traditional Indochina, women were passed from fathers to husbands, while widows either remarried or lived with their son's families. Yet many refugees are widowed women with children. As these women exercise responsibility and authority, unemployed males in the community may lose prestige. Even in families with two adults, the woman may be employed while the man is not. Moreover, many women have formed support groups and economic cooperatives to market traditional crafts. The impact of these changes in refugee neighbourhoods is reflected in the growing physical abuse of women and children, for the first time a major problem in Southeast Asian communities.

Older refugees are particularly at risk. They may stay inside for weeks at a time, afraid to venture onto streets where crime rates are high and most people speak only English. Even those who try to make friends may feel isolated and lonely, particularly as traditional Indochinese family life is disrupted. Children often learn English more quickly than adults, and so take on major responsibility for contact with English speakers and institutions. They also may adopt new behaviours and values, such as lack of respect for teachers and indifference towards religion. Thus children gain exceptional power through their ability to speak English, while adults lose authority and resent the changes they see taking place within families increasingly out of their control.

Even when there are other Southeast Asians at school, children may be unwilling to speak their own language, owing to disapproval from teachers and other students. Their language difficulties are compounded by the unwillingness of many English-speaking students to befriend people from other cultures.

The result is that many Southeast Asian children are isolated within themselves, unable to speak English fluently and afraid to speak their own language in public (*Children of Change* 1983). Some turn to other children for support, often in youth gangs. The result is a high rate of crime, particularly among young Vietnamese males.

The collapse of traditional social structures and economic roles, particularly within changing family life, leads to an extraordinary rate of psychological problems. Post-traumatic stress disorder is widespread, as are drug abuse, uncharacteristic aggression and hostility, and the effects of grief such as failure to maintain good nutrition (Tepper 1980; Lin 1984; Williams and Westermeyer 1986). Many survivors of Khmer Rouge rule in Cambodia, as well as Vietnamese boat refugees who experienced 'pirate' attacks and starvation, feel they are stalked by an evil presence throughout their lives (Brende and Parson 1985, p. 126; Cohon, Lucey, Paul and Penning 1986). One study found that over half of all Vietnamese refugees are depressed (Lin 1984). Moreover, nearly all of these individuals were diagnosed as depressed only after reporting to clinics for physical ailments such as headaches, stomach pains, and rashes. This may be due in part to a reluctance among most Southeast Asians to talk about psychological problems, but also to the fact that such therapy requires a high degree of communicative competence. Thus treatment is difficult when it is attempted within traditional Western psychological paradigms that emphasize talking about one's problems.

To stem their concern that they will live out their lives in permanent alienation, many Southeast Asians seek a single key to open the door to a new home where they can truly feel that they belong. Most believe that this key is learning to speak English. They are encouraged in this belief by the US government and service agencies; indeed, it is a central assumption of the educational programme (Tollefson 1989).

According to the federal programme, acquiring English depends above all on individual motivation. Refugees who successfully acquire English are assumed to be those who work hard, while those who complete ESL but do not speak English well are considered to be unmotivated and thus responsible for their own failure. Moreover, the ability to speak English is seen as an important measure of loyalty to the United States (Tollefson 1989). In fact, speaking English is defined by the US Immigration and Naturalization Service as a 'basic citizenship skill' (Gutstein 1988).

Thus the refugee education programme, particularly ESL, does not end the desperate economic circumstances or the social and psychological problems associated with economic crisis and resettlement. Classes for refugees generally do not lead to jobs paying a liveable wage; they do not lead to jobs that provide an opportunity to improve language or employment skills; and they do not improve prospects for upward mobility for most graduates. Instead, classes seek to convince refugees that they have no alternative but to accept minimum-wage employment; they train refugees for these jobs by teaching entry-level employment skills, attitudes of subservience, and limited survival English competencies such as apologizing and following orders (Tollefson 1986a).

THE EDUCATION OF INDOCHINESE REFUGEES

Since the late 1970s, a special educational programme for refugees has had the stated purpose of solving the problems facing resettled Southeast Asians. An extensive network of federally funded refugee programmes in the United States offers courses in survival English for 'entry level' employment. In addition, in 1980, specially built processing centres in the Philippines, Thailand, and Indonesia were established in order to reduce the cost of educating refugees in the United States. (The centre in Indonesia closed in 1987.) At these centres, refugees receive six months of intensive training in English language, cultural orientation, and pre-employment skills such as attending job interviews and filling out applications. Since 1980, 300,000 people have completed this programme, while hundreds of thousands of their family members depend upon them for survival. Like most refugees, Binh completed all of these classes.

Supported by federal funds earmarked for special refugee assistance, these programmes are intended solely to speed refugees' entry into the labour market. As the former Deputy Coordinator for Refugee Programs at the United States Embassy in Manila declared in 1984, the purpose of classes is to keep refugees on a track into employment rather than on to government assistance programmes (Waggoner 1984). Domestic educational programmes are required by federal funding agencies to focus upon the goal of early employment in entry-level jobs (Office of Refugee Resettlement 1984). Language, cultural orientation, and skills training are designed so that refugees obtain jobs quickly and exhibit 'appropriate' workplace behaviour on the job. The term used to describe employed refugees earning at least a minimum wage is 'self-sufficient' (e.g., see International Catholic Migration Commission 1985).

Refugee education is part of a larger effort to prepare both legal and illegal immigrants for employment. Since 1985, approximately 270,000 immigrants and 60,000 refugees have entered the USA every year. An uncertain number of undocumented immigrants – perhaps as many as three to five million – have also entered the country since the late 1970s (Kritz 1983; Reimers 1985). Though some officials have demanded that severe restrictions be placed on immigration (e.g., Lamm and Imhoff 1985), US policy generally has encouraged legal and illegal immigrants as a means of increasing the pool of cheap labour available to the growing number of service industries and light manufacturing plants, particularly in California and the Sunbelt states in the South and Southwest (Muller and Espenshade 1985). As the United States has shifted from a largely industrial economy to one of high technology and service-oriented industries, employers have increasingly used large numbers of immigrant workers to fill available positions (Jiobu 1988; Latkiewicz and Anderson 1983). In addition, immigrants and refugees provide a category of labour that is especially susceptible to shifts in the economy: during periods of economic slowdowns, they are the first to lose their jobs. Thus they provide a kind of buffer that cushions other groups from the boom and recession swings of the modern economy (Marshall 1986).

The primary goal of refugee education is to reduce the cost of public assistance by forcing refugees and other immigrants to accept low-paying jobs or be declared ineligible for public assistance. The importance of this goal is underlined in testimony by programme officials before Congress. For instance, H. Eugene Douglas, US Coordinator for Refugee Affairs in 1983, complained before Congress that refugee welfare costs remain high, despite special programmes (Douglas 1983). Two years later, in a statement before the House Judiciary Committee, Douglas suggested that a consensus had been reached that the refugee welfare rate was far too high: 'We are all familiar with the major disappointment of the past few years in the domestic program – the utilization and expense of the public assistance programs which provide financial assistance and resettlement services to refugees' (Douglas 1986, p. 15). Both refugees themselves and the voluntary agencies (primarily religious groups) which assist refugees are blamed for their use of public assistance funds: 'There is little that the [refugee] program can do to significantly reduce the rate of refugee welfare dependency as long as public assistance is available to refugees and as long as friends, relatives, and others encourage them to enroll.' (Tannenbaum 1985, p. 81) The implication of such statements is that steps must be taken to limit eligibility for welfare.

Regulations promulgated by the Office of Refugee Resettlement (ORR) of the US Department of Health and Human Services, which disburses funds to refugee programmes, prohibit advanced language education for jobs other than entry-level employment. State programmes require refugees to accept minimum-wage jobs, and they restrict services for refugees only to those that contribute directly to economic self-sufficiency (ORR 1984). In practice, these regulations have been interpreted as forbidding child care, translation services (e.g., in police and judicial hearings), transportation assistance, and other services that might facilitate but not contribute directly to employment. The highest priority of the regulations is strictly applying sanctions against refugees who refuse to register for or accept entry-level and minimum-wage jobs. It is this regulation which forces Binh to take a job and lose the chance to learn enough English to be a mechanic.

In 1988, the ORR adopted additional rules designed to reduce costs and to provide newly arriving refugees 'stronger incentives' to accept entry-level jobs. Under these rules, eligibility for special refugee cash assistance was cut from 18 to 12 months, thereby forcing more refugees into general assistance programmes, which in some states are considered as loans that must be repaid by doing work for local governments (*Federal Register* 1987; *Refugee Reports* 1987).

The effect of these rules is that ESL programmes must emphasize 'survival' English, regardless of the previous education, training, and job skills of refugees. Refugees with experience as nurses and doctors, engineers, office staff, teachers, technicians, or mechanics cannot rely upon federal refugee assistance for ESL courses appropriate for these professions, but instead must enter general ESL classes at colleges and universities outside of work hours and at their own expense. In addition, most states refuse to recognize advanced degrees and professional certification from the countries of Indochina. Many medical doctors from Vietnam, for instance, have had to complete medical school in the United States before being permitted to practise medicine. Thus, by discouraging courses other than those considered suitable for minimum-wage work, policy-making agencies ensure that the educational programme prepares most refugees for minimum-wage jobs. (For a different situation, see the discussion of Australia, in Chapter 7.)

Refugees concerned that they will not learn English once they accept a minimum-wage job are assured that they will be able to learn English on the job. Lessons teach that on-the-job training is one of the best ways to increase English proficiency (Department of State 1984, p. 275). Refugees are also assured that American co-workers will be willing to help them learn English (Department of State 1984, p. 331). Yet studies demonstrate that refugees rarely learn English or other skills on the job (Arter, Hadley, and Reder 1984; Cox 1983; Finnan 1981; Strand 1984). This is because most minimum-wage jobs for which they are hired provide no opportunity to use English or to receive additional training. One study found that refugees who work *fewer* hours normally learn English faster, perhaps because they are more likely to be enrolled in ESL classes (Arter, Hadley, and Reder 1984).

MEDIA EXAMPLE 5.1

In an article about ESL classes on the job, Carol Smith Monkman praises the decision of the Westin Hotel chain to begin ESL classes for its employees who work as housekeepers, laundry workers, and dishwashers.

> The Westin is . . . among the first [companies] in the country to mount a formal literacy program for its non-English-speaking employees. Of all the basic workplace skills, the most basic is English. For . . . recent immigrants . . . not speaking English is a barrier to getting employment. Once on the job, problems with English can hinder advancement. (Monkman 1989)
> (Source: *Seattle Post-Intelligencer*, 20 January 1989)

Questions

1. The language programme offered at the Westin Hotel meets four hours per week, with participants being paid their wages for two hours of that time. The first cycle of classes lasted two months, for a total of 32 hours of instruction. What effect is 32 hours of ESL likely to have upon the ability of employees currently working as house-keepers and dishwashers to find better jobs?

2. If the ESL programme will not effectively qualify workers for more advanced jobs, what might be the purpose of the programme, from the perspective of the company offering it? How might it benefit the company?

Employed refugees

What are the effects of the federal policy of providing refugees with a specialized educational programme to prepare them for entry-level employment? Does an ESL programme emphasizing minimum-wage jobs effectively prepare refugees for living in the United States? One way to answer these questions is to look at the most successful graduates of the programme – those refugees who find jobs. Having accomplished the goal which the educational programme has set for them, they are the most successful graduates. Yet a major ORR study of resettled refugees found that a job does not resolve the economic problems confronting refugees (*Southeast Asian Refugee Self-Sufficiency Study* 1985).

The ORR study, conducted by the University of Michigan Institute for Social Research, found that refugees' unemployment rate drops as they spend a longer time in the United States. While nine out of ten refugees are unemployed after four months, only about a third are unemployed after three years. Yet, while about a fifth of all refugee families live above the poverty line after four months in the United States, only about 57 per cent do so after three years. In other words, a rise in the refugee employment rate is not accompanied by an equivalent drop in the poverty rate. Getting a job does not necessarily end poverty (*Southeast Asian Refugee Self-Sufficiency Study* 1985, p. 180).

An explanation for these findings is to be found in the types of jobs refugees obtain. The ORR study found that four out of five employed refugees find jobs in the lowest paid category of work ('operatives, service workers, and laborers'), although in Southeast Asia only 14 per cent had jobs of this type. The study also found that more than half of all refugees who work are employed in peripheral jobs, which are part time, irregular, or seasonal, and which pay low salaries and provide little opportunity for advancement. For the great majority of Southeast Asian refugees, resettlement in the United States entailed significant downward mobility.

The ORR study also showed that few refugees find employment appropriate to their previous experience, education, and skills. Although refugees who were professionals and office managers in Southeast Asia are the most likely group to find work in the United States, they are employed primarily in unskilled or semiskilled jobs paying low wages. Fewer than 4 per cent find work as professionals and managers in the United States, while most work as janitors, maids, and assemblers. Half of this group do not find any job (*Southeast Asian Refugee Self-Sufficiency Study* 1985, pp. 121–9). Only 25 per cent of those with experience as skilled machine operators are employed in any job in the United States.

The average hourly wage for employed refugees in the study was only $4.90, with most earning somewhere between $3.07 and $6.77 per hour. Because this amount is barely adequate to support an individual's essential needs, refugees with families must pool earnings from several wage earners. The ORR study found that one in ten refugee households held at least four jobs, while only a third had just one employed individual. A job does not mean financial security, however: those who are employed are likely to be among the first to lose their jobs during slow economic times. In the recession of the early 1980s, for instance, the unemployment rate for refugees who arrived during 1975–78 increased dramatically (Bach 1984).

Because the bleak salary structure and the high probability of losing their jobs places refugees at great economic risk, the ORR study concluded: 'In addition to being unemployed and underemployed, the refugees tend to hold dead-end jobs. . . Even where jobs are held by refugees, they tend to be low in wages, status, and any possibility for upward mobility.' (*Southeast Asian Refugee Self-Sufficiency Study* 1985, pp. 133, 139)

Unemployed refugees

Despite the evidence that a job does not mean an end to serious economic problems, officials who support existing policy argue that the policy is successful. The only problem, they claim, is the number of refugees who *choose* to remain on welfare. For instance, in 1985 James Purcell, then Director of the Bureau for Refugee Programs, argued before the Subcommittee on Immigration, Refugees, and International Law of the House Judiciary Committee that refugees are reluctant to accept jobs because they are attracted by the high benefit structure of the welfare system in some states. As a result, he complained that refugees' social and cultural assimilation is delayed (Purcell 1985, pp. 3–4).

Though officials condemn refugees' 'welfare dependency', all studies of resettled refugees suggest that it is a myth. Neither the ORR study nor one by the Church World Service found any evidence that refugees have a 'dependency mentality' characterized by attitudes and values that discourage work (*Southeast Asian Refugee Self-Sufficiency Survey* 1985, pp. 244-5). The Church World Service found that real service needs rather than refugees' attitudes are behind refugees' high use of welfare (Church World Service 1983, p. 7). In both studies, most refugees who stopped looking for work did so for reasons that are widely considered to be acceptable. Most of the adults at home were mothers with young children, usually in families with at least one other employed adult, while most other refugees not seeking work were in school. Only 2 per cent of all sponsors surveyed by the Church World Service reported that they know refugees who do not want to work; only 1 per cent stated that public assistance discourages them from seeking work. Moreover, refugees have a good reason to delay work in order to enrol in school for language education or job training: over a third of all refugees who had ever been employed had lost their jobs.

Additional research by Robert Bach suggests that refugees are much less likely than the US population generally to cite household responsibilities as a justification for not looking for a job (Bach 1984). Bach found that employment problems for refugees resemble those facing other immigrants and linguistic minorities, and have nothing to do with attitudes and values. He concluded instead that the use of public assistance among refugees will decline when they find jobs, not that people will find jobs when they are cut from the welfare rolls. The reason for high use of public assistance seems to be straightforward. Refugees need, on average, eleven months to find their first jobs. The process of gaining employment paying a liveable wage takes a great deal of additional effort over at least two to four years. Moreover, those refugees who do not obtain welfare experience serious health, nutrition, and safety problems, as public assistance provides virtually the only source of food, shelter, and clothing for new arrivals. Thus, public assistance plays a crucial role in the early stages of resettlement, and self-sufficiency is possible only after enormous dedication and effort over a period of several years, including much more than the 180 hours of ESL teaching provided by federal regulations. In its insistence that an entry-level job will provide the opportunity to gain language and employment skills that will lead to upward mobility, the educational programme does not address refugees' continuing economic, social, and psychological needs.

Yet the myth of welfare dependency persists. One reason may be that it helps to sustain a deeply held ideology of American success that claims that a unique American character is respons-ible for the nation's riches. By implication, the poor must be responsible for their own poverty, due to the choices they have made based upon their values and attitudes. To admit that refugees are unemployed despite their hard work means that hard-working people may remain impoverished (Lears 1981; Tollefson 1989).

Industries employing refugees support high quotas for refugee admissions as well as the current educational programme, praising its graduates as good employees in part because they follow orders and do not emphasize wages (Latkiewicz and Anderson 1983). Yet in the US population as a whole, there is growing resistance to immigration and to special educational programmes for refugees and immigrants. This resistance has culminated in the movement to amend the US Constitution to declare English the sole official language. If adopted, this measure could further the political and economic disenfranchisement of people like Binh Nguyen and millions of others who do not speak English well enough to participate in the dominant institutions of American society.

peripheral

THE ENGLISH LANGUAGE AMENDMENT

In the general election in the United States in November 1988, three states had voter-initiated measures on the ballot to declare English the official language in those states. In Florida and Colorado the measures passed by large majorities, while in Arizona the measure passed by a narrow margin. These citizen efforts to impose language policy followed the important 1984 California initiative declaring that English is the sole official language of that state, and similar actions in Indiana, Kentucky, Illinois, Nebraska, and Virginia. By early 1989, seventeen states had adopted such measures.

These state-by-state actions are part of a national movement, coordinated by an organization called US English, which enjoys strong support across the country. The main goal of US English is to amend the US Constitution so that English will become the official national language. To reach this goal, US English has supported a range of language policy measures to enhance the privileges enjoyed by speakers of English. Although I will discuss the movement in the United States, it is important to keep in mind that similar movements exist in other English-speaking countries, and that even countries which support minority languages have powerful pressure groups that resist pluralist policies.

MEDIA EXAMPLE 5.2

During summer 1988, superstar pop singer Linda Ronstadt embarked on a nationwide tour across the United States singing songs from her album of Mexican folk songs, 'Canciones de mi Padre,' ('Songs of my Father'). News services reported that at her concert in the Boston area, unhappy fans shouted for her to sing in English and left midway through the concert to demand their money back. (*Seattle Post-Intelligencer*, 15 August 1988)

Questions

1. Why do you think those who attended the Ronstadt concert were so upset that she sang songs in Spanish?

2. Do you think the owner of the theatre should refund the price of tickets to unsatisfied members of the audience?

Proposals to declare English the official language

Proposals to declare English the official language have been made at state and federal levels. At the state level, the 1984 California 'English Ballot Initiative', which voters overwhelmingly approved in November, 1984, is typical:

> Section 1. Findings and Declarations
> We the People of the State of California do hereby find and declare that:
> (a) The United States has been and will continue to be enriched by the cultural contributions of immigrants from many countries with many different traditions.
> (b) A common language, English, unites our immigrant residents, fosters harmony among our people, promotes political stability, permits interchange of ideas at many levels and encourages societal integration.
> (c) The United States Government should foster similarities that unite our people, the most important of which is the use of the English language.
> (d) Multilingual ballots are unnecessary since immigrants seeking citizenship must pass an examination for literacy and proficiency in English.
>
> Section 2. Transmittal
> The Governor of the State of California, within thirty (30) days of enactment of this statute, shall sign and cause to be delivered to the President of the United States, the Attorney General of the United States, and to all members of the United States Congress a written communication which incorporates the findings and declarations in Section 1 and includes the following language: The People of the State of California recognizing the importance of a common language in unifying our diverse nation hereby urge that Federal law be amended so that ballots, voters' pamphlets and all other official voting materials shall be printed in English only.

Measures in other states are similar in their rejection of multilingual ballots and voting materials, and their assumption that a single language is necessary for political stability and social integration.

Because bilingual education programmes and elections are federally funded and thus governed by federal law, these state ballot measures have had relatively little practical effect on elections. In other ways, however, they have had a direct practical impact. In Arizona, the state Board of Pardons and Paroles has denied hearings to non-English-speaking prisoners until confusion over the new official English law is cleared up. In Florida, a cashier in a Coral Gables supermarket was suspended from work for ten days for asking a co-worker a question in Spanish (Combs 1989).

Because state laws do not apply universally across the country, however, supporters of the English language movement are pressing for a federal constitutional amendment. Beginning in 1981, when Senator S.I. Hayakawa of California introduced the first English Language Amendment (ELA), proposals to amend the Constitution have been submitted at least five times. Though varying somewhat from year to year, all these proposals declare that English shall be the official language of the United States and that no law or regulation may require the use of any language other than English. By mid-1989, no ELA proposal had passed the US Congress, though state measures continued to be proposed and organizations supporting the ELA claimed rapidly increasing membership.

Should the ELA eventually be adopted, the implications for language policy would be profound. In a detailed analysis of its likely effects, a Congressional study concluded that bilingual voters' pamphlets and ballots would be banned nationwide and that bilingual education programmes could use languages other than English only for the specific purpose of fostering fluency in English (Dale 1983; also see Marshall 1986). A wide range of programmes using languages other than English would also be eliminated: interpreters in the physical and mental examination of immigrants; translators in federal civil and criminal proceedings; and foreign-language personnel in community health, alcohol, and drug-abuse programmes. Universities would not be permitted to establish foreign-language degree requirements (Dale 1983). Other effects would vary from state to state. Those states having long traditions of bilingualism in testing and certification, education, and other areas of public life (e.g., New Mexico and Hawaii) would be forced to abandon practices that use languages other than English. In some states, health and safety may be impaired. Under current New Mexico law, for instance, pesticide warning labels must be in English and Spanish in order to protect agricultural workers who speak only Spanish.

The perspective on language that motivates the ELA movement has been explored by Marshall (1986) and Donahue (1985). In addition, US English has published many documents presenting pro-ELA arguments, and the director of US English, Gerda Bikales, has testified before Congress (Bikales 1985) and published a rationale for the amendment (Bikales 1986).

Perhaps the most common assumption among proponents of the ELA is that the United States has always been a monolingual English-speaking country. Writing in 1986, for instance, Bikales argued that the USA is essentially monolingual, but that bilingual education and bilingual voting rights threaten for the first time in US history to introduce language divisions (Bikales 1986, pp. 84–5). From this perspective, the historically dominant position of English is seen as being under attack from supporters of bilingual education and other measures. Bikales warns that most Americans will oppose the threatened displacement of English by other languages (1986, p. 81).

Fear that English is in retreat is linked to another argument, namely, that use of languages other than English is inherently disunifying, and therefore politically dangerous. This argument has two parts: first, that the United States requires a single language for public debate and political discourse; second, that use of languages other than English will delay the assimilation of immigrants and others who do not speak English as a first language. In part, this concern reflects a belief that people speak other languages because they do not want to learn English: they are too lazy, poorly motivated, indifferent to its benefits, or possess other personal and cultural characteristics that make them poor learners of English (see Donahue 1985, p. 104). This view is deeply suspicious of the cultural distinctiveness of today's immigrants and warns that they are different from those of the past: Latin American and Asian rather than European. Bikales warns that today there are far greater religious, cultural, and racial differences between immigrants and what she called 'indigenous groups' (Bikales 1986, p. 78).

The declared intention of the ELA is to encourage immigrants to learn English by removing the benefits accorded them under bilingual policies. ELA supporters suggest that this is for the good of immigrants. Bikales argues that jobs for unskilled workers are in short supply, and thus immigrants see little reason to learn English in order to obtain such jobs. Lacking this economic incentive, immigrants must be forced to learn English through educational and political means, in order that they will be able to enjoy the benefits of speaking English (Bikales 1986, p. 83). To summarize the arguments of the proponents of the ELA:

1. The USA has always been a monolingual, English-speaking country.
2. For the first time in US history, this monolingualism is threatened by bilingual education, bilingual voting, and other measures that help languages gradually displace English.
3. Today's immigrants differ from those in the past in that they come from Latin America and Asia rather than Europe, and often are unwilling to learn English.
4. Use of languages other than English delays the economic, cultural, and linguistic assimilation of immigrants.
5. Multilingualism threatens the political and cultural unity of the US.

MEDIA EXAMPLE 5.3

One of the strongest supporters of the measure to declare English the official language in California was Guy Wright, an influential columnist for the daily *San Francisco Examiner*. Wright argued in his columns that those who support bilingual voting and other measures are guilty of threatening to divide the United States along ethnic lines. He demanded that everyone residing in the United States should be required to learn English, and he celebrated in 1984 when California's voters adopted Proposition 38 by an overwhelming 71 per cent to 29 per cent.

Yet Wright did not support increased funding for ESL programmes for those immigrants who want to learn English, even though he correctly predicted a serious shortage of ESL classes: 'The Legislature will balk when it realizes how much it would cost to hire enough credentialed teachers and professional administrators to cope with the waiting lists for English classes' (Wright 1986). Instead, as the media example shows, he proposed that Boy Scouts and members of the Junior League volunteer to teach English.

Let's Teach English
BY GUY WRIGHT

Once the holidays are out of the way, I plan to spend one evening a week teaching English to immigrants. I hope some of you reading this will do the same thing. Lots of people with strange-sounding names are waiting in line to learn.

I'm not going into this as a sacrifice. Quite the contrary, I expect to meet new friends, have some fun, maybe even get an occasional column out of it.

But beyond that, it just makes sense that those of us who campaigned to make English the official language of California should help new Californians learn it. By volunteering to teach them, perhaps we can dispose of the charge that we were plotting to freeze them out.

If I may dream a little, I would like to see a great statewide grass-roots network of English classes for immigrants, staffed by volunteers.

Instead, there is talk of tapping the state treasury to finance more classes through the regular school system. I doubt that's the best way to go. The Legislature will balk when it realizes how much it would cost to hire enough credentialed teachers and professional administrators to cope with the waiting lists for English classes.

Besides, it isn't necessary to take that route. The immigrant doesn't need to learn perfect English, desirable though that would be. He needs survival English. And fortunately there are many of us who can teach him that.

What's missing is an organized recruitment program for volunteers. That's what the state should provide.

For retired people with time on their hands, here is a chance to do something worthwhile. For service clubs hunting new activities, here is a natural.

Why shouldn't Boy Scouts teach English to immigrant kids? And the Junior League to immigrant women? Why shouldn't pastors get their congregations involved?

Most working people can spare one evening a week. If bowling and bridge and Monday night football have become a bore, sign on to teach an English class to immigrants.

Years ago I taught radio for a while. It was technical stuff, and often I had to struggle to get it across. But I'll never forget how gratifying it was to see that light suddenly turn on in a student's eyes. I felt like Steve McQueen in 'The Sand Pebbles' when his Chinese helper finally realized how a steam engine worked. I hope to recapture that feeling by teaching English.

If my dream of a grass-roots network of classes should become reality, we'll need a clean, well-lighted place – and lots of them. Schools, empty at night, are a logical choice if the red tape can be cut. If not, let's use church basements, lodge halls, union halls, corporate conference rooms, vacant store fronts.

Volunteers will need some guidance from the state. But not too much. A simple briefing and a handbook that set out the lessons should do. I'm not keen on having conventional educators in control. They get hung up on grammar rules and stuff like that.

Better we should draw on the Berlitz method and the techniques of the Defense Language School at Monterey – and try to find out how European schools teach every kid a second language.

But I'm willing to start with whatever tools are at hand, knowing that each time an immigrant learns a new word his future brightens and the tensions caused by heavy immigration are lowered.

I shall still work for repeal of the bilingual ballot law and for defeat of politicians who peddle ethnic separatism. But I also believe that we who recognize the value of English as a unifying force in our nation should take a more active role in sharing it with those who want to learn.

(Source: *San Francisco Examiner*, 23 November 1986)

Questions

1. How effective do you think Guy Wright's proposals will be?
2. Wright argues that English is a 'unifying force' in the nation and he insists that English should be the only language used for official purposes. Yet he does not support increased funding for ESL. What does this indicate about the underlying aim of the ELA movement?

Growing opposition to the English language movement

As more states adopt measures supporting English as the official language, opposition to the English language movement has begun to grow. The TESOL organization passed a resolution at its 1987 conference to oppose all measures to declare English the official language. The American Civil Liberties Union, the Center for Applied Linguistics, and 30 other organizations have adopted an 'English Plus' resolution supporting the use of diverse languages in business, government, and private affairs. In his speech accepting the Democratic Party nomination for President in 1988, Michael Dukakis spoke Spanish when praising efforts to register new voters and bring 'new people' into politics, thereby implying that Spanish was an appropriate language for public political discourse.

Opposition to the ELA has focused its efforts primarily upon discrediting the major assumptions of ELA proponents. The English-Plus (anti-ELA) position may be summarized as follows:

1. The USA is not and never has been a monolingual country. Kloss (1977) has demonstrated that multilingualism and policies supporting languages other than English have been a central feature of the American language situation since colonial times. Viewed in historical perspective, bilingual education and voting

are consistent with practices that extend back to the early eighteenth century.

2. English is not being displaced by other languages; in fact, English is dominant today as no other language in recent history. Although its population has always been multilingual, the United States has long tended towards reduced multilingualism (Gorlach 1986). In other words, the trend is towards greater and greater domination by English speakers, not vice versa as supporters of the ELA would argue.

3. Use of languages other than English aids the integration of immigrant groups into the political and economic life of the nation by making it easier for them to participate in political activity, receive an education, and find employment. For example, Spolsky (1972, 1978) has shown that English-only policies present a serious barrier to the education of linguistic minorities. Similar linguistic barriers enacted by the ELA would limit for many people their full participation in the political and economic life of the nation.

4. Today's immigrants pose no more of a challenge to US institutions than those immigrants who entered the country during the last great period of immigration between 1880 and 1920. Indeed, at that time, many argued that the new immigrants from southern and eastern Europe were different from those who had arrived from northern Europe earlier in the nineteenth century, and therefore that special educational programmes to assimilate them should be enacted along with tight limits on immigration (Tollefson 1989). In fact, efforts to penalize immigrants for not speaking English are likely to slow their movement out of low-paying jobs in the peripheral economy. Heath and Krasner (1986) point out that today's immigrants are isolated socially, their communities having little access to dominant institutions. Moreover, Marshall (1986) points out that racial, cultural, and religious differences among US immigrants, which are the source of such concern among ELA proponents, will not be changed by policies that block immigrants' full participation in American life.

5. The use of more than one language does not threaten national unity. Indeed, the attempt to restrict languages is a far greater threat to stability in that it presents a direct political and economic challenge to specific ethnic and linguistic groups. Milan (1986) argues that earlier immigrants, who are now praised for

their contribution to the industrialization of the country and their willingness to learn English, required two or three generations to shift from their native languages to English. As Binh Nguyen's case suggests, a similar period may be necessary for today's immigrants. Under the proposed ELA, immigrants would be unnecessarily penalized during this period of language shift.

The underlying issues

Despite opposition arguments, the ELA movement to legislate language policy continues to gain momentum, with US English reporting a membership of 350,000 supporters, including prominent individuals such as former CBS news anchor Walter Cronkite, Linda Chavez (the former director of the US Civil Rights Commission), Saul Bellow, Bruno Bettelheim, and Alistair Cooke (*Time*, 1988). Influential members of Congress, state legislatures, and citizens' groups throughout the country are pushing for a policy of officially granting English preferential status. Clearly, many individuals in positions of authority support the ELA.

The false but commonplace assumption that English can be mastered by anyone with sufficient motivation permits policy-makers to claim that they are only encouraging people to do what is in their own interest as well as the nation's. But the unwillingness of ELA supporters to fund ESL classes suggests that the real aim of these policies is something else. As Deutsch (1975, p. 7) points out, language is a signalling system second only to race in identifying targets for privilege and discrimination. Indeed, other periods in which immigrant communities have been involved in a gradual shift to English have also included discriminatory policies adopted against them (Loescher and Scanlan 1986).

Thus policies limiting the use of languages other than English must be viewed as an effort to restrict immigrants' access to political power and economic resources. The potential role of the ELA in this process can be seen clearly in the following list of its likely effects:

1. The ELA will further stratify immigrants, who are already among groups with the lowest average income in the USA (Jiobu 1988).
2. Immigrants will be less likely to vote or otherwise participate

in the political process (Marshall 1986).
3. The dropout rate is likely to increase among children who do not speak English, while those who remain in school will fall further behind as they are denied mother-tongue classes in arithmetic, social studies, writing, and other subjects (*New Voices* 1988).
4. Immigrants will continue to be employed primarily in low-paying jobs in the peripheral economy (Marshall 1986).

Bikales (1986, p. 78) argues that multilingualism is not a threat in itself; rather, it becomes a threat to national unity when it is combined with religious, cultural, and 'racial' differences between immigrants and 'indigenous groups'. McArthur (1986, p. 91) points out that this view expresses fear of Spanish speakers from Latin America, who are often perceived as 'illiterate, impoverished, dirty, backward, criminally inclined, residually Roman Catholic, prone to Communist infiltration, dark-complexioned, and now pushing cocaine and marijuana north for all they are worth'. Because restricting the language of immigrants will not change their religious, cultural, and ethnic characteristics, Marshall (1986) concludes that the agenda of those who support the ELA must be something other than language, namely, restricting access of non-English speakers to economic resources and political institutions.

In 1986, ELA opponents uncovered a memo from John Tanton, co-founder of US English, in which he warned that high birth rates among Spanish speakers in the USA threatened the future of the country: 'Perhaps this is the first instance in which those with their pants up are going to get caught by those with their pants down' (*Time*, 1988). In the ensuing uproar, several prominent supporters of US, English, including Walter Cronkite, resigned from the organization and Tanton was forced to step down. The incident demonstrates that the movement to disenfranchise immigrants cannot be separated from the question of racism.

MEDIA EXAMPLE 5.4

The cartoon in this example depicts control of the large Teamsters Union by organized crime. In the cartoon, a criminal professes his innocence as he forces a rank-and-file member of the union to agree with him.

(Source: *Seattle Post-Intelligencer*, 30 June 1988)

Questions

1. How do we know which speaker is a criminal? Notice in particular the use of specialized spelling to indicate language. In what way does the cartoon imply that language diversity is a symbol of deviancy?

2. The cartoon assumes that the language of mobsters is different from that of law-abiding citizens and that criminality is reflected in language. Is the language of criminals different from that of other speakers? If so, how? If not, then why does the cartoon use specialized language for the mobsters?

3. Does the cartoon depend upon ethnic stereotypes? Of what group(s)?

THE IMMIGRATION REFORM AND CONTROL ACT OF 1986

Closely related to the ELA movement is the Immigration Reform and Control Act of 1986 (IRCA), which includes special provisions requiring certain immigrants to learn English (although the Act does not provide funds for teaching English to these individuals). The IRCA established procedures for the legalization of undocumented aliens who have lived in the United States since before 1 January 1982. An important legislation that continues to evoke controversy, the IRCA was passed by Congress in an attempt to document illegal aliens who had become permanent residents in the United States, and thereby to make it more difficult for employers to hire undocumented aliens in the future. Although legalization offered the chance for several million people to become permanent legal residents, it also required that those who have lived for many years in fear of being discovered must turn themselves in to the authorities. While many immigrants who could provide proof that they meet the requirements of the Act were willing to come forward, many others were afraid that they would be arrested, imprisoned, and deported. Others objected to the implication of the Act that they were criminals who needed to be forgiven. Despite these problems, as many as 1.8 million people came forward under the provisions of the IRCA.

The IRCA spelled out a two-step process for legalization. First, illegal aliens meeting the residency requirement had to complete an application for amnesty and temporary residency before 4 May 1988. Second, applicants must fulfil certain residency, health, and education requirements in order to be granted permanent residence. These requirements include: continuously residing in the United States for 18 months from the time of the original amnesty application until application for permanent residency; being tested for HIV antibodies (AIDS); and demonstrating basic citizenship skills, defined by the US Immigration and Naturalization Service (INS) as knowledge of English and of American history and government (Gutstein 1988). In 1988, proposed federal rules governing the educational requirement stated that applicants must either demonstrate minimal understanding of English, civics, and government as measured by an INS citizenship examination, or be enrolled in a course of study to meet this goal.

INS regulations provide for six specific educational options: (1) completing 40 hours out of a 60-hour course, and showing a 'certificate of satisfactory pursuit' issued by the course to verify continuing progress; (2) presenting a high-school diploma or completing the general equivalency diploma (GED) exam; (3) attending a state-accredited institution, which must verify attendance; (4) attending courses offered by employers or private service agencies certified by the INS; (5) passing the INS proficiency test; (6) passing a proficiency test administered by the Educational Testing Service (ETS) or other approved agency (*Federal Register* 1988). Immigrants who failed to meet the November 1990 deadline for these requirements were to be subject to deportation.

These requirements have led to a huge increase in the demand for ESL classes. Though this demand is the direct result of federal immigration policy, federal funds have not been allocated to enable ESL programmes to meet the demand. In areas with especially large numbers of immigrants, ESL programmes have been flooded with new students (Associated Press 1988). The Evans Community Adult School in Los Angeles, for example, must hold classes 24 hours a day to accommodate everyone who wants to enrol. In El Paso, Texas, the public schools offer day classes while Roman Catholic churches offer classes at night. In the Dallas–Ft Worth area, where 65,000 people applied for amnesty, the waiting period for classes in 1989 was two to three months. The result is that immigrants who signed up under the amnesty programme find themselves at risk of being unable to meet its requirements through no fault of their own.

The content of classes presents additional problems. The INS initially required the classes to use the 1987 edition of the Federal Citizenship Textbook, which is written at both fourth- and eighth-grade reading levels. Realizing that many immigrants could not read at these levels, the INS asked the Center for Applied Linguistics to prepare appropriate materials, using the Federal Citizenship Textbook to determine content.

Perhaps the greatest difficulty is that the heavy content of the Federal Citizenship Textbook (history, government, geography, and society) cannot be adequately taught in 40–60 hours. Moreover, the text is designed for immigrants who plan to assimilate permanently into US society, yet many of those registered under the IRCA hope to return to their homes in Latin America some time in the future. For them, much of the information about citizenship is irrelevant.

THE IDEOLOGY OF LANGUAGE IN THE UNITED STATES

In the debate over US language policy, the impact of policy alternatives on real people is often forgotten. The failure to consider the struggle of people like Binh Nguyen to learn English and to support a family under difficult economic circumstances is due to the ideology of language in the United States.

Sonntag and Pool (1987) believe that all sides in the debate over language policy, refugee policy, the ELA, and the IRCA accept certain ideological assumptions, and that only individuals and groups who accept these assumptions are accorded serious consideration in the policy debate. These assumptions, which reflect a neoclassical perspective (see Chapter 2) are as follows:

1. Language diversity is inherently disunifying.
2. English language competence is a measure of loyalty to the nation.
3. The key to learning English is motivation. Anyone who truly wants to learn English – who has adequate willpower – will be able to acquire English.
4. English language competence leads to upward mobility.
5. Language is rightfully excluded from protection under laws barring discrimination.

Although these neoclassical assumptions are widely accepted, Binh's case calls many of them into question. First, there is no evidence that language diversity is inherently disunifying or that English language competence is an indicator of national loyalty. Indeed, Binh Nguyen's limited English proficiency has nothing to do with loyalty to the nation, but rather to the intrinsic difficulty involved in acquiring a new language. Second, Binh is highly motivated, but faces a formidable task with inadequate support from the programme established to help him. Moreover, there is no evidence that ESL (apart from education generally) leads to upward mobility, or that employment leads to increased English proficiency (Tollefson 1986a).

The final assumption of the American ideology of language involves the question of language rights. Should language, like race, nationality, ethnicity, and gender, be protected under laws barring discrimination? Though the United States has not yet seriously considered such laws, Chapter 7 will examine two countries which have begun to take steps to provide such protection.

CONCLUSION: BINH'S DECISION

Binh Nguyen's decision about whether to continue studying English while his son drops out of school to work is filled with risk. Even if Binh learns English quickly, will he find a job as a mechanic or will he meet other barriers in his path to self-sufficiency? What kind of job will his son find? Will he lose interest in school? What if his son finds a job, only to lose it later?

Neoclassical theory analyses Binh's decision in a straight-forward manner: he must weigh the costs (including the risks) against the potential benefits. The risks are great – his son dropping out of school permanently, the possibility of losing his job, the difficulties involved in learning English, and the uncertainty of being able to find a mechanic's job in the future. The benefits to his son leaving school include time for Binh to study ESL, the possibility of a better job in the future, and security for the family. According to neoclassical theory, Binh's difficulty in making a decision is due only to the degree of uncertainty: he cannot know with certainty that a particular decision will lead to a particular outcome.

In contrast, historical–structural analysis examines Binh's dilemma within the context of broader policy issues, in particular the state's unwillingness to support long-term ESL or to provide adequate funding for existing ESL programmes, a federal labour policy that demands large numbers of minimum-wage employees, and the federal goal of integrating refugees into the peripheral economy. Historical–structural analysis explains current policies with reference to the beneficiaries of those policies, primarily employers of refugees. Thus Binh's difficult decision is seen not as a result of uncertainty, but rather as a direct and intentional effect of policies designed not in his interest, but rather in the interest of those who most influence the policy-making process.

Binh successfully completed both the overseas and domestic educational programmes. He has done everything asked of him. From the historical–structural perspective, Binh's choices are constrained by policies which he has not chosen and over which he has no control. The effect of those policies is now manifest in the fact that he and his family, regardless of what decision he eventually makes, almost certainly will face permanent economic crisis.

FOR DISCUSSION

1. Compare the following two ESL texts: Walsh (1984), and Auerbach and Wallerstein (1987). Notice that Walsh provides recipes for success, including directions for how to dress and act at work. In contrast, Auerbach and Wallerstein pose problems for discussion, expecting students to define their own problems and derive their own solutions. What other differences do you observe between the two texts?

2. Some opponents of the ELA have proposed a Cultural Rights Amendment (CRA). One such CRA, proposed by the Federation of American Cultural and Language Communities, is as follows (Marshall 1986, p. 39):

> Section 1. The right of the people to preserve, foster, and promote their respective historical, linguistic and cultural origins is recognized. No person shall be denied the equal protection of the laws because of culture or language.
> Section 2. The Congress shall have the power to enforce this Article by appropriate legislation.

What might be the effects of such a Constitutional amendment? Do you think a CRA will be adopted?

FOR ACTION

1. Observe an ESL class for refugees or immigrants near your home. If possible, talk with the teacher after class. What is the purpose of the course? How much time will students study English? What will happen to the students after they leave the programme?

2. Find out where refugees, immigrants, or other ethnic minorities are employed in your home town. You can talk with someone at a government employment office, a welfare office, or a social service agency such as a church that provides assistance to these groups. You can also observe people at work in low-

paying jobs in your community. Who fills these jobs?
3. Contact the office responsible for voters' information pamphlets in your area. Find out what laws and regulations determine which materials, if any, are specially prepared for voters who do not speak English.

FURTHER READING

In their survey of survival ESL texts, Auerbach and Burgess (1985) found that most texts prepare students for entry-level jobs by emphasizing limited English competencies such as asking questions, apologizing, and clarifying understanding. Tollefson (1989) is a critical analysis of the US refugee education programme, with emphasis upon its role in channelling refugees into minimum-wage jobs that lead to long-term economic crisis. Marshall (1986) includes an essay by Gerda Bikales and commentaries by many prominent analysts of US language policy.

SIX

Revolutionary language policy

PREVIEW

Chapter 6 examines the impact of language education upon inequality in the Philippines. It argues that economic, political, and social inequality are reinforced by language policies that require people to learn a second language in order to obtain work. In the Philippines, English is necessary for most good jobs, but because most people are unable to acquire English fluently, they find themselves locked into poorly paid, marginal employment offering little room for advancement. The chapter concludes that language policies requiring widespread second language acquisition may help to sustain a system in which language is a key marker of socioeconomic class and power. When such a system is sustained over time, individuals whose economic advance is blocked may increasingly support revolutionary changes in language policy.

Although refugees in the United States face formidable linguistic barriers to employment, the dominant ideology claims that they can overcome these barriers by learning English. This belief underestimates the difficulties of learning a new language, particularly the structural barriers that confront some groups. When language is a gatekeeper for employment and higher education, it may become a powerful tool for sustaining inequality and hegemony. One of the clearest examples is the Philippines, where English is associated with a rigid class structure characterized by extremes of wealth and poverty.

CASE: HECTOR AND MAJA ADOLPHO

Hector Adolpho drives a taxi in Metro Manila. He works twelve hours a day, seven days a week, and earns less than $30 per month. He lives with his wife, Maja, and three children in Tondo, the district in Manila that has been called the largest slum in Asia. The Adolpho home in Tondo is less than fifteen square metres. It is made of scraps of lumber, sheet metal, and tin. During the rainy season, the dirt floor floods with filthy water which pours in from the muddy road outside. Maja walks 300 metres to the nearest pump for drinking water, which often is contaminated with sewage. Their children wash in the drainage ditch which runs alongside the railroad tracks behind their home.

Yet the Adolphos are more fortunate than most of their neighbours. Hector has a job that provides a steady income with which they can buy rice for their family and shoes for their children. Equally important, the children do not have to work all day, like most other Tondo children, selling candy and cigarettes, running in and out of the lines of cars stuck in Manila's infamous traffic jams. Instead, they attend school, which Hector and Maja hope will provide them with a way out of the misery of Tondo.

Like many of his neighbours, Hector is fairly well educated. He completed seven years of elementary school in his rural province of Bataan, and, when his family first moved to Manila, a full year at an English-language public high school. As a child he studied hard, because his mother had repeatedly told him that education – especially the English language – was the key to finding a good job. Hector had been an excellent student, earning top marks in his classes every year. His ability to speak English had helped him get his job with the taxi company when it hired drivers to serve the growing number of foreigners who came to Manila after President Marcos declared Martial Law in 1972. Like many poor women, Maja completed only three years of schooling.

Yet Hector has little chance of finding a better job or otherwise improving his family's economic situation. Although his English proficiency is reasonably good, it is not sufficient for anything other than work as a taxi driver, a money changer, or a hustler selling goods on the streets of Ermita, the Metro Manila 'tourist belt'. His education prepared him for limited contact with foreigners in his taxi, but not for extended interactions requiring fluency and stylistic variation, reading and writing, and a broad range of vocabulary. For the Adolphos, their children are the hope for the future. Their dream is that their children will be able to build for themselves a better life than they can provide for them. With this hope, Hector and Maja insist that they go to school every day in the Manila public schools, that they do their homework diligently, and that they earn top marks.

At night, after their children are asleep, Hector and Maja talk about their children's future. They worry that their children will do well in school, only to find that they are unqualified for jobs paying a liveable wage. They know that they will never be able to afford to send their children to private institutions where pupils truly become fluent in English. So they fear that their children, despite the family's best efforts, will be doomed to a life in the slums of Tondo.

Three years ago, Hector and Maja attended their first meeting of the local 'Zone One Tenants' Organization' (ZOTO). At first, they knew nothing about the group's political ideology. They had never been especially political themselves, but they could see that their children would have great difficulty escaping a fate like their own. They were desperate for an alternative, and so they accompanied a friend to the first meeting.

At that meeting, one speaker denounced the government for failing to provide a medical clinic for the neighbourhood; then a priest said that the community had a right to a supply of safe drinking water. Finally, a Catholic nun told the small gathering that there were really two educational systems in the Philippines, one for the wealthy and one for the poor, and that schools for poor children prepared graduates only for poorly paid jobs. The Adolphos knew that their schooling had not helped them earn enough to move their family out of Tondo. So they returned for the next ZOTO meeting to find out more about this group's plans.

ZOTO's five thousand members represent a 56-hectare area in the Tondo Foreshoreland, a narrow landfill reported to contain the largest squatter district in Southeast Asia (Bagadion 1986). After Martial Law was declared in 1972, the government wanted to lease the Tondo Foreshoreland to international firms planning a new port to be funded by the World Bank. Despite Martial Law prohibitions against political demonstrations, ZOTO members marched on the presidential palace at Malacanang to demand that demolition crews be stopped. In subsequent meetings with government officials and representatives of the World Bank, ZOTO successfully negotiated rights to nearby land for resettlement of the residents and a schedule of demolitions coordinated to resettlement plans (Bagadion 1986). Though ZOTO could not stop the demolition of homes in the Tondo Foreshoreland, it obtained land for new homes and a more humane procedure for resettlement.

Although ZOTO is the model for community-based organizations elsewhere in the Philippines, it differs from most other groups in its willingness to discuss the economic and political context of squatters' problems. Most squatters' organizations restrict their activism to the specific issues of eviction, demolition of housing, and resettlement, without confronting the broader issues of land ownership, distribution of wealth, and access to economic and political resources. When these groups attempt to expand their involvement, local clergy may resist, perhaps setting up competing organizations. Often, they are dominated by local political officials, particularly the *barangay* captains, and federal bureaucrats (Pinches 1985). Those that persist may be labelled communist or subversive, their leaders arrested, tortured, or murdered. Unlike many organizations that become ineffective in these ways, ZOTO sustained its activism, even under Martial Law.

As they continued to go to meetings, Hector and Maja gained a better understanding of how their children's education may limit rather than expand their options for the future. Indeed, some people at ZOTO meetings argued that English, the language which Hector and Maja considered to be the key to their children's future, was also one source of the inequality which ensured that their future would be no better. Hector and Maja began to wonder whether their children would ever be able to work their way out of Tondo as long as English proficiency was essential for most of the good jobs in the Philippines. Though they did not know what to do to help their children, they began to question whether English was a *solution* to their children's poverty, or part of its *cause*.

MEDIA EXAMPLE 6.1

The Philippine government explicitly recognizes the importance of English in attracting foreign investment. In advertisements placed in foreign newspapers during the 1970s, the Marcos government listed the English language competence of the Philippine labour force, along with low labour costs, as special reasons for foreign companies to invest in the Philippines. Media example 6.1 is an excerpt from such an ad, placed in the *New York Times* in July, 1974.

Philippine Government Advertisement, *New York Times*

We've put our house in order. You can't afford to overlook the new Philippines in surveying your Asian prospect this year. For the authoritarian government in Manila has put an end to political factionalism and social anarchy. Restored peace and order. Purged the bureaucracy of the inept and the corrupt. Freed economic policy-making from the constraints of extremist rhetoric. Result: The renewed optimism of 40 million people and the resurgence of the national economy. . .

We like multinationals . . . Local staff? Clerks with a college education start at $35 . . Accountants come for $67, executive secretaries for $148 . . .

Our labor force speaks your language. Whether you're talking electronic components, garments or car-manufacturing. National literacy was placed at 83.4% in 1973 (English is the medium of instruction) . . .

Questions

1. What is the audience for this ad? What concerns of the audience are addressed by the ad?
2. Why are the salaries listed for various job categories?
3. According to the ad, how widespread is the use of English within the Philippine labour force?
4. Why does the ad emphasize that Philippine workers speak English?

As the ad suggests, English is required for a broad range of jobs in the Philippines. That employers are able to require second language competency as a condition for employment suggests not only that English is widespread, but that there is a labour surplus. Urban unemployment is estimated at 20 to 25 per cent (Ramos 1987). In addition, there is widespread 'underemployment', as large numbers of people earn meagre wages in such jobs as washing car windows at traffic lights, carrying messages for businesses, and selling cigarettes one by one on the street. A huge pool of labour is unoccupied, and those who are fortunate enough to be employed cannot risk seeking to improve their wages or working conditions through labour organizing. From the beginning of Martial Law until 1986, trade unions, collective bargaining, and other forms of organized labour were under severe restrictions. Although the Aquino government has been more willing than Marcos to permit collective bargaining, the huge labour surplus continues to favour employers. As a result, English proficiency is likely to continue as a condition of employment, even in positions where English may be marginal to workplace duties.

LANGUAGE IN THE PHILIPPINE POLITICAL DEBATE

The Philippines is characterized by extraordinary language complexity. With seven thousand islands spread over thousands of square miles of the South China Sea, the country has developed perhaps 80 different languages and major dialects (Smolicz, 1984). In addition, since the nineteenth century there has been continuing conflict over the issue of the national language. This conflict persists today in the Philippine civil war.

The key question in the politics of language in the Philippines is: what language(s) should be used in education and in the exercise of commerce, mass media, politics and government? For more than 50 years, three distinct answers to this question have dominated political debate. One group favours continuing the central role for English in government, higher education, and key areas of elementary and secondary education. Supporters of English argue that it is the major language of science and technology, publishing, commerce, and world trade, and thus links the Philippines to the English-speaking world and aids economic development and the transfer of technology (Valdepeñas 1977).

A second group supports Pilipino, also called Tagalog, a native language of many Filipinos living on the main island of Luzon. The key argument of this group is that Tagalog is widely spoken, particularly in the Metro Manila area; that non-Tagalog speakers can learn it more quickly than English; and that it offers an indigenous national symbol of unity and identity.

A final group argues that Pilipino spoken in Metro Manila has been changed by the impact of migration into an amalgam of the main indigenous languages of the country. As a result, this group claims that the Manila variety is preferable to standard Tagalog, which would offer native Tagalog speakers significant advantages in employment, education, and government. Many who favour this amalgam language support English until such time as the new language can be further developed and standardized. Yabes (1972), a prominent supporter of an amalgam language, argues that English should remain the sole official language of the government, the sole medium of instruction in secondary schools and higher education, and an auxiliary medium of instruction in primary and intermediate schools. Although supporters of an amalgam recognize that English would continue to offer significant advantages to some Filipinos during this undefined period of transition, they are more concerned about blocking domination by Tagalog. Thus Yabes admits that English has developed a new educated elite class, but he believes it is acceptable because it cuts across ethnolinguistic boundaries (Yabes 1972, p. 43).

The standard analysis of this debate is that English has instrumental value due to its advantages as a major world language of science and technology, publishing, and commerce, its ability to link the country to the developed English-speaking world, and its utility in economic development programmes. The standard analysis also claims that those who support Pilipino do so because it has the potential of serving as an indigenous symbol of national identity and unity, but that it has proved to be inadequate because it has not been accepted by the non-Tagalog population. Finally, this standard analysis concludes that English will continue to be used because its instrumental value remains strong, until either Pilipino or a developed amalgam becomes broadly acceptable as an integrative national linguistic symbol. In this view, opposition to English is interpreted as an effort to rally nationalist forces with a largely symbolic policy of supporting an indigenous language. (For examples of the standard analysis, see Bowen 1977; Gonzalez 1984; Llamzon 1977, 1984; Pascasio 1977, 1984; Valdepeñas 1977).

Yet the standard analysis fails to consider the relationship between the language question and broader conflicts over Philippine social organization, economic development, and political power. As Hector and Maja Adolpho know, the choice of an official language in the Philippines has crucial impact upon access to economic resources, to policy-making institutions, and to political power. It is no accident that the most powerful revolutionary group in the Philippine civil war today advocates a fundamental change in Philippine language policy.

THE LANGUAGE POLICY OF THE NEW PEOPLE'S ARMY

In 1965, the Philippines was the most prosperous country in Asia after Japan. By the time of the fall of Ferdinand Marcos in 1986, the Philippines had become the poorest country in the region after war-torn Laos and Cambodia (Richter 1987). The social and economic problems facing the Philippines today are enormous. First, the nation's people face massive poverty, along with spectacular inequities in the distribution of wealth. Second, most Filipinos do not own land; the agricultural system is essentially a medieval system of farming by landless peasants hired by owners of huge plantations (Koppel 1987). Third, rural poverty has forced millions of people into the cities, where they face homelessness, unemployment, and underemployment (Lindsey 1987). Fourth, for decades, the political process has been dominated by a few wealthy families with private armies which enforce their will upon masses of people without legal protections (Koppel 1987). Finally, a phenomenal population growth rate has exacerbated all of these social, political, and economic problems. The resulting disillusionment and desperation of millions of Filipinos has led to a rapid growth in the popularity of groups which support significant political change through, if necessary, violent revolution. The most important of these new groups is the New People's Army (NPA). Among the NPA's goals is a fundamental change in the role of English in the Philippines.

In the months immediately preceding the formation of the NPA on 29 March 1969, remnants of the Communist Party of the Philippines (CPP) struggled over control of the Party apparatus. Finally, a group headed by Jose Maria Sison succeeded in adopting its Program for a People's Democratic Revolution, with the NPA as the military organization charged with carrying out a prolonged armed struggle. A number of documents describing the organization of the NPA and its policies have been circulated by the NPA or discovered in raids by the Armed Forces of the Philippines (AFP). The most important statements of language policy are those in the Program for a People's Democratic Revolution, found by AFP forces in Capas, Tarlac, in June 1969, and allegedly written by Sison. This document (available in Lachica 1971) outlines NPA principles in politics, economics, culture, and education, as well as specific policies in these areas.

Two sections, entitled 'The Problem of Culture, Education, and the Intellectuals' and 'Our Specific Program', deal explicitly with the language question. According to these sections, the main goals of NPA policy are to expand rapidly the use of Pilipino in all areas of Philippine life and to give it 'revolutionary content'. Specific statements are as follows:

> A people's democratic revolution . . . shall promote the national language as the principal medium of communication in Philippine society. . . It shall see to it that the national language, art, and literature shall be given revolutionary content (Lachica 1971, p. 289).

> [In 'Our Specific Program – the Cultural Field', the third of ten points is:] Propagate the national language as the principal medium of instruction and communication (Lachica 1971, p. 292).

Other statements in the programme indicate that mass education and literacy are to replace elitist policies.

Like Marcos and Aquino, the CPP–NPA does not propose the spread of the vernacular languages into official status. In part, this reflects the constricted nature of the Philippine language debate, in which there is little discussion of a broad movement toward vernacular language rights, such as takes place in other countries (see Chapter 7). A section on national minorities, for instance, does not mention language, but rather states that land is the main concern of the national minorities (Lachica 1971, p. 290). The NPA document consistently argues that economic measures such as land reform and redistribution of wealth will solve the language issue, and that largely symbolic issues of language are unimportant. The NPA views the use of Pilipino not as essentially symbolic, but rather as important in eliminating the economic inequalities created by use of English. Clearly, NPA policy favours an end to the use of English for most purposes, though some role may continue insofar as Pilipino is favoured as the 'principal', but not the sole language of education and communication.

Other CPP–NPA documents, such as the official history of the formation of the NPA, 'The New People's Army' (Lachica 1971, p. 302) and the operational rules of the organization, 'Basic Rules of the New People's Army' (Lachica 1971, pp. 317–25), do not explicitly mention language. But the official history, like the Program for a People's Democratic Revolution, rejects alliances with liberal reformist groups, such as the Liberal Party, which support English–Pilipino bilingualism; while they permit tactical alliance with the Movement for the Advancement of Nationalism (MAN), a Socialist organization with support among intellectuals, whose language policy is identical to that of the CPP–NPA (see Movement for the Advancement of Nationalism 1969). In contrast to the Socialist/Communist opposition, support for English–Pilipino bilingualism is generally widespread within pro-business groups, the Aquino government, and the Catholic Church, whose key publications, such as *Mr. and Ms.*, are published in English. In order to understand why the NPA would oppose the use of English in education and government, we must look at the historical background to the NPA policy.

Historical antecedents of NPA language policy

As the most recent in a long line of leftist insurgencies, the NPA has its roots in the HUK rebellion in central Luzon in the 1940s and the 1950s, which developed from the remnants of the Socialist and Communist parties that thrived briefly in the 1930s.

The founder of the Philippine Socialist Party was Pedro Abad Santos, an intellectual who reportedly read German, English, Russian, Spanish, Greek, and Tagalog. A central tactic in Santos's early attempts to educate and mobilize workers and peasants was the use of vernaculars for meetings, speeches, and dramatic skits (Tan 1984). Socialist language policy condemned the use of colonial languages, as well as English and Spanish literacy requirements for voting, and the Party actively encouraged newspapers published in vernaculars. Lino Dizon, one of Santos's key associates and a noted poet, delivered speeches and wrote in his Pampango dialect of central Luzon. All of these steps had important tactical value: since few peasants and workers were educated in English, local varieties and Tagalog were most likely to involve them in Party politics. The Socialist Party had little time to develop beyond its original base in central Luzon, however, because it merged with, and was quickly dominated by, the Communist Party of the Philippines (CPP) in 1938.

Major information about CPP language policy and practice during the 1930s is available in the memoirs of James S. Allen (1985) of the Communist Party-USA, who travelled extensively in the Philippines and advised the CPP, which was administratively tied to the American Party because the Philippines was an

American colony. Allen attended the important CPP convention in Manila in October 1939, which carried out the merger with the Socialist Party. He reports that discussion took place in Tagalog and that his speech supporting the Socialist–CPP merger was translated into Tagalog from his native English. Allen's reports provide substantial evidence that use of Tagalog was widespread and that English was avoided by most CPP leaders. Gregorio Aglipay, for instance, founder of the schismatic Philippine Independent Church, which split from Roman Catholicism over political abuses by Spanish priests, refused to speak English as a matter of principle when the Americans took over (Allen 1985, p. 16). A cleric, Aglipay was highly influential in the CPP and had even fought as a guerrilla in 1899. Though originally concerned with reducing the political influence of the Spanish clergy, he often spoke Spanish, believing that it was more important to demonstrate his opposition to American colonization of the Philippines. At the many social events Aglipay hosted for Allen, Tagalog dominated.

CPP publication in the 1930s was primarily in Tagalog, though the eight-page CPP weekly *Kalayaan* contained some articles in English and English supplements. In contrast, other leftist publications appeared mainly in English, reflecting the English-language education of most intellectuals and writers. For instance, the antifascist League for the Defense of Democracy, formed by opposition writers and professionals, published a monthly magazine, *The Vanguard*, in English with a Tagalog supplement. 'The Beer Club', a group of leftist writers who opposed the government, criticized the imposition of English as an official language, but nevertheless wrote and conducted their weekly meetings in English, claiming that their 'unmodernized native dialects' were inadequate for their purposes (Allen 1985, p. 25). Allen summarizes his view of this group: 'For the most part, they still had to overcome their elitism and bridge the wide [linguistic] gap that separated them from the masses of Filipinos. . . Their inner conflicts [over language use] were sharp, often excruciating, in the last analysis the result of colonialism (Allen 1985, pp. 25–6).

CPP policy in the 1930s opposed use of English in education and government and supported use of Tagalog. This policy expressed CPP opposition to intellectuals and other elites who were educated in English and who used it for most official and commercial interactions. Moreover, the policy aided CPP efforts to educate and organize peasants and workers, who generally had little education and therefore were unable to speak English. Beginning in the 1930s, the CPP focused its efforts on opposition to Japanese expansion, for a time cooperating with American and Philippine officials despite the fact that the CPP was not a legal organization. During the Second World War, many CPP leaders led the armed opposition to Japanese occupation, forming in 1942 the famous Hukbo ng Bayan Laban sa Hapon (Hukbalahap), the People's Anti-Japanese Army. Finding themselves blocked from political power by the pro-American government of independence in 1946, many Hukbalahap fighters retained their arms, eventually forming the Hukbong Mapagpalaya ng Bayan (HMB), the People's Liberation Army, which conducted its military campaign into the 1950s, primarily in central Luzon.

The by-laws of the Hukbalahap (available in Saulo 1969), as well as the Constitution of the HMB (also in Saulo 1969) do not spell out policies for a post-revolutionary government, as do NPA documents. Nevertheless, HUK language policy can be derived from major statements by its leaders as well as analyses of the HUK revolt. For instance, Alfredo Saulo, in the field with HUK fighters from 1950 to 1958 and imprisoned from 1958 to 1966, emphasized the importance of Tagalog as opposed to English in his history of the CPP published in Manila newspapers in English and Tagalog in 1969 (reprinted in Saulo 1969). Lachica's sympathetic study of the HUK movement criticizes the impact of English in central Luzon and argues that the 'essence of Hukism' is lost in English translations. Lachica traces the oral literature of leftist politics in central Luzon and suggests that erosion of Pampango and Tagalog by English was associated with the demise of the HUKs (Lachica 1971). Lachica's analysis stresses that, in addition to ideological, economic, and tactical reasons for opposition to English, the HUK movement strongly identified with the Pampango vernacular as a symbol of resistance to the English-speaking government.

Thus, in general, the language policy and practice of the Philippine Left since the 1930s has consistently opposed use of English and favoured use of Pilipino (Tagalog), with vernaculars also having tactical value. The question, therefore, is why opposition to English has persisted for five decades, from the

Socialist and Communist parties of the 1930s, through the HUK organizations of the 1940s and 1950s, to the New People's Army of the 1970s and 1980s.

The standard view of the Philippine language question emphasizes the symbolic, integrative value of Pilipino in contrast to the economic, instrumental value of English. The weakness of the standard view is that it fails to explain why the NPA, as well as its antecedents among the HUKs, the Socialists, and the Communists, would be concerned primarily with the symbolic role of Pilipino rather than the economic value of English, especially since NPA policies in other areas, such as minorities, consistently emphasize economic rather than symbolic solutions to political problems. An alternative to the standard explanation for NPA opposition to English must focus on the role of English in structuring economic relations and in favouring particular economic interests. From this perspective, the Philippine language issue is seen not as a struggle between the instrumental value of English and the symbolic/integrative value of Pilipino, but rather as one aspect of a struggle between competing economic interests, with English and Pilipino serving the aims of fundamentally different groups. The key to understanding this perspective is the role of English in the Philippine economy since Martial Law was imposed in 1972.

LANGUAGE POLICY UNDER MARCOS

The crucial importance of language decisions made by the Philippine government was especially striking in the period of increasing political conflict just prior to the imposition of Martial Law and immediately after it was imposed in September 1972.

Gonzalez (1980) reports that many student leaders and publications discontinued use of English in the late 1960s and early 1970s. The student paper of the University of the Philippines was published in Pilipino beginning in 1970, while at universities which continued to publish student papers in English (e.g., Ateneo de Manila University), alternative papers appeared in Pilipino. In addition, speakers and signs at demonstrations and rallies switched to Pilipino, as opposition to American policies and to the Marcos government increasingly became associated with refusal to use English. As Gonzalez states (1980, p. 13):

Above all, the rhetoric of the streets . . . was totally in Pilipino. To speak English at these rallies was to court ridicule and jeers. . . Furthermore, to establish one's credential as a student leader and a militant nationalist, one had to learn to do public speaking in Pilipino.

The shift to Pilipino meant that the composition of the student leadership shifted from English-speaking students at the elite institutions to Pilipino-speaking students at the state-run colleges.

When Martial Law was declared in September 1972, however, the movement for Pilipino was abruptly halted, and with it the temporary rise to power of working-class students from state schools. Martial Law continued under President Marcos from 1972 to 1981. Even after it was lifted, most policies which had been adopted under Martial Law by presidential decree continued until February 1986, when Corazon Aquino replaced Marcos.

The effects of Martial Law have been extensively documented by Philippine and foreign observers (e.g., Civil Liberties Union 1984; L.R. Constantino 1984a, 1984b; Enriquez and Marcelino 1984; Kerkvleit 1986; Piñeda-Ofreneo 1985; Ramos 1987; Richter 1987; Shalom 1985). Though the official justification for imposition of Martial Law was a general breakdown in law and order, the major impact was severe political repression accompanied by redirection of the economy towards export-oriented, labour-intensive light industry financed by foreign capital. With the exception of political allies of the Marcos family, local Filipino businesses and agriculture suffered great losses, as a huge influx of foreign investment and borrowing led to the establishment of light manufacturing industries, assembly plants, and a host of foreign subsidiaries producing consumer goods.

The impact on the educational system was immense. Various presidential decrees transformed the elementary and high-school curricula into 'work-oriented' programmes to prepare youth for participation in commercial and industrial enterprises (De Leon and Lugue 1984, p. 438). The goal was to ensure that the educational system would 'equip high school students with specific skills needed for industry and agriculture' (De Leon and Lugue 1984, p. 438). In addition, beginning in 1976, the World Bank funded publication and distribution of millions of new textbooks and manuals through the Ministry of Education, Culture, and Sports that were designed to help the system of education respond to the new economic policy (L.R. Constantino 1982, 1984a; De Leon and Lugue 1984).

In language education, the policy meant a renewed emphasis on English and a shift towards vocational and technical English training. The Marcos government's strong support of English was due primarily to its crucial role in meeting the labour requirements of the Philippine economy. Under the policy of export-oriented, labour-intensive light industry financed by foreign capital, there were three main labour needs (Civil Liberties Union 1984; R. Constantino 1976; Lichauco 1973; Piñeda-Ofreneo 1985):

1. A pool of workers qualified for light manufacturing, assembly, and similar unskilled and semi-technical jobs.
2. Office staff and middle managers able to work under managers of corporations investing in the Philippines.
3. A service industry for foreign businesses, including maintenance crews, hotel staff, and domestic workers.

Under Martial Law, the educational system was managed in order to turn out the appropriate number of workers for these types of jobs. This meant that most students had to be educated for low-paying jobs requiring a little English. Masses of poor youth, particularly in rural areas outside central Luzon, provided the bulk of this group. Because they receive inferior English language education in state-supported schools and drop out of school early (*Times Journal* 1985), they become only marginally literate in English or Pilipino. Indeed, in schools outside Manila and the Tagalog-speaking areas of Luzon, children learn to speak English only haltingly, and Pilipino only to a basic level of proficiency (Gonzalez 1988a). Since 1981, the government Bureau of Secondary Education has administered achievement tests in maths, science, English, Pilipino, social studies, and youth development training to all fourth-year high-school students in public and private schools. Test results show that the lowest scores are consistently associated with students in economically impoverished rural areas in Bicol, Central Mindanao, and the Eastern Visayas (National Census and Statistics Office 1986). These are all areas in which the NPA enjoys widespread support. Moreover, because their native languages are not used in schools, poor youth remain illiterate or only semiliterate in their native languages as well (Smolicz 1984). In this way, the educational system has helped to ensure that the masses of rural poor and impoverished urban families provide a huge pool of cheap unskilled and semiskilled labour (R. Constantino 1974).

Since the imposition of Martial Law, the educational system has also successfully produced a sufficient number of competent English speakers to staff office and service positions cheaply. In general, better-paid jobs are filled by graduates of a small number of elite schools (Ateneo de Manila, Assumption College, Maryknoll College, the College of the Holy Spirit, and Saint Paul College), whose students become reasonably proficient in English (Muego 1987). Cory Aquino herself attended the elite Assumption Convent in Manila and the College of Mount St. Vincent in the United States. R. Constantino (1982, p. 13) describes the situation since 1972 as one in which there is a small group capable of using English for a wide range of purposes, a larger group able to read and speak in fairly comprehensible English, and a great mass largely incapable of speaking English. The policy of using English in schools thus serves a dual purpose: it helps to ensure that a great number of students fail, and it produces the necessary number of graduates with appropriate English skills.

Even after Martial Law ended, the government continued policies to ensure that workers had the necessary qualifications, including English ability, and that they did not demand high wages. The Marcos government took many steps to achieve these goals, including marginalization of farmers forced into urban labour markets, restrictions on labour unions, and favourable economic benefits to foreign firms investing in the country. Emphasis on limited 'English for specific purposes' (primarily technical and vocational English) was also an essential part of this labour policy. The government's success in carrying out its policy can be seen at the American military bases. One of the main reasons the United States wants to keep them in the Philippines is that their highly skilled Filipino workers are paid wages a fraction of those in the United States (see *Newsweek* 1985).

Government officials explicitly emphasized the role of English in supporting state economic policies long after Martial Law ended. Political Affairs Minister Leonard B. Perez urged in 1985 that English should be the sole medium of instruction in all maths, science, technology, and related subjects in elementary and high schools, and in all subjects in college (Villa 1985a, p. 1). Criticizing nationalists who demand the use of an indigenous language and 'Tagalistas' who support Tagalog, Education Minister Jaime C. Laya warned in 1985 that the rest of the world is learning English while Filipinos seem too attached to their mother tongues (Villa 1985b, p. 1). Laya also blamed old laws on bilingualism for a 'deterioriation' of English. Minister of Tourism Jose D. Aspiras blamed 'chauvinistic nationalism' for what he termed a decline of English and argued that foreign tourism and business require upgrading of English (Villa 1985c, p. 6). In 1983, Demetrio Quirino, Jr, of the Technological Institute of the Philippines pleaded for a monolingual English system of education (Gonzalez 1984, p. 50). Marcos himself supported English as the medium of instruction, declaring that under his rule no Filipino educator dared to support a policy of using Pilipino as the language of instruction (see Enriquez and Marcelino 1984, p. 4).

The support for English by the Marcos administration resembled that of US English and other organizations in the United States that favour a constitutional amendment declaring English the official language (see Chapter 5). Although English is not a native language in the Philippines, the essential issue is the same as in the United States, Britain, and elsewhere: who benefits from continued dominance by English? Those who support English are those who speak it, thereby claiming for themselves significant advantages in competition for education, employment, and political power. Thus, though the rhetoric may vary, the effort to sustain a privileged position for English has a similar motivation in the United States, Britain, and the Philippines, namely, the advantages that one gains when one's language is used for official purposes.

The only major official action supporting Pilipino during the Marcos era was an announcement by the Ministry of Education, Culture, and Sports in 1974 that Pilipino should be used as a medium of instruction in all subjects except science and mathematics. Little was done, however, to carry out this goal. Only two universities developed any programmes in which Pilipino was the medium of instruction, while a consortium of universities and colleges produced a syllabus for teaching sociology, and Philippine Normal College and the National Teachers' College required the use of Pilipino in theses and dissertations for graduate degrees in Pilipino language departments (Sibayan 1985). Thus Pilipino has failed to challenge English for dominance in any area of higher education outside Pilipino language studies. According to Bonifacio Sibayan, a respected Philippine educator and linguist, few Filipino intellectuals can write in Pilipino, and those who do have no readers (Sibayan 1985, p. 48). With the educational system geared to producing its best educated students in English, it was inevitable that English under Marcos would be a major criterion for employment, as well as for access to the key institutions dominating Philippine economic and political life.

LANGUAGE POLICY UNDER AQUINO

When Cory Aquino replaced Marcos in February 1986, there was widespread hope that the 'People Power' which brought her to office would lead to mass political participation and an expansion in grass-roots democracy, as well as an end to the paralysing political polarization and deepening economic crisis which gripped the country. For a few months, that seemed to be the case, as open debate about the country's future included, for the first time in many years, representatives from across the political spectrum. In June 1986, for instance, a seminar entitled 'Trends in the Philippines III' brought together Aquino supporters, former Marcos supporters, including Arturo Tolentino, leader of the Kilusang Bagong Lipunan (KBL, Marcos's political party), and Jose Sison, founder of the NPA. At this remarkable gathering of political enemies, Sison argued that the semifeudal economic and sociopolitical system of the Philippines was in rapid disintegration, and he warned that Aquino would ultimately be unable to achieve the kind of redistribution of political power necessary for her government to survive (Sison 1986; Youngblood 1988). Although in 1989 Aquino remained popular with the majority of Filipinos, a series of attempted military coups, an upsurge in political murders, and the failure by the government to deal with the underlying causes of the NPA insurgency suggest that political violence and economic crisis will continue to dominate Philippine politics for some time to come.

Although she faces significant internal opposition, Aquino has a reliable base of support consisting of the business community, the Catholic Church, international financial institutions, and foreign governments (Overholt 1987, p. 106). In her analysis of the Aquino government, Richter (1987) reminds us that Aquino is a member of a large land-holding family, and that her policies have been successful in winning support of the business community, which has encouraged her administration to secure foreign aid, favour private industry, and restructure the Philippine debt (Richter 1987, p. 66; also see Concepcion 1986; Hooley 1987; C. Jones 1987).

Thus there is widespread concern that Aquino's government is dominated by interests which oppose significant change (Rajaretnam 1986). In his analysis of Aquino's programme of economic policies announced in early fall 1986, Lindsey (1987, p. 139) noted that much of it is similar to the positions of the technocrats under Marcos. One reason may be that Cory and her murdered husband, Benigno Aquino, along with Laurel and other leaders of UNIDO and Laban, the main groups which opposed Marcos, constitute an 'old elite' which sought a change of individual leadership, but not a change in policy or in the political process itself (Druckman and Green 1986; Komisar 1987). Examples of Aquino's reluctance to reform may be drawn from many areas of public policy, including the slow pace of land reform, the return to a military solution for the NPA insurgency, the renewed appearance of government-approved vigilante groups (*Manila Bulletin* 1987) – and language policy.

Like members of the Marcos government, Aquino and her major advisers continue to use English in many speeches, and English remains the dominant language of the media, government, education, and business. Prior to Aquino's rise to power, the main pro-Aquino, anti-Marcos press was published in English, including the Catholic Church publication *Veritas* (though one Pilipino tabloid, *Malaya*, appeared during the boycott of government papers after the Aquino assassination). Under Aquino, newspapers which once printed English-language editions controlled by Marcos and his supporters instead publish English-language editions that praise or criticize Aquino. As Doronila (1985) has shown, Aquino supporters include wealthy business interests with major holdings in the press, radio, and television, who favoured a change in leadership from Marcos to Aquino, but do not favour a change in policy. They continue to support English as the language of mass media, government, and business.

In government and administration under Aquino, almost all bureaucrats speak English; indeed, proficiency in English is a requirement for most positions. For this reason, multinational corporations and financial institutions praise the Philippine bureaucracy for ease of communication (Richter 1987).

In education, Aquino's support for English sustains the dual system in which elite colleges and universities provide graduates for most upper- and middle-level posts in business, industry, and government, while state universities provide workers for low-paid positions. At state universities on Luzon, for instance, most college students speak English only in classes and consider bilingualism to mean mixing English and their native language in a single sentence. Because state universities have teachers who do not speak English well, few textbooks, virtually no funds to purchase or develop instructional materials, no language labs, and huge English classes (from 40 to 65 students), administrators at state institutions must seek copies of old texts and other assistance from individual colleagues abroad.

The increased political consciousness and participation initiated by People Power, however, has led to greater awareness of the gap between private and state-supported education. Students from the University of the Philippines and other state universities have become more critical of the Aquino government than students in the elite institutions such as Ateneo and Maryknoll College. In 1986, protests in the state institutions over the rising costs of tuition and other educational expenses demonstrated the increased militancy among Pilipino-dominant students. The issue of the rising cost of education is so explosive precisely because students and graduates are aware of the poor quality of most state universities, where faculty remain poorly trained, facilities are inadequate, and graduates are unable to compete in the job market and the professions against graduates of elite institutions (Muego 1987). One observer predicts that the gap between students at state and private institutions will continue to widen, leading to a class-based split within the student movement (Muego 1987, p. 256). With more than half of the nation's population under thirty, and one of the highest proportions of university students in the total population anywhere in the world, the Philippines can ill afford a fracturing of the student population, which is likely to be reflected more broadly in an increasingly polarized citizenry. Although language policy is not the only reason for this problem, as long as current language policy in education is unchanged, the process of polarization can be expected to continue.

An explanation for Aquino's policy of supporting English can be found in the advantages the language provides for her supporters. In an analysis of Marcos's support for English, Miller (1981, p. 149) noted that elites resisted surrendering the dominance of English because they owed a major part of their professional success to their proficiency in English. Similarly, leading members of the Aquino government graduated from elite universities where they became fluent in English, and they enjoy the benefits of their education in relatively well-paid jobs requiring advanced English proficiency. The most recent scores on high-school achievement tests indicate that a wide gap remains between the quality of education available at elite and poor schools at the secondary level as well (National Census and Statistics Office 1986). For the government to shift toward an indigenous language in key areas of Philippine life, Aquino and her supporters would have to be willing to give up the enormous advantages provided by their proficiency in English. In doing so, they would risk encouraging the rise to power of a new elite, much as the shift toward Pilipino within the student movement led to a shift in the composition of the student leadership in the late 1960s and early 1970s.

In addition, there remains the question of the status of indigenous languages other than Pilipino. These languages are largely left out of the debate. Though some schools use them during the first three elementary grades, virtually no one argues for a policy of official status for the many vernaculars. If Pilipino were to replace English, the metropolised population in Luzon would benefit, while speakers of the vernaculars outside central Luzon would still have to acquire Pilipino. They would find it easier to learn Pilipino than English, but they would nevertheless be disadvantaged in relation to those who speak the dominant variety of Pilipino in the Metro Manila area. Of course, language is not the only factor determining who has political power in the Philippines, but it is important not to underestimate the enormous practical advantages enjoyed by those with exclusive control over the means to communicate within the domains of government, business, technology, and education. To open the door to languages other than English or Pilipino is to admit masses of people now excluded from participation in the dominant institutions of Philippine public life.

The new Constitution of 1986–87

A new constitution, written at a constitutional convention in 1986 and adopted by popular vote in February 1987, was a significant step in legitimizing Aquino's government and the movement toward democracy implicit in 'People Power'. The constitution specifies the major social and political goals of 'the new Philippines', as well as a remarkably detailed plan for achieving those goals. Nowhere in this blueprint for the future of the country is there any indication that English will lose its privileged position.

Unlike constitutions in some other multilingual countries (e.g., Yugoslavia, see Chapter 7), the Philippine constitution does not include linguistic guarantees in specific areas of Philippine life (see *The Constitution of the Republic of the Philippines*, in Blaustein and Flanz 1988). For instance, article II, the 'Declaration of Principles and State Policies', includes the assurance that the nation 'recognizes and promotes the rights of indigenous cultural communities' (sec. 22), but it does not specifically guarantee language rights for cultural or linguistic minorities. Neither the Bill of Rights nor sections on literacy (art. V, sec. 2), courts and the rights of the accused (art. VIII), or the civil service (art. IXB) include any statements about language. Sections dealing with congressional records, publication and dissemination of laws, and elections do not specify the language(s) to be used in these key areas. A section providing for autonomous regions in Muslim Mindanao and the Cordilleras (art. X) does not mention language. A section entitled 'National Economy and Patrimony' (art. XII) guarantees that 'the State . . . shall protect the rights of indigenous cultural communities to their ancestral lands' (sec. 5), but it does not commit the government to the protection of linguistic rights. Article XIII, 'Social Justice and Human Rights', asserts that 'the Congress shall give highest priority to the enactment of measures that protect and enhance the right of all people to human dignity, reduce social, economic, and political inequalities, and remove cultural inequities by equally diffusing wealth and political power for the common good' (sec. 1), but it does not commit the Congress to ensuring language rights. Article XIV, 'Education, Science and Technology, Arts, Culture, and Sports', commits the country to free public education, but not to any specific language policy in schools. This article also states that 'the state shall recognize, respect, and protect the rights of indigenous cultural communities to preserve and develop their cultures, traditions, and institutions' (art XIV, sec. 17), but it does not commit the government to direct protection of cultures, traditions, and institutions – only to ensuring that cultural groups are permitted to do so themselves. Moreover, the section does not commit the state to any policy of language maintenance. In short, the constitution falls far short of a declaration of language rights (see Chapter 7).

Rather than a list of specific statements about language, the 1987 constitution includes a single section on language within Article XIV, 'Education, Science and Technology, Arts, Culture, and Sports'. This section reads as follows:

> Sec. 6. The national language of the Philippines is Filipino. As it evolves, it shall be further developed and enriched on the basis of existing Philippine and other languages.
> Subject to provisions of law and as the Congress may deem appropriate, the Government shall take steps to initiate and sustain the use of Filipino as a medium of official communication and as language of instruction in the educational system.
> Sec. 7. For the purposes of communication and instruction, the official languages of the Philippines are Filipino and, until otherwise provided by law, English.
> The regional languages are the auxiliary official languages in the regions and shall serve as auxiliary media of instruction therein. Spanish and Arabic shall be promoted on a voluntary and optional basis.
> Sec. 8. This Constitution shall be promulgated in Filipino and English and shall be translated into major regional languages, Arabic, and Spanish.
> Sec. 9. The Congress shall establish a national language commission composed of representatives of various regions and disciplines which shall undertake, coordinate, and promote researches for the development, propagation, and preservation of Filipino and other languages.

At first glance, these statements seem to support a move toward Filipino (Pilipino)–English bilingualism in official language use. Within the historical context of Philippine language policy, however, it is a strongly pro-English statement.

One way in which the constitution supports English is that it distinguishes between 'national' and 'official' languages. The 'national' language is Filipino. Although the constitution implies that Filipino should be used for official communication and education, the article implicitly recognizes that Filipino does not yet play that role, by promising that the government shall take steps to 'initiate' the use of Filipino in these areas. Moreover, the constitution recognizes both Filipino and English as 'official' languages 'for purposes of communication and instruction'. The only constitutional basis for an expansion in the use of Filipino is the symbolic value of a national integrative symbol. Yet that basis has existed for many decades, and there is no reason to expect it to lead now to dominance of Filipino in government, business, or education.

The support for English implicit in the 1987 constitution is especially clear if we compare it with the earlier constitutions of 1935 and 1973. The 1935 constitution was written in English and Pilipino (Tagalog), with the English text to prevail in case of conflict. In the debate during the constitutional convention, anti-Tagalog forces proposed amendments granting official status to Ilocano and Bicol as well as to English and Tagalog (Sibayan 1985). Though these amendments were defeated, the anti-Tagalog forces were sufficiently strong to ensure that Tagalog would not prevail. Thus the constitution gave official status to Pilipino (Tagalog), English, and Spanish.

The 1935 constitution also called for steps to adopt a common national tongue based on one of the existing native languages (art. 13, sec. 3; see Miller 1981). In response, legislation created the Institute of National Languages to study the problem and recommend what action should be taken to implement this constitutional provision. The Institute eventually recommended Tagalog, and in 1940 it completed a grammar which became the basis for what President Quezon declared to be the national language (Miller 1981). Despite the President's statement, the impact of the Institute's recommendation was minimal, as fierce resistance to Tagalog ensured that it would not replace English.

The 1973 constitution implicitly rejected Pilipino (Tagalog) as the national language. Instead, it directed the National Assembly to take steps towards the development of and adoption of a national language to be known as Filipino (art. 15, sec. 3). Nearly 40 years after the first constitutional mandate for the development of a national language, this constitution insisted that an amalgam language could be developed to replace English. With the National Assembly suspended under Martial Law, however, implementing legislation was not enacted.

Under the constitution of 1986–87, pro-Tagalog forces continue to insist that Pilipino should be the national language, though their updated view is that the still developing variety in Metro Manila is primarily Tagalog/Pilipino. Their argument is that Tagalog/Pilipino is particularly adept at borrowing from other Philippine languages as well as from English and Spanish (cf. Perez 1983). Thus the politico-linguistic debate between Tagalog and anti-Tagalog forces which characterized the constitutional convention of 1935 persists today, with the same result: the new constitution avoids granting privileged status to Pilipino/Tagalog by holding out the hope that a newly developed variety will someday become a reasonable alternative to English and Pilipino. As it has for the past half-century, this policy ensures that English will continue in its dominant position.

Other policy actions under Aquino

In 1987, the Department of Education, Culture, and Sports of the Aquino government adopted two 'department orders' regulating language in education. These orders have come to be known as the '1987 Policy on Bilingual Eduation' (Gonzalez 1988b). This policy states that Filipino and English should be used at the primary and secondary levels, with science and mathematics reserved for English, though Filipino is permitted an unspecified future role in these subject areas. The orders also encourage the use of regional languages for beginning literacy and recommend increased funding for teaching Filipino, greater use of Filipino in teacher education programmes, and improved materials and syllabuses. Of special importance for our purposes is the recommendation that university faculty who are proficient in Filipino should use the language for their content areas in the hope that, as Filipino becomes increasingly appropriate for use in higher education, it will move down through the educational system – a 'trickle down' approach to language change (Gonzalez 1988b).

Two points about this current policy suggest its limitations. First, the policy implicitly recognizes that efforts have failed to expand Filipino through the educational system from the bottom up. The suggested top-down approach does not specify how faculty members whose work has been conducted in English for many years should carry out this shift to a new language. Second, the policy defines Filipino as Tagalog-based Pilipino enriched with vocabulary from other languages of the Philippines as well as English (Gonzalez 1988b, p. 3). Thus the policy reiterates the old hope that an amalgam language will replace Pilipino as the best alternative to English.

Pro-Tagalog forces remain strong. The tendency to equate Tagalog and Filipino is reflected in the programme of the Institute of National Language, now renamed Linangan ng mg Wikang Pilipino (Centre for Philippine Languages). In late 1987, the Centre held a symposium entitled 'Simposyum Pangwika Tungkol sa Pinasiglang Pagpapuanlad at Papgpapayaman ng Wikang Filipino Batay sa Konstitusyon ng 1986' – Language Symposium on the Development and Cultivation of Filipino based on the 1986 Constitution. The implication of the symposium was that Tagalog is the basis for the new Filipino. One Pilipino supporter believes that Pilipino will eventually be adopted as the national language simply by renaming it Filipino (Sibayan 1985). Yet past experience suggests that, as Tagalog forces seek to make Filipino their own, the resistance among non-Tagalog groups is likely to increase. If that happens, there may be greater pressure to recognize the vernaculars and admit languages other than Tagalog to official status.

Although much has changed in the Philippines since February 1986, much also remains the same. In language policy, the Tagalog forces are seeking to expand its use. Meanwhile, English continues to be the language of secondary and higher education, government, business, and the influential mass media. English is also used for the thousands of interactions every day between Filipinos and the huge number of foreigners involved in matters of business, the military, and international relations. As the Philippine national debt continues to grow and international financial institutions play an increasingly important role in the daily life of the Philippines, these contacts in English will become more numerous and more important. The new constitution and current educational policy ensure that English will sustain its dominant role. Moreover, individual members of the Aquino government, as well as its most influential supporters in business, industry, and the media, owe much of their success to English. There is, therefore, no reason to expect English to lose its critical position in Philippine life.

LANGUAGE AND COMMUNITY ORGANIZATION

In the absence of a national language policy that offers Filipinos the chance to be educated in their first languages and employed at jobs paying a living wage, Hector and Maja Adolpho's decision to turn to a local community group is a small first step in the long struggle to open doors now closed to most linguistic groups. Through ZOTO, Tondo residents, like other poor people throughout the country, can seek to have impact within a sociopolitical system in which economic resources and political power are in the hands of a few. ZOTO and similar groups provide a mechanism with which the poor can exert some influence over important decisions affecting their families and their futures.

At its meetings, ZOTO uses Tagalog and Cebuano, the main languages of the residents of Tondo. In this way, people can understand events at meetings and express themselves when decisions are discussed. In contrast, state organizations and institutions, including planning agencies, institutions of higher education, and banks and major corporations, all use English for key areas of policy debate and decision making. As a result, only those Filipinos who speak English are able to participate in the state policy-making apparatus.

One result of the widespread inability of the masses of Filipinos to participate in making decisions that affect their lives is a rapid growth in their support for groups promising a radical alternative. Though it was estimated to have no more than 2,000 members when Martial Law was declared in 1972, the NPA is now estimated to have more than 20,000 fighters operating in about 60 of the nation's 72 provinces, with hundreds of thousands of sympathizers offering food, shelter, and logistical support (Richter 1987). The phenomenal growth of the NPA is a direct result of the exclusion of most Filipinos from the policy-making process. The NPA language policy of ending the dominance of English promises that rural peasants, poor urban workers, and the unemployed and underemployed everywhere will be involved in decision making and have access to government discussion and debate, education, mass media, and other areas of national life. This policy does not address, however, the possibility that speakers of vernaculars will have difficulty competing with native speakers of Tagalog, the likely national language. Although there is widespread uncertainty about what life would truly be like under a government dominated by the NPA, the NPA's stated goal of opening access to Philippine institutions has attracted scores of Filipinos who have lost faith in their government's willingness to let them have a say in their futures.

CONCLUSION: HECTOR AND MAJA ADOLPHO'S CHOICES

The impact of using English as the language of government, education, business, technology, and the media is to sustain economic inequalities within Philippine society. Elites under Aquino, like elites under Marcos, are those who speak, read, and write English. English proficiency continues to be a major criterion for access to higher education, better jobs, and a full range of institutions and decision-making processes. Aquino's willingness to continue the pro-English policy symbolizes her government's reluctance to restructure Philippine society. Thus Philippine language policy reinforces inequalities in land distribution, education, and employment, all of which continue to force people to support moderate community groups such as ZOTO and more radical groups such as the NPA in a struggle to open popular access to quality education, reasonable employment, and the institutions of power. The period of hope which began with Aquino's inauguration in February 1986 is ending, to be replaced by a renewed, prolonged, and increasingly violent political struggle.

Thus Hector and Maja Adolpho's effort to provide their children with the opportunity for a better life beyond the poverty of Tondo takes place within a context which tightly constrains their choices. A neoclassical analysis of Hector's 'failure' to learn English well enough to better support his family emphasizes such factors as his motivation, the quality of teaching in the public schools, the limited time he has available for language study, and other variables associated with his and his teachers' individual behaviour. In contrast, a historical–structural analysis emphasizes the paradoxical nature of his quest. His family's effort to learn English, while intended to provide an avenue for escaping Tondo, in a sense contributes to their difficulties, in so far as it involves cooperating with a language policy that is partly responsible for their impoverishment. Their immediate economic needs force them to become participants in a policy which is not in their interests.

Thus Hector and Maja Adolpho's alternatives offer only limited hope. They could, like the socialists and communists in the 1930s, refuse to speak English as a matter of principle, but in the short run – perhaps in the life of their children – such principled behaviour would have little visible impact upon their economic circumstances, and indeed would hurt Hector's work as a taxi driver. Continued efforts to build a strong local community through ZOTO and similar organizations can ease the impact of forced dislocations and inadequate services. In the long run, however, community organizations must exert an impact on policy in order for a change to take place in the historical and structural conditions underlying economic inequality in the Philippines. In this sense, ZOTO is caught in a paradoxical situation: if it wants to have access to policy-making bodies, it must meet the requirements for admission, including having a cadre of fluent speakers of English able to manipulate the mass media, negotiate, and lobby. Yet this accommodation requires that ZOTO cooperate with the dominance of English.

Ultimately, the resolution to the Adolpho's poverty will depend upon intensified struggle leading to a new set of structural conditions in Philippine society. Though the shape of these conditions will depend upon the outcome of the continuing political and military conflict in the Philippines, it is clear that the future of Hector and Maja's children will be best served by a system in which they can live, learn, and work in a language they speak fluently. Short of that, they must have an effective means for gaining the language competence and literacy skills necessary to meet their economic needs. At present, that appears to be impossible without major changes in the social, political, and economic structure of Philippine society.

FOR DISCUSSION

1. Hector and Maja Adolpho face a difficult decision. On the one hand, their children are not likely to learn English adequately in the public schools, nor complete their education. On the other

hand, they must learn English to find a job, even as taxi drivers; and if they hope to earn a wage that is adequate to support a family, they must become fluent in English. What would you do, if you were Hector or Maja? What would you do, if you were one of their children?

2. The hope that Filipino can be developed as an amalgam of Tagalog and other languages indigenous to the Philippines has been a key part of the Philippine language debate for many decades. Do you believe this proposal is realistic? What examples can you find, if any, of other languages that have been developed in this way?

3. Many jobs that require English involve only speaking and understanding a restricted variety of English. As a result, English for Specific Purposes (ESP) has been widely adopted in many countries. What kinds of jobs require only simple speaking and listening? Are they widely available? What salaries are paid for these jobs? What opportunities do they present for advancement into better jobs?

4. Read the constitutions of the Philippines (in Blaustein and Flanz 1988) and your country. Compare specific statements about language. What are the advantages and disadvantages of making *constitutional* statements about language? In the constitution of your country, what provisions protect – or fail to protect – linguistic minorities?

FOR ACTION

1. Thousands of Filipinos have emigrated to other countries in a search for employment. In many cases, individual men and women send home their paychecks to support extended families in the Philippines. If there is a Filipino community in your area, interview an individual to find out about his or her family back home. You might begin by contacting the local Filipino community association or church. If there is no Filipino community nearby, you can do this for another immigrant community in your area.

2. Go to an ESL centre in a local state-supported school in your community. Interview a teacher and a student. Where do most ESL students live in town? What do you think is the average income of families of ESL students? Try to learn whether the

student and teacher believe most ESL students will attend academic courses of study, vocational classes, or other 'tracks' after they finish ESL.

FURTHER READING

R. Constantino (1984) is an analysis of Philippine nationalism written before the fall of Marcos by the foremost spokesperson for the nationalist solution to the problems of the Philippines. Gonzalez (1980) presents a traditional perspective toward the Philippine language issue written by a supporter of Pilipino who is one of the most well-known linguists in the Philippines. Green (1987) outlines the aims of the writers of the new Philippine constitution as well as the problems facing the struggle for social justice and economic equality. San Juan (1986) presents a sympathetic portrait of the NPA's response to the social and political problems facing the Philippines.

SEVEN

Education and language rights

PREVIEW

Chapter 7 examines the movement to assert language rights, particularly in education. Two countries with an especially strong commitment to language rights are Australia and Yugoslavia. In Australia, the recently adopted national language policy (Lo Bianco 1987) specifies the right to government information and services in the native language, as well as native-language education for students who do not speak English. Australian policy demonstrates the value of official recognition of language rights. Yugoslavia, with a long commitment to extensive language rights for many nationalities, is currently undergoing a political crisis in which many rights are being withdrawn. This important development suggests that the foundation for rights is *power* and that constant *struggle* is necessary to sustain language rights.

In the Philippines, the use of English has been associated for several decades with economic inequality, unequal educational systems, and a rigid class structure that has elicited an increasingly desperate response from the rural and urban poor. Other countries, however, have recognized the dangers of sustained linguistic inequality and therefore have sought ways to reduce linguistic barriers to education, employment, and political power. Though this effort involves ongoing struggle, it has resulted in a new strategy for reducing hegemonic domination by privileged groups. This new strategy is the assertion of language rights.

CASE: SHARON KENDRICK AND JANEZ OREŠNIK

Sharon Kendrick and Janez Orešnik are elementary-school principals on opposite sides of the earth, Kendrick in a neighbourhood
in central Sydney in Australia, and Orešnik in Piran, a small town
on the Adriatic coast in the republic of Slovenia in Yugoslavia.
Though separated by both geography and politics, both principals
direct schools with a large number of pupils who do not speak the
dominant language well (English in Sydney, Slovenian in
Slovenia). In Sydney, many pupils are recently arrived refugees
and immigrants from Asia, while in Piran, many are children of
Italian families who have lived in the area for many years.

Under the educational policies of the two countries, Kendrick
and Orešnik must work toward three language-related goals. First,
they must make certain that all children receive a good education in
required subjects. To achieve this goal, pupils who do not speak
the dominant language may attend classes taught in their native
language. Second, both principals must prepare children for
further education and eventually for employment. Since most
educational institutions and jobs require fluency in the dominant
language, Kendrick and Orešnik believe they have a responsibility
to ensure that all children become fluent in it. Finally, their schools
are expected to reduce the tension and conflict that exist among
the different ethnic groups, not only within the school itself, but
also within the larger society. To achieve these goals, both
Kendrick and Orešnik have instituted new classes in English or
Slovenian as a second language, in minority languages for speakers
of the dominant language, and in cross-cultural understanding;
they have also offered workshops for teachers to help them become
more effective in dealing with students from different linguistic
backgrounds; and they have hired bilingual teachers for a wide
range of subjects.

Kendrick and Orešnik work in countries in which mother-
tongue education is widely considered to be a right. In Yugoslavia,
this right applies to most, but not all groups. As a general rule, the
right to mother-tongue education – and other language rights as
well – is protected within the geographical area in which a
particular linguistic group lives in significant numbers. (There is no
fixed minimum; in some districts, groups comprising less than 10
per cent of the population have schools in their mother tongue.)
When the right to native-language education is granted, it may

extend from elementary school through to postgraduate university study. Yet for some groups, there are practical limits. For the 20,000 Italians in Slovenia, elementary and secondary schools are available in localities with heavy concentrations of Italians, but unavailable elsewhere. Higher education and most good jobs require fluency in Slovenian.

In Australia, mother-tongue education is seen as a right for children who do not speak English well. The principle behind it is that education is so important for employment and other life processes that it must be effective. Because children who do not understand the language of the school will be seriously disadvantaged, federal policy supports mother-tongue education for these children.

Although federal policy supports their efforts, Kendrick and Orešnik face a continuing dilemma. Despite new courses and programmes, children in their schools seem no more tolerant of each other than in past years. They eat lunch mainly with others from their own language group, they use derogatory names when talking about other groups, and their disagreements and fights often occur along linguistic lines. More importantly, ethnic-minority children continue to drop out of school at a higher rate than those who speak the dominant language, fewer go on to higher education, and they have greater difficulty finding good jobs. Also, teachers complain that they spend more time dealing with language problems and ethnic tensions than with 'real teaching'. Thus both principals are frustrated in their efforts to solve the social problems of inequality, intolerance, and misunderstanding. Nevertheless, they remain deeply committed to the goals of tolerance and linguistic and cultural diversity. They believe that their pupils have a right to use their own language, and that the school can play an important role in helping them to exercise that right. They continue to search for programmes that will help them achieve these goals.

LANGUAGE RIGHTS

In recent years, one of the ways linguistic minorities have sought to expand the range of use of their language is through the assertion of language rights. The claim that individuals have a right to speak their native language in education, government, the media, and other areas is an effective strategy in the effort to resist domination by more powerful groups. Australia and Yugoslavia are among the few countries that have incorporated the principle of language rights into official policy.

Though separated by both distance and ideology, education officials in Australia and Yugoslavia face similar linguistic pressures. On the one hand, the schools are expected to integrate linguistic minorities into the economic, social, and political institutions of both countries. In Australia especially, it is widely believed that learning the *dominant language* plays a central role in this process. On the other hand, schools in both countries are expected to reduce economic and social problems among linguistic minorities, including high dropout rates, unemployment, and lack of political participation. Official policy in both countries asserts that *mother-tongue education* is useful in this effort.

Outside education, both Australia and Yugoslavia claim enlightened policies with regard to minority languages and cultures. Both use several languages for official purposes, and language minorities are guaranteed equal access to government agencies and services in their native languages. Yet both countries are currently undergoing a serious re-evaluation of language policy, particularly in the area of education – a re-evaluation which entails political conflict and, in the case of Yugoslavia, widespread violence.

Australia and Yugoslavia have different systems for achieving the goal of reducing language-based inequality. Australia supports a policy called *multiculturalism* or *cultural pluralism* with English dominance, while Yugoslavia supports a policy of regional autonomy for different language groups. As we shall see, these policies are subject to powerful economic and political forces. Although the movement to extend and to protect language rights is a positive one for linguistic minorities in both countries, the experience of Australia and Yugoslavia suggests that language rights are subordinate to the structure of power and domination, and that language policy, even when it protects language rights, is a form of covert state control.

MEDIA EXAMPLE 7.1: THE DECLARATION OF RECIFE

In October 1987, the Association Internationale pour le Developpement de la Communication Interculturelle (AIMAV), a UNESCO agency, held its 22nd seminar on Human Rights and Cultural Rights in Recife, Brazil. Concerned with widespread discrimination and inequality associated with language, AIMAV adopted a statement asserting the existence of universal language rights and calling on the United Nations to adopt a Universal Declaration of Linguistic Rights.

The Declaration of Recife

The XXII Seminar of AIMAV on Human Rights and Cultural Rights held at the School of Law of the Universidade Federal de Pernambuco (Recife, Brasil), October 7–9, 1987, chaired by Francisco Comes de Matos,

Considering that the ideals and principles of equality, solidarity, freedom, justice, peace, and understanding, which have inspired national and international legislation and instruments on human rights, share a crucial linguistic dimension,

Recognizing that the learning and use, maintenance and promotion of languages contribute significantly to the intellectual, educational, sociocultural, economic, and political development of individuals, groups, and States,

Noting that the Universal Declaration of Human Rights, the International Covenants related to human rights and other international universal instruments make provision for cultural rights,

Mindful of the need to arouse and foster awareness, within and across cultures, of the recognition and promotion of the linguistic rights of individuals and groups,

Asserting that linguistic rights should be acknowledged, promoted and observed nationally, regionally, and internationally, so as to bring about and assure the dignity and equity of all languages,

Aware of the need for legislation to eliminate linguistic prejudice and discrimination, and all forms of linguistic domination, injustice, and oppression, in such contexts as services to the public, the place of work, the educational system, the courtroom, and the mass media,

Stressing the need to sensitize individuals, groups, and States to linguistic rights, to promote positive societal attitudes toward plurilingualism and to change societal structures toward equality between users of different languages and varieties of languages,

Hence, conscious of the need for explicit legal guarantees of the linguistic rights of individuals and groups to be provided by the appropriate bodies of the member states of the United Nations,

RECOMMENDS that steps be taken by the United Nations to adopt and implement a UNIVERSAL DECLARATION OF LINGUISTIC RIGHTS which would require a reformulation of national, regional, and international language policies.

Questions

1. The Declaration of Recife assumes that 'linguistic prejudice and discrimination' are widespread. Can you think of some examples in your country? Consider minority languages in places of work, at school, in courts, and in the mass media.

2. The Declaration calls on the United Nations to adopt a Universal Declaration of Linguistic Rights. With your classmates or friends, write a Declaration of Linguistic Rights for your home town or city. Consider any linguistic minorities in your area, and what specific measures would guarantee their 'linguistic rights'. You might use as a starting point the following statement written by those in attendance at the Recife seminar, adapting it to the specific languages in your town or city.

> Statement of the XXIInd AIMAV Seminar
> Every social group has the right to positively identify with a language or languages and have its identification accepted and respected by others.
> Every child has a right to learn fully the language or languages of his/her group.
> Everyone has the right to use any language of his/her group in any official situation.
> Everyone has the right to learn fully at least one of the official languages in the country where she/he is resident, according to his/her own choice.

3. The Statement in question 2 asserts that everyone has the right to use his or her native language in any 'official situation'. This refers to situations involving government agencies, including the courts. For this policy to be implemented in your home town or city, what changes would be necessary in the way government agencies operate? Consider specific agencies such as the schools, legislative bodies, government media, and offices that provide utilities, handle complaints, and offer social services such as welfare, health, and public housing.

LANGUAGE RIGHTS IN AUSTRALIA

After many decades in which immigration policy favoured English speakers and educational policy favoured rapid assimilation, Australia has moved recently toward an official declaration of language rights. The Australian conception of language rights calls into question the assumption implicit in British policy (see Chapter 3) that language learning and cross-cultural contact can effectively reduce economic, political, and social inequality.

The language situation in Australia

One of the most striking features of the Australian language situation is the number and diversity of native languages in use throughout the country. In addition to several varieties of English, there are approximately 150 Aboriginal languages (50 of which have more than 100 speakers) and between 75 and 100 immigrant languages, 11 of which are used in the home by more than 50,000 speakers. The largest immigrant languages are Italian (416,000), Greek (277,000) Serbo-Croatian (141,000), Chinese (139,000), Arabic (119,000), German (111,000), Spanish (74,000), Polish (68,700), Vietnamese (66,000), Dutch (62,000), Maltese (60,000), and French (53,000) (Clyne 1988). In 1983, 17.3 per cent of the citizenry was reported to speak first languages other than English (Senate Standing Committee 1984); one out of eight residents is estimated to regularly use a language other than English (Ozolins 1988).

Prior to the Second World War, government policy favoured immigration from Britain and other European countries. Between the end of the war and the 1960s, immigration from other countries increased, while official policy remained assimilationist. Immigrant families were encouraged to learn English quickly so that children would adopt English as their primary language. Official ideology assumed that assimilation would be rapid and successful.

In the 1960s and 1970s, the number of immigrants from southern Europe, the Middle East, and Asia increased dramatically. Although the policy of assimilation was abandoned in favour of 'integration', the dominant explanation for immigrants' economic, educational, and social problems continued to be that they did not speak English and had not integrated into the dominant Australian culture. Thus it was assumed that immigrants' problems would disappear when they were properly educated in English and in the Australian way of life.

Despite official confidence that education could lead to integration, many immigrants continued to live in ethnic enclaves, work in low-paying jobs, and have educational levels below those of the English-speaking population. In order to address growing concerns about these problems, in September 1977, Prime Minister Malcolm Fraser appointed a committee headed by Frank Galbally, an attorney, to review programmes and services for them.

The Galbally Report, 1978

Completed in late 1978, the Galbally Report (Galbally 1978) was issued in English, Arabic, Dutch, German, Greek, Italian, Serbo-Croatian, Spanish, Turkish, and Vietnamese (though the appendixes were printed in English only). The decision to publish the Report in these languages reflected the committee's recommendation that federal policy should end the decades-long emphasis on assimilation, and instead change to a policy that eventually came to be called *multiculturalism* or *cultural pluralism*.

The policy of multiculturalism articulated by the Galbally Report meant that the government should foster 'the retention of the cultural heritage of different ethnic groups and [promote] intercultural understanding' (section 1.38). The policy was to be implemented through an array of measures in initial settlement programmes; in English-language education; in information, communication and the media; in the legal system; in social security and employment; and in health services. In addition, the Report recommended special programmes for young children, women, the handicapped, and the aged.

The committee adopted the principle that every individual has the right to access to government programmes and services and to 'maintain his or her culture without prejudice or disadvantage' (1.7). Nevertheless, believing that migrants with the greatest difficulties were those with little or no English proficiency, the committee viewed language as the root of most problems facing migrants (1.9–1.10). Therefore the committee recommended significantly increased government funding for ESL classes, teacher training, and translation and interpretation, and for expansion of media in migrants' languages. Although the committee argued that migrants who never become fluent in English should not be placed at a disadvantage (4.2), it suggested only that non-English speakers should have equal access to government services; no similar recommendation was made for education and employment. Nevertheless, the committee recognized that migrants are often subject to unfair treatment by employers and the legal system, and that special efforts should be made to ensure that migrants understand their rights and privileges under Australian law (5.17).

Like the US refugee programme (see Chapter 5), the Galbally Report pointed to cultural and linguistic differences between migrants and English-speaking Australians as the primary cause of the social and economic problems facing migrants. Thus the report emphasized education as the solution to migrants' economic difficulties. Unlike the US programme, however, the Galbally Report also argued that preservation of cultural and linguistic minorities could strengthen Australian society and need not be a source of divisiveness. Therefore the report proposed increased federal funding for programmes designed to maintain community languages. Clearly favouring English, however, the committee made a weak case for the universal value of multiculturalism. Arguing that all Australians 'should be encouraged to understand and embrace other cultures' (section 1.7), the committee claimed that specific benefits would ensue from multiculturalism: native-born Australians would be better prepared to learn other languages and to 'gain a greater understanding of social problems, history, art, etc.'; children of migrants would be more likely to learn the language of their parents; and the 'unity of the family' would be reinforced (9.9). In comparison to these limited benefits, however, the Report placed much greater emphasis upon the migrants' many difficulties stemming from their differences from the dominant culture. With this emphasis on migrants' cultural and linguistic differences (see 1.10), a logical solution to their problems was to reduce their linguistic and cultural diversity. Indeed, many conservatives opposed the recommendations in the Galbally Report on the grounds that the committee's own argument defined cultural diversity as the problem rather than the solution (see Bullivant 1982).

Although it shifted language policy debate to a discussion of the meaning and value of pluralism, the Galbally Report left unresolved the question of whether the government should formally adopt a new language policy. As a result of lobbying by various social groups for a more formal policy, the Senate Standing Committee on Education and the Arts decided to tackle the issue. (For a summary of the lobbying effort, see Ozolins 1988.) The result was its 1984 report, *A National Language Policy* (Senate Standing Committee 1984).

Senate Committee Report on a National Language Policy, 1984

The Senate Committee on Education and the Arts met for two-and-a-half years, holding public meetings throughout the country and accepting 420 written submissions and documents from concerned individuals and organizations. Its Report included 117 recommendations on official language use, language and bilingual education, libraries, and the media.

Although the stated purpose of the Report was to develop a coordinated language policy for Australia, the Committee was quite cautious in its recommendations regarding official status for migrant languages and English language education. While supporting increased primary-school language training, improved teacher education, and other measures, the Report generally reinforced the dominant role for English by arguing that no language policy should 'devalue English as Australia's national language nor deny its role as our common language, nor suggest that non-standard variants of English should become the norm' (p. 1). Competence in English was declared the primary policy goal, with secondary support for 'maintenance and development of languages other than English' as well as for public services in other languages and increased opportunity for learning second languages (p. 4). The Committee recommended that 'at all levels of Government it is recognised that English is, and will remain, Australia's national language' (p. 18). The Report accepted the assumption that learning English is essential for good jobs, and therefore it viewed the major responsibility of the state as being to provide English language education for non-English speakers, including migrants and Aboriginal peoples (p. 39).

In its analysis of the Australian language situation as well as in its recommendations, the Senate Committee expressed a neo-classical view of language learning and language change. Like the Swann Report in Britain (see Chapter 3), it accepted the argument that language policy cannot determine the survival of Aboriginal or community languages: 'People will be making individual decisions on whether they want to maintain their language . . . and no language policy is going to do that . . . it is an individual decision.' (p. 2) The Report emphasized intermarriage and community 'cultural values' as being more important than policy in this regard (p. 139). The Committee also ignored the role of power and conquest in European domination of Aboriginal peoples, blandly stating that English was given predominance by the settlers, as if they might just as easily have chosen one of the Aboriginal languages as the major means of communication. The Report asserted simply that 'the pre-eminence of the English language reflects the fact that European settlement . . . has been chiefly by English-speaking people' (p. 8), while ignoring widespread bilingualism in nineteenth-century Australia, as well as the destruction of Aboriginal culture and the domination of Aboriginal languages that this 'settlement' entailed. Indeed, the Report played down Aboriginal multilingualism by noting that 'restricted mobility' limited the number of languages most Aboriginal people knew.

Neoclassical assumptions were expressed also by the Committee's failure to critically examine the low status of ESL teaching and its low priority in government budgets, despite its alleged importance in reducing inequality. Noting, for instance, that adult literacy teaching relied primarily upon unprofessional volunteer tutors, the Committee recommended that this system continue because 'students who . . . have low self-esteem and lack confidence will in many cases not embark on a literacy course with even one other student in the same room as the tutor' (p. 69). In other words, unprofessional, unpaid tutors should be used because that is what non-English speakers prefer. The Committee did not address the question of whether such programmes reflect a half-hearted effort to achieve the claimed goal of full adult literacy for migrants, and instead placed responsibility for illiteracy on the culture of illiterate individuals, listing the primary causes of illiteracy as 'broken schooling/illness/ changes of school; emotional upset/pressure/instability; cultural deprivation/illiterate parents' (p. 66). The poor performance of Aboriginal pupils in Australian schools was explained with reference to their frequent ill health, Aboriginal 'cultural values', including an alleged antagonism towards English and low expectations among parents, as well as 'the history of repression of Aboriginal languages and culture since European settlement' (p. 84). The Committee did not consider a connection between Aboriginal school performance and, for instance, the fact that no Australian university taught an Aboriginal language at the time the Report was prepared (p. 168).

Perhaps the most significant neoclassical assumptions in the

Report involved the Committee's acceptance of certain 'common sense' explanations for policies: everyone should learn English because it is necessary for jobs; it is not feasible to provide translation and interpretation services for all of the languages in Australia; dominance by English is more practical than other systems for organizing language in Australian society; and people who do not speak English must inevitably suffer in many ways throughout their lives. By accepting these unchangeable 'truths', the Committee ensured that it would make no proposals to significantly alter the language situation in Australia.

The Senate Committee Report set forth many recommendations that would require agency action. Nevertheless, during its long deliberations, the public debate over language policy largely passed it by, particularly as state governments began to adopt language policies of their own and as the debate intensified over the desirability of Asian immigration. Therefore in 1986 the Minister of Education commissioned Joseph Lo Bianco to prepare a document on a national language policy. Completed in November 1986, the *National Policy on Languages* (Lo Bianco 1987) is the most important official statement to date about language policy in Australia. One of the major foundations for its policy recommendations is an assertion of language rights.

The Lo Bianco Report, 1987

The difference between the Lo Bianco Report and earlier statements of federal language policy can be seen in its version of the history of language in Australia. While the 1984 Senate Report accepted the myth that 'English was given predominance' by early settlers who mainly spoke English (p. 8), the Lo Bianco Report emphasized that 'from the mid-nineteenth century, large sections of the population used a non-Aboriginal language other than English for virtually all their social, familial, economic, and educational purposes' (Lo Bianco 1987, p. 9). In so describing early Australia, Lo Bianco located multilingualism and multiculturalism at the core of Australian history and identity. From its opening pages, the Report emphasized language pluralism as a national resource rather than a problem to be overcome.

Language is a core value, according to the Report, because it is associated with the identity of individuals, ethnic groups, and nations, and it is 'a source of human identity' (p. 1). The Report supported societal multilingualism because of its value in enriching culture (p. 44), its contribution to the Australian economy (p. 48), its importance in social justice (p. 56), and its enhancement of the country's role in the Pacific region (p. 60). Yet the Report accepted the practical need to learn English, trying to balance it against the right to speak native languages. In Lo Bianco's view, the reasons for learning English are obvious. English is a 'cohesive and unifying element in Australian society' (p. 71) and it has overwhelming practical value for higher education and advancement in employment. Thus the highest priority in the language education policy outlined in the Report is 'English for all' (p. 146). In this regard, Lo Bianco accepted the basic principle outlined in both the Senate Committee Report and the Galbally Report that English should continue to play a dominant role in Australian life.

Unlike the earlier reports, Lo Bianco gave equal weight to the problems that English domination creates for many Australians. Recognizing that English is 'the language of power and influence', Lo Bianco argued that 'to be without English is to be without the means of participating effectively in public life' (p. 72). In response to concern for those who do not speak English fluently, Lo Bianco proposed two sets of actions: information and government services in languages other than English, including Aboriginal languages; and educational programmes to ensure that as many Australians as possible are able to acquire English. Emphasizing that English should be an *added* language rather than a replacement for other languages, the Report recommended funds for programmes to preserve Aboriginal languages and to teach school content subjects to children in their native language if they are not fluent in English. Acknowledging that some people will never acquire English, the Report asserted that the government should reach out to its citizens in languages that they understand. Thus Lo Bianco recognized that English as a second language does not solve all of the language-related problems of the country.

Lo Bianco envisioned an end to the 'malaise in language education in Australia which is deep and pervasive' (p. 138) and a rejuvenated society in which most people are bilingual in English and another language, language learning is universal and widely effective, and all languages and cultures are respected. His report painted an appealing portrait of a society characterized by respect for difference, by understanding born of cross-cultural experience, and by interaction among peoples of diverse cultures, with English remaining the language of advanced education, the most powerful institutions of business and finance, and the highest-paying jobs.

Striving for such a society, the Lo Bianco Report proposed a language policy with two broad social aims: universal English language learning, and social justice for those who do not speak English. The first goal is reached through English as a second language. The second goal is reached in two ways: *directly* through native language education for children and special governmental efforts to provide information and services for those who do not speak English; and *indirectly* through the enhanced tolerance and understanding of cultural diversity that is supposed to result from increased contact among cultures and from universal language learning.

Lo Bianco's dual concern for ensuring that all Australians have the opportunity to learn English, and that the government does not unnecessarily disadvantage those who do not speak it, is expressed in the list of programmes created to implement his recommendations. With the advice of the Australian Advisory Council on Languages and Multicultural Education (AACLAME), which Lo Bianco chairs, the federal government has supported six major initiatives: the Australian Second Language Learning Program, the Adult Literacy Action Campaign, the Multicultural and Cross-Cultural Supplementation Program, the National Aboriginal Languages Program, Asian Studies, and the New Arrivals Program in English as a Second Language (Australian Advisory Council on Languages and Multicultural Education 1988). While ESL remains the most heavily supported programme, the others reflect Lo Bianco's strong support for Aboriginal language maintenance, adult literacy, and second language education for all Australians.

Lo Bianco's belief that language policy can contribute to greater social justice raises the issue of the educational value of language learning and cross-cultural contact. Can government-supported language and culture programmes reduce inequality? We now turn to an examination of the value of language education for achieving social justice.

Education and inequality

To some extent, the Lo Bianco Report claimed a connection between education and social justice. For instance, Lo Bianco argued that English-speaking Australians will understand 'Aboriginal cultural values' by studying the structure, 'socio-linguistic patterns', and 'rich store of myths and stories' of Aboriginal languages (p. 117). Similarly, when second language learning in schools is widespread, 'intercultural understanding' is enhanced (p. 123). The Report also argued that education can be part of a broad process leading to changes in attitude. Lo Bianco's analysis of the economic, social, and political problems of non-English speakers claimed that education could contribute to a solution to those problems. For instance, he justified the priority given to ESL as follows:

> Lack of proficiency in Standard English correlates closely with occupancy of lower paid employment and, to a great degree, occupational mobility in Australia depends on skill in the English language. Advanced technologies are displacing workers from some jobs which have, in the post-war decades, usually been occupied by non-English speakers. Retraining is hampered without English, as are most aspects of labour market participation (Lo Bianco 1987, pp. 56–7).

Thus Lo Bianco summarized the importance of English education by claiming that 'English is not just one variable among others, but the base-line variable in determining unemployment risk.' (p. 58)

Yet, unlike some supporters of cross-cultural education, Lo Bianco acknowledged its limitations. He admitted that attitudes towards other cultures will not necessarily change simply because of language contact and learning. He also recognized that language and education policy are unlikely to be sufficient to maintain languages threatened by powerful economic and social forces (p. 68). Given such an analysis, the solution to problems of social justice is complex, involving 'expansion and improvement of appropriate opportunities for adults to gain literacy and skills in Standard Australian English' (p. 59), mother-tongue education for children still learning English, and other non-educational changes in social policy.

Lo Bianco's recognition that education alone cannot solve

problems of economic inequality and social injustice is unusual, for the belief that education can reduce social inequality is a powerful one with a long history. It depends upon the assumption that education is the cause of affluence rather than its effect (see Bullivant 1987). Since the nineteenth century, educational reformers in the United States and England have proposed ways of using the educational system to reduce inequality, change values and attitudes, and alleviate social problems (for a discussion of such efforts in the USA, see Tollefson 1989). Nowhere has this belief been more strongly expressed than in the attempt to reduce ethnic and linguistic conflict through cultural and language contact.

Culture contact theory (which includes language learning) asserts that minority students can overcome inequalities through curricula and teaching practices, and that prejudice and discrimination by the members of the dominant culture will be reduced if they study other languages and cultures. Exposure, in other words, leads to tolerance. In an extensive review of research in this area, Bullivant (1987) found that there is little empirical support for this belief. Research studies on inter-group awareness and prejudice in schools show that culture contact has little impact on prejudice and minority school performance (Amir 1969, 1972, 1976, cited in Bullivant 1987). Indeed, some studies have found that contact increases intolerance and racist attitudes (Bochner 1982; Fitch 1984). Bullivant concludes that the optimism of culture contact theory is not supported by data.

Critics of culture contact theory argue that its persistence is not simply an example of a good idea without empirical support. Instead, they suggest that it is part of an ideology that sustains inequality. This is because culture contact programmes assume that the problem that needs to be fixed is within individual children. Thus culture contact theory 'sanitizes' inequality by making it seem just a matter of individual ignorance, which education can overcome, rather than an effect of historical and structural factors that are overcome only through political struggle. An example is the denial of employment to immigrants in the United States under the Immigration Reform and Control Act (see Chapter 5). Although the Act includes sanctions against employers who discriminate against immigrants who have legal permission to work, a 1988 survey of employers in New York City found that 22,000 aliens or citizens who look or sound foreign were denied employment or had employment delayed, despite being qualified for jobs and having completed required training (*New York Times* 1989). The inability of these individuals to find work was clearly unrelated to their lack of education. Moreover, most employers who denied employment to them had frequently hired other immigrants, and so had had a great deal of contact with other languages and cultures. The banal suggestion that these employers need further education to make them more tolerant of diversity fails to confront alternative explanations for their hiring practices.

An alternative to culture contact theory is the view that inequality is rooted in system and structure – historical, social class, economic, and political forces – which are *reflected* in the educational system, and therefore are not amenable to change by it. From this perspective, the claim that language itself can be a source of inequality distorts the role of language. Language itself leads neither to equality nor inequality, but instead is a tool to further them. The important question is: how is language used to structure social relations? In Australia, this perspective leads to questions such as: why are Aboriginal languages ineffective tools for gaining high-paying jobs? Why are the languages of Asian immigrants useless for higher education in Australia? Such questions focus on the history of language inequality as a source of injustice rather than upon the attitudes or feelings of individual children in school. The emphasis on language education as the key to economic and social justice risks oversimplifying the problem by ignoring historical and structural factors.

In contrast to culture contact theory, historical–structural analysis attempts to explain how language is used to determine which individuals and groups have access to economic resources and political power. Consider the example of high unemployment and low wages among migrants in Australia. Culture contact theory predicts that cross-cultural classes will reduce discrimination, and that ESL will provide migrants with the language skills they need to find better jobs. The assumption is that the pattern of migrants' employment is due to poor attitudes among both migrants and members of the dominant group, and to migrants' lack of language skills.

But is this the case? In a study of migration and social class, Tait and Gibson (1987) argue that certain segments of the Australian economy benefit from migrants' inability to find good jobs, and thus there is powerful economic pressure sustaining their unemployment, low wages, and associated problems in education, housing, health, and transportation. This analysis depends upon an understanding of the historical connection of language minorities to the Australian labour market.

Migration to Australia has been essential for more than forty years of post-Second World War economic expansion. Until the 1980s, this expansion was largely in manufacturing, with migrants entering the labour force primarily as factory workers. When manufacturing declined in the 1970s, migrants bore the brunt of increased unemployment. Then, as new, non-unionized service industries expanded in the 1980s, a large number of workers were needed to fill unskilled jobs paying low wages in hotels, restaurants, finance, real estate, telecommunications, and entertainment. Such jobs are low in wages, subject to the swings of boom and recession, and labour intensive. Thus, migrants' employment resembles that of industrial workers in the Third World. (For similar labour needs in the Philippines, see Chapter 6.)

Migrants are particularly attractive workers for these jobs because they cannot easily organize or fight for their economic rights. As Tait and Gibson point out, 'migrant labour is attractive because it is cheap and easily controlled' (p. 17). Among the mechanisms for control available to the state are the overt control of contract labour migration and the covert control of language barriers and migrants' lack of knowledge about their political rights.

Tait and Gibson's analysis emphasizes the central importance of Australian immigration policy in government efforts to manage the growth and specialization of the labour force and to determine which segments of the population will suffer during periods of economic restructuring. Because Australian society requires English proficiency for effective exercise of political power, non-English-speaking migrants have greater difficulty changing their economic circumstances than English-speaking migrants facing similar challenges. Thus they are a more easily managed segment of the labour force and they serve as a buffer during industry recessions, thereby protecting politically more powerful English-speaking Australians. In this way, language is a form of covert state control of labour. Tait and Gibson conclude that immigrant workers who do not speak English are in a fundamentally different situation from English-speaking immigrants, whose connection to the labour market more closely resembles that of English-speaking Australians. Thus it is extraordinarily difficult for migrants who do not speak English to improve their education or employment in Australia. Indeed, migrants who speak English are similar to native-born, English-speaking Australians in their rate of employment, while migrants who do not speak English remain in peripheral jobs characterized by low pay, poor benefits, and great insecurity, and which are likely to be the first cut in a recession. In addition, due to lack of child care, poor transportation and other problems, they find it difficult to attend school to gain new skills that might offer better prospects for work.

It is within this context that the role of education must be evaluated. Immigrant and Aboriginal education in Australia cannot be expected to eliminate economic inequalities by preparing minorities to work in an English-speaking environment and fostering respect for all cultures. As Tate and Gibson demonstrate, Australian economic expansion requires large numbers of people without skills, without advanced education, and without the capacity for organized struggle. At present, a key criterion for determining which people will fill this position is lack of proficiency in English language. The correlation between language and economic status means that this system for allocating workers to jobs has been effectively implemented. This analysis implies that the educational system is largely irrelevant to the processes that determine the economic fate of people who do not speak English, and that the schools will be unable to resolve minorities' economic problems.

MEDIA EXAMPLE 7.2

This example suggests that nonstandard varieties of a dominant language may face the same barriers to official recognition as other languages. Linguists have long recognized that pronunciation of *ask* as [aks] ('axe') and use of *be* as in 'He be sick' are features of certain nonstandard dialects, including Black English. Yet, according to the following article from the *New York Times*, in 1988 the Mayor of New York asked the New York City public school system to rid its students of these 'offensive features'.

Purging 'What-Cha' and 'Ain't'
New York students will be taught to avoid New Yorkese
BY NEIL A. LEWIS
Special to the New York Times

NEW YORK, Feb. 27 – New York City's Schools Chancellor, Richard R. Green, is beginning a campaign to purge New York of New Yorkese and other offending speech patterns.

In a memorandum to Mayor Edward I. Koch released today, Dr. Green identified 20 phrases or mispronunciations, some peculiar to New York, he is determined to eliminate from the speech of city students.

Listing 'Speech Demons'

The items supposed to be corrected include the cheery 'what-cha doin?' ('what are you doing?,' students will be be taught to say) to the hoary bane of English teachers, ain't. Malefactors being questioned should learn not to say: 'I don't know nuttin about it.' Instead, they should respond with a proper: 'I don't know anything about it.'

The Chancellor's list of 'speech demons' and his detailed program to eradicate them from the speech of schoolchildren are a response to Mayor Koch's repeated prodding and complaining about poor speech habits of the city's youth. Although Dr. Green has suggested that many of the Mayor's educational proposals are superficial, he has responded to the complaints about speech patterns with apparent alacrity.

In his memorandum to the Mayor, Dr. Green said he was beginning a full-scale assault.

His list of speech demons will be distributed to each student and a poster contest will be held to 'focus on common errors in the oral use of language.'

Dr. Green said he would convene in April 'a working group of outstanding educators, including representatives of the university community, the New York Public Libraries and Central Office experts' to develop a long-term plan, Dr. Green wrote.

Plan Called 'Superb'

In realising the Chancellor's program today, Mr. Koch pronounced it 'superb.'

Included on the list are some of the speech patterns the Mayor singled out in a letter to Dr. Green as particularly offensive – saying 'axe' for 'ask,' for example, and the misuse of the verb 'to be' as in 'He be sick.'

Among the 20 problems cited by the Chancellor is the mispronunciation of the word 'library' as 'liberry,' a mistake the Mayor has acknowledged he occasionally makes himself.

Demons Possessing Student Tongues

May I *axe* a question?	May I ask a question?
Hang the *pitcher* on the wall.	Hang the picture on the wall.
He's *goin'* home	He's going home.
He *be* sick.	He is sick.
I *ain't* got none.	I don't have any.

Can I leave the room?	May I leave the room?
I was *like* tired, *you know*?	I was tired.
Where is the ball *at*?	Where is the ball?
What-*cha doin'*?	What are you doing?
I'll *meetcha* at the *cau-nuh*.	I'll meet you at the corner.
What do *youse* want?	What do you want?
Let's go to *da* center.	Let's go to the center.
I *brang* my date along.	I brought my date along.
The *books is* in the *liberry*.	The books are in the library.
Yup, you *betcha*!	Yes, you're right.
Pacifically, . . .	Specifically, . . .
I don't know *nuttin* about it.	I don't know anything about it.
I'm not the *on'y* one.	I'm not the only one.
We *was only foolin' 'round*.	We were only fooling around.
So, I *says* to him . . .	So, I said to him . . .

(source: Lewis 1989)

Questions

1. Do you think the schools will be successful in their effort to end students' use of these features? Do you think students will stop using these forms in classes? On the playground? At home? Why?

2. What message does the Mayor's action convey to speakers of dialects that include these features?

Language rights in Australia

We now return to the assertion of language rights in Australia. Rights are granted when those who support them have the power to insist that they be enacted. In other words, the foundation for language rights is power. Like language rights, access to quality education also is associated with power. This is not to deny that education may also increase power, but people without power are unlikely to have access to education, or they may have access only to limited education that prepares them for low-paying jobs. It is unlikely that education offers a solution to problems of inequality that are fundamentally rooted in differences in power.

But it would be oversimplified to suggest that language rights are enjoyed only by those with power. There is instead a dynamic relationship between rights and power. When a relatively weak linguistic minority gains some rights, the group may have a more secure foundation for improving its economic circumstances, increasing its power, and eventually gaining greater rights. That is, language rights are grounded in struggle. To achieve some measure of rights does not end the struggle; it merely changes its nature. This is because language rights that are granted can also be taken away. If Australia shows that language rights depend upon economic status and power, Yugoslavia shows that rights are won and sustained only through struggle, and that changes in the structure of power can lead to changes in language rights.

LANGUAGE RIGHTS AND POWER IN YUGOSLAVIA

Yugoslavia has a much longer experience than Australia with language rights at the federal level. For nearly three decades Yugoslavia has sought to minimize linguistic inequality by protecting basic language rights and ensuring that most people will be able to live their lives using their home language for most purposes. But since the early 1980s, the country has faced a serious challenge to this policy. As we shall see, Yugoslavia faces a choice between, on the one hand, continued support for a pluralist system in which official policy seeks to minimize the linguistic barriers to full participation in society, and, on the other hand, the increasing likelihood of a bureaucratic dictatorship in which language is an overt mechanism for state control. The current crisis in Yugoslavia reveals the need for constant struggle if language rights are to be a means for reducing social inequality.

The language situation in Yugoslavia

Like Australia, Yugoslavia is characterized by great linguistic and cultural diversity. Divided by religion, history, and language, the peoples in the region have often been historical enemies. In order to accommodate this diversity, the country is divided into six republics (Slovenia, Serbia, Croatia, Montenegro, Macedonia, and Bosnia-Hercegovina) and two provinces within the republic of Serbia (Kosovo and Vojvodina). The constitution of Yugoslavia divides the country's nationalities into two categories: *nation* and *nationality*, the official translations of *narod* and *narodnost*. (There is some ambiguity in official usage, as 'nationality' is used both for the generic category, including nations and nationalities, and for the specific category in contrast to *nation*.) The six nations are Serbs, Croatians, Macedonians, Montenegrins, Slovenes, and

Moslems, corresponding to the six republics. By official definition, 'Moslem' denotes a national or ethnic group rather than a religious one, residing primarily in Bosnia-Hercegovina. These groups have 'nation' status because Yugoslavia is their homeland. The 'nationalities' are groups whose parent nations are elsewhere. These include Albanian, Bulgarian, Czech, Hungarian, Italian, and many others.

Two variants of Serbo-Croatian (Serbian and Croatian) are spoken as a first language by over 16,000,000 Serbs and Croatians, as well as by Montenegrins and Moslems. The four other major languages are Slovenian (1.75 million), Albanian (1.73 million), Macedonian (1.34 million), and Hungarian (0.42 million). Nearly everyone speaks Serbo-Croatian as a second language, which is normally the language of communication between members of different nationalities.

The boundaries of the republics are drawn so that the nations are located largely within their home republics. This means that major language groups are concentrated in particular republics or provinces. For instance, over 96 per cent of all Slovenes live in Slovenia, 96 per cent of all Macedonians live in Macedonia, and about 75 per cent of all Albanians live in Kosovo. Yet concentration is not equal for all groups. The most dispersed are the Serbs, about 40 per cent of whom reside in other republics. As we shall see, this has important consequences for language policy.

The relative dominance of the various groups within specific regions permits even small groups to exercise a high degree of autonomy within the decentralized political-administrative system. For instance, the nations control their own political institutions, economic policy, and local police. The ability of the nations to exercise this power has been, since the 1960s, the central feature of Yugoslav political organization. Moreover, the Albanian and Hungarian nationalities have enjoyed a great deal of control over their own affairs in the semi-autonomous provinces of Vojvodina (Hungarian) and Kosovo (Albanian). The current crisis is partly over Serbian efforts to rescind Albanian and Hungarian autonomy.

At the root of the current crisis is the unequal economic development of the republics. Although Slovenia contains less than 9 per cent of the total population of the country, it has enjoyed 15–20 per cent of the gross national product for many years, and has had in recent years an average income of three to six times that of the poorest areas in the south. Although slightly less affluent than Slovenia, Croatia enjoys a similar standard of living. This huge gap between the wealthy areas of Slovenia and Croatia in the north and Montenegro, Macedonia, Kosovo, Bosnia-Hercegovina, and Serbia in the south, leads to vast differences in education, literacy and other measures of development. For instance, by 1971, the literacy rate in Slovenia was about 98 per cent, while in Kosovo it was less than 70 per cent (*Statistični koledar Jugoslavije, 1976* 1976). A major effect of this unequal development is that thousands of guestworkers from southern regions live and work as temporary residents in the north (*Statistični koledar Jugoslavije, 1988* 1988).

For the first 20 years or so after the Second World War, the League of Communists of Yugoslavia (LCY) played a dominant role in republic economic policy, but the LCY was unable through strict centralization to solve the problem of unequal development of the republics. Meanwhile, the republics continued to assert their own interests within the federal structure, often identifying their nationality interests with those of the working class. As the LCY under Tito came to acknowledge that it could not resolve regional differences, it supported constitutional measures to grant ever-increasing economic and political power – and language rights – to the nations and nationalities. The primary mechanism for delegating power and rights is the constitution (see Jončić 1974).

The constitutions of Yugoslavia

Language policy is spelled out in great detail in the Yugoslav constitutions. Rather than being an unchanging document with a set of amendments, the federal constitution has been rewritten periodically since the Second World War. The first constitution in 1947 was basically a centralizing document designed to unite the country after the division and destruction of the war, and to assert the domination of the LCY over political life. In 1953, constitutional changes reflected Tito's split with Stalin, and began the country on the road to its decentralized brand of socialism. From 1953 to 1974, the trend was generally toward decentralization of authority and transfer of politico-administrative functions from the federal to the republic level (see Jovanović 1969; Lah 1972; Shoup 1968).

In addition to the federal constitution, each republic adopts its constitution in accordance with federal principles, with detailed provisions relating to the language situation in the republic. Each of the more than 500 communes also adopts a communal statute, or local constitution, which spells out in great detail the language policies and practices for the local area.

The 1974 constitutions adopted at the federal, republic, and communal levels enshrined as constitutional principle the trend toward decentralization that had begun years earlier. The policies spelled out in 1974 generally granted the power to establish laws protecting languages to those groups that dominate the individual republics, as well as to smaller nationalities that are the majorities within specific communes (Tollefson 1981b). This means that the languages of the nations gain full equality at the federal level and pre-eminence at the republic level, while other languages are protected within their autonomous provinces or communes. Thus the federal constitution declares the official languages at the federal level to be two varieties of Serbo-Croatian, as well as Slovenian and Macedonian. (There has also been a move in recent years to distinguish a variety of Serbo-Croatian spoken by Moslems in Bosnia-Hercegovina.) In addition, the federal constitution includes general statements guaranteeing the right of the nations and nationalities to use their home languages for many official purposes and to form organizations to promote their languages.

The Slovene constitution is typical of republic language policies. It declares that everyone has the right to express loyalty to a nation or nationality, to promote one's own culture, and to use one's native language and script (article 212). It also specifically guarantees equality with the Slovene language to Italian and Hungarian in areas inhabited by these groups (article 250). This guarantee applies to the courts and other official hearings, to publication and dissemination of laws and all public announcements, to education, and to the media. The federal constitution guarantees the right to judicial hearings in the languages of the nations; the Slovene constitution specifically declares that Slovene will be used in Slovenia, except in Italian and Hungarian communes, where those languages are used.

In education, the constitutions ensure that the nations may establish their own school systems, with their own languages as media of instruction. Many small nationalities operate their own primary and secondary schools in specific communes. Until recently, Albanian was used at all educational levels in the province of Kosovo. At the communal level, the Italian communes in Slovenia take many steps to ensure the use of Italian: all signs posted on kiosks and bulletin boards must be bilingual in Italian and Slovenian, all street signs are bilingual, the local radio station broadcasts in Italian, and elementary and secondary schools use Italian as the medium of instruction.

Between the early 1960s and 1988, the steady increase in the importance of the republics meant that they eventually became the only legal expression of linguistic nationalism. Thus regional autonomy protected language rights. Under the decentralized system, the republics developed elaborate institutional support for Slovenian, Croatian, Serbian, and Macedonian, while also protecting Hungarian, Albanian, Italian and other minority languages within the two autonomous provinces and bilingual communes. For more than 20 years, most language groups have been committed to the state federation because it provided an effective structure within which they could further their own interests and to a large extent control their own destinies.

The 1974 federal constitution, however, did not create an effective central body to deal with inter-republic conflict, particularly that resulting from the problem of unequal regional development. As long as Tito was alive, disputes were resolved through the force of his personal authority. But after his death, it was impossible to achieve consensus among the republics, since real power was dispersed in the hands of elites who were effective only within their own republics. Without extension of popular democracy, republican and provincial elites became entrenched within their regional areas, thereby making party and federal politics increasingly subject to state-led nationalism (Magaš 1989). The result is the current economic and political crisis, which entails serious threats to long-protected language rights.

The economic crisis

The economic crisis has been building since 1979, when the first shortages of food appeared in 20 years. By the mid-1980s, the country had a foreign debt of $20 billion and industrial growth had fallen to the minus range. The rate of inflation reached nearly

300 per cent in 1988, while some housing multiplied 40 times in price between 1986 and 1988, and interest rates on variable-rate mortgages came to be revised monthly. By 1989, living standards had fallen to those of the early 1960s, while unemployment had risen dramatically, especially as many Yugoslav guestworkers in Western Europe were sent home. Three administrative units (Kosovo, Macedonia, and Montenegro) declared that they were bankrupt. As a result of these problems, the gap increased visibly between rich and poor, a serious blow to Yugoslavs who had long prided themselves on achieving a relatively low level of class differentiation.

Political consequences

Two major responses to the worsening economic crisis took place. In Slovenia alone of all the republics, an important democratization occurred, with unofficial groups gaining wide public support, and official organizations, particularly the Alliance of Socialist Youth of Slovenia, bringing these alternative movements into the decision-making system (Lee 1989). The other response to the crisis was a movement to rescind the decentralized system, led by Serbia and the Army, which is dominated by Serbian officers. These two trends came into conflict at a trial that took place in Slovenia in the summer of 1988. That trial, in which language policy played a major role, has become the focus for a major crisis involving constitutionally-protected language rights.

In the trial, a military court in Ljubljana, the capital of Slovenia, sentenced to prison a sergeant major in the Army and three journalists from *Mladina*, the journal of the official Alliance of Socialist Youth of Slovenia. The four were found guilty of revealing secret military documents, and sentenced to prison terms ranging from 5 months to 4 years. The secret that they had revealed was that Defence Minister Mamula had built a private villa using active-duty military personnel. The trial was important because it was conducted in Serbo-Croatian, in direct violation of the Slovene republic constitution. Moreover, the transcript was then poorly translated into what one commentator complained 'can only be described as Slovene with an abundance of good will' (Mastnak 1989, p. 47). The use of Serbo-Croatian and the careless translation conveyed the Army's message that it was not subject to constitutional provisions guaranteeing Slovene language rights.

Of course the trial did not only involve a struggle over language rights. In part, it reflected a debate over the country's future, with the defendants arguing for decentralization and market reforms and the Army favouring centralized authority centred in Belgrade. In order to demonstrate its power to impose its view, the Army used the explosive issue of language. As a sign of the Army's success in conveying its message, many Slovenes concluded that the trial threatened the federal system itself, given the fact that the legitimacy of the federal government has been based for three decades or so upon its capacity to provide a framework within which the nations and nationalities are protected and can pursue their interests. To Slovenes, who demonstrated in huge numbers outside the courthouse, the trial meant that the political system was no longer capable of safeguarding their language and nationality rights. In effect, the decentralized system of regional autonomy that Tito had implemented was overturned by the Army's ability to conduct the trial in Serbo-Croatian.

But why would the Army, which since the early years of Tito's rule had remained largely outside politics, risk public outrage to pursue a policy of centralization? Could not a policy of centralized control of the economy and the political system be combined with protection of language and nationality rights? The answer lies in the close connection between language rights and political power. In Yugoslavia, political power is shifting to Serbian nationalists. The movement to establish Serbian hegemony throughout Yugoslavia reveals that power is the foundation for winning and sustaining language rights.

Serbian nationalism

At the time of writing, the Serbian nationalist movement is led by Slobodan Milošević, the head of the Serbian League of Communists, who has been able to mobilize a populist movement that now dominates politics in Yugoslavia (see Lee 1989). Milošević sided with the military in the trial in Slovenia. In addition, he has taken steps to fundamentally change language policy in Serbia. The initial focus of this change involves the Albanian population in the province of Kosovo, where Serbs and Albanians have coexisted uneasily since the seventeenth century.

For many years, the main political pressure exerted by the

Albanians on the Serbian republic government was the demand for republic status. The impetus for this goal was that republics have substantially more representation than provinces in the federal government (Pipa and Repishti 1989). During the 1950s, Tito was generally unfavourable to the Albanians, but with the movement toward decentralization in the 1960s, federal policy appeased the Albanians by: (1) providing the highest rate of federal funding in the country; (2) permitting the Albanians to operate schools, radio, newspapers, publishing, and the courts in Albanian; and (3) placing ethnic Albanians in the police and administrative positions. When the federal constitution of 1974 granted autonomy to Kosovo within the republic of Serbia, even the Serbian leadership favoured increased autonomy for Albanians because running the province, the poorest region in the country, was a serious drain on the Serbian treasury.

But recently, in his effort to gain power within the state federation, Milošević has exploited the historical tensions between Albanians and Serbs, shifting Serbia away from a politics of economic issues toward a politics of nationalism, in which the key issues are homeland, Slavic identity, and historical rights. He accomplished this change by forming a coalition within Serbia to reduce the language rights of Albanians.

In this effort, Milošević was actually following a pattern first used successfully by his supporters in the Macedonian leadership, over which he had gained control through an orchestrated series of demonstrations that led to purges in the Macedonian League of Communists. In Macedonia, Milošević's supporters responded to economic collapse in that republic by stirring up anti-Albanian feelings among workers, thereby making the Albanians a scapegoat for the economic problems of the republic. Bilingual street signs in Albanian districts were eliminated; secondary education in the Albanian language was cut back; many Albanian administrators and teachers in the schools were purged; and students who protested the shift to the Macedonian language were expelled (Lee 1989).

In Serbia, Milošević used mass demonstrations to force the resignation of some provincial leaders in Vojvodina and Kosovo in order to install a new leadership that was more favourable to Serbian interests. In this effort, he had the support of Serbs who had left Kosovo in the 1960s, as well as those remaining in Kosovo who feared republic status. When he succeeded in engineering a purge of the Serbian party in 1987, Milošević was able to place his own people in power. After that, criticism of his policies came only from other republics, which he then used as evidence that attacks against him were motivated by nationality, and constituted attacks against all Serbs.

The campaign against Albanians was designed to force the Kosovo provincial leadership and then the federal leadership to acquiesce in accepting the full integration of Kosovo into the Serbian republic, under full Serbian control. Through a series of demonstrations and strikes designed to show that he had the power to mobilize huge numbers of supporters, Milošević convinced the federal leadership to accept this change. In November 1988, federal leaders agreed to replace the Albanian leaders in Kosovo who had resisted Milošević.

Despite protests by Albanians, Slovenes, and other smaller nations and nationalities, at the end of March 1989, the Serbian parliament cancelled the autonomy granted to Kosovo and Vojvodina under the 1974 Constitution. This meant that the Serbian Parliament had control over the Kosovo police, courts, and civil defence, and the power to make all official appointments. Moreover, Serbia was free to impose further restrictions on Kosovo without having to gain approval from the federal Parliament, where Slovenes and other linguistic minorities could resist. In response, Albanians attacked police stations in several towns in Kosovo, leading to more than twenty deaths and hundreds of injured. The day after the worst violence, a curfew was imposed in Kosovo, while schools, the university, theatres, and markets were closed, and people were banned from walking in groups of more than three persons.

In April 1989, Serbia began to carry out policy changes in Kosovo. New policies rolled back the use of the Albanian language in government and the courts. Purges began in the educational system, as officials announced that hundreds of Albanians would be removed from their positions as administrators, university lecturers, school principals and teachers. Serbs replaced Albanians in labour unions and administrative positions throughout the province.

These events suggest that the power vacuum which has existed at the centre of Yugoslav politics since Tito's death in 1980 is now being filled by Milošević as leader of the Serbs, who have historically dominated the region. This shift in power has been expressed within the arena of language policy. By their ability to rescind fundamental language rights in Slovenia, Macedonia, and Kosovo, Milošević and his supporters have shown that they are capable of dominating decision making at the federal level. Yet Serbian hegemony entails great risks. Due to their important role in the army and the federal government, migration to seek employment, and the relative ease with which they can live and work anywhere, Serbs are dispersed outside Serbia. (Indeed, Milošević's popularity is due in part to his rhetorical skills at exploiting Serbian concern for Serbs outside the republic.) Thus they are especially susceptible to the dangerous consequences of 'Balkanization', the splitting of the country into separate and competing political units within a weak federal structure. In a Balkanized Yugoslavia, Serbs outside Serbia would be at great risk. Yet the mobilization of Serbs along nationalist lines increases the risk of Balkanization. Therefore to advance Serbian hegemony, Milošević must counter the inevitable resistance of other nationalities with increasingly repressive measures. Thus, unless this movement toward centralized Serbian power is reversed, additional changes in policy are likely to further weaken the language rights of minorities (see Magaš 1989).

Implications for multilingual societies

The rise of Serbian nationalism within a top-down party structure in control of the state has two important implications for the study of language policy in multilingual societies elsewhere. First, it reveals that language rights are a fragile basis for language policy, and that constant struggle is necessary to protect rights, even in a country with a long historical commitment to – and a federal structure which supports – a pluralist language policy. Yugoslavia demonstrates that language rights reflect power relationships, and that rights which are granted can be taken away.

The second implication of the Yugoslav experience is that hegemonic policies may not bring the stability which the dominant groups desire. Indeed, the effort by one language group to seek hegemony may contain within it the seeds of a cycle of resistance and repression. Hegemonic policies make compromise increasingly difficult and polarization increasingly extreme. The resulting struggle is not 'ethnic conflict' grounded in linguistic or cultural differences, but rather a conflict over power and policy resulting from the effort of one group to establish hegemony over others. In the long run, therefore, the choice is between, on the one hand, escalating conflict and the likelihood of a repressive bureaucratic dictatorship, or, on the other hand, an assertion of language rights. In Yugoslavia as elsewhere, this choice will be made through the struggle for power.

CONCLUSION: LANGUAGE RIGHTS AND EDUCATION

Both Yugoslavia and Australia support language rights for national minorities. In their effort to reduce linguistic and economic inequality, they emphasize the importance of education. In Australia, mother-tongue education and ESL are expected to provide migrants with skills they need to succeed economically, while multicultural education is expected to reduce tension and change attitudes that contribute to inequality. Yugoslavia's long historical commitment to mother-tongue education is currently being challenged by a movement to centralize decision making. In both countries, education is the focus for the debate over language rights.

As school principals, Sharon Kendrick and Janez Orešnik must deal with the consequences of policies designed to protect rights and reduce inequality through education. In a sense, the task they face is an endless one involving constant struggle: resolving the economic, social and political problems of linguistic minorities. Without doubt, education is vitally important for minorities, as well as for everyone else, but the belief that education can resolve inequality is based upon the false assumption that the school system itself is not part of the institutional and historical patterns that sustain inequality. Schools are not extra-societal forces for cultural change; they are a part of society. Even if Kendrick's and Orešnik's schools are able to operate with appreciation and respect for diversity, minority-language children who attend them will find that their prospects for employment and higher education are influenced by many factors besides the curriculum and teachers.

The movement to articulate language rights is an important advance in the effort to reduce the consequences of linguistic inequality, and it has profoundly affected educational programmes. Yet recent events in Yugoslavia show that language rights can be protected only through the effective exercise of power. Orešnik believes deeply that his school should protect the language rights of its Italian minority children, but the constitutional principles which express this belief may soon be rescinded. Already, school principals in other parts of the country have been replaced for supporting minority language rights. If current trends continue, Orešnik's school will some day face a powerful, perhaps violent challenge to its commitment to language rights. In that struggle, language rights may be one of the first casualties.

FOR DISCUSSION

1. Consider the issue of language rights in your community. Is the term ever used? Is there any support for language rights? What groups support or oppose language rights?
2. The United Nations has not yet enacted a Universal Declaration of Linguistic Rights. What provisions should be included in such a declaration?
3. Bilingual education programmes are normally divided into those that are intended to shift minority-language students into the dominant language as soon as possible ('transitional' programmes) and those designed to support the minority language ('maintenance' programmes). What kinds of programmes exist in your community? Do you support transitional or maintenance programmes? For whom?

FOR ACTION

1. Visit an elementary or high school in your community. Talk to school officials about minority-language students in the school. Find out whether there are special classes for them. If so, what is the purpose of these classes? Ask whether the school has any data comparing the graduation rates of students speaking different languages.
2. Visit a company that employs people who do not speak the dominant language in your community. Find out whether there are language classes offered to these employees. How do

managers communicate with them? What are their prospects for advancing to better jobs within the company?

FURTHER READING

Clyne (1976, 1982, 1985) include a wealth of information about the language situation and language policy in Australia. Bullivant (1987) examines the experience of both English-speaking Australians and minority students in an inner city and a suburban high school in Australia. Devetak (1988), written by the Director of the Institute for Ethnic Studies in Lubljana, examines the relationship between language rights in Yugoslavia and workers' self-management within the decentralized state system. *Nations and Nationalities of Yugoslavia* (1974) includes Yugoslav analysis of the history of language rights since 1945, as well as key constitutional and legal documents pertaining to language policy. Tollefson (1981b) examines efforts to implement the declarations of language rights in the 1974 federal and republic constitutions and communal statutes of Yugoslavia.

EIGHT

Conclusion: Language policy and democracy

KEY POINTS OF THIS BOOK

The hegemony of English, or of other languages, is not merely tolerated by the 'developing' world; it is considered a legitimate model for society. In many newly independent states, a tiny English-speaking elite controls state policy-making organs while the masses of people remain excluded. In the developed world, linguistic minorities are often prevented from enjoying economic equality by powerful linguistic barriers. A world system that is more just and equitable depends upon an understanding of how people can gain control of their own institutions. A key issue is the role of language in organizing and reproducing those institutions.

To understand the impact of language policy upon the organization and function of society, language policy must be interpreted within a framework which emphasizes power and competing interests. That is, policy must be seen within the context of its role in serving the interests of the state and the groups that dominate it.

Because language policy is a function of the state, language groups which are excluded from the institutions of state power are likely to see policy as a threat. Yet the dominant paradigm in language policy research (the neoclassical approach) persists in seeing language planning as the benevolent arm of the state serving 'national' interests (Williams 1986). Thus it cannot analyse the role of language planning in creating and sustaining economic inequality through the mechanism of language education. Indeed, neoclassical theory misses altogether the role that language policy plays in exploitation (see Giddens 1982a). As a powerful tool for exclusion, language policy in many states is fundamental to exploitation.

201

Because language policy is embedded in the rise of the state, research must evaluate policies with reference to their role in the exercise of state power and their effect upon the lives of individuals. What role does language policy play in the function of the state? How do states employ language policy to further their aims? What are the consequences of language policies in the lives of individuals? These should be the fundamental questions that guide the effort to understand the relationships between language policy, social organization, and political power.

When language policy is analysed with reference to relationships of power, then research must focus on the mechanisms by which minority languages are restricted to specific domains. To restrict minority languages to specific domains is to legitimize the domination of specific groups and to institutionalize the marginal status of some members of the population (i.e., those who speak minority languages). In contrast, the struggle to adopt minority languages within dominant institutions such as education, the law, and government, as well as the struggle over language rights, constitute efforts to legitimize the minority group itself and to alter its relationship to the state. Thus while language planning reflects relationships of power, it can also be used to transform them.

As a theory of human behaviour, the historical–structural approach regards human actions as socially determined by class, gender, ethnicity, or other factors. But behaviour is also creative, which does not mean unconstrained. Choices such as those facing the people described in the cases in this book will be more creative if they are rooted in consciousness of the social relationships that give meaning to actions. It must be the purpose of a theory of language planning to explain human creativity as well as historical and structural constraints.

Thus we return to the paradox outlined in the introduction. At a time when vast resources are devoted to language teaching and learning, tens of millions of people, desperate to learn the languages they need to improve their economic circumstances, are unable to accomplish this essential goal. Though states may fund language programmes and proclaim the importance of language learning, they simultaneously create conditions which make it virtually impossible for some citizens to acquire the language competence they need. This occurs when groups that hold power enjoy economic and political advantages based upon their exclusive language proficiency. In Namibia, masses of poor people have little or no opportunity to attend school to acquire the language skills they need for jobs and political power. In the Philippines, the dominance of English plays a key role in sustaining unequal educational systems that ensure that the masses of Filipinos have little chance to enjoy the wealth and political power open only to those who speak English fluently. As a result, an increasing number of Filipinos support revolutionary changes in social organization. In Britain, state policy is reasserting the dominance of standard English in the school system, while restricting mother-tongue education. The result is that pupils who do not speak the standard variety face special disadvantage in school. In the United States, educational pro-grammes for refugees and immigrants channel graduates into minimum-wage jobs in the peripheral economy where they have little opportunity for upward mobility. Meanwhile, a powerful movement to declare English the official language of the USA threatens to further disenfranchise people who do not speak English. In Iran and China, as in other countries in Asia and Africa, English has been associated with 'modernization' pro-grammes that depend upon Western institutions and practices and a Westernized elite. In 'modernizing' countries, ESL profes-sionals are agents of 'modernization', bringing methods and materials that claim to empower citizens but in fact help to sustain existing power relationships. This is true as well in many immigrant language programmes in 'developed' countries.

In contrast to the monolingual ideology that dominates the USA and Britain, both Australia and Yugoslavia have sought to protect the language rights of minorities and to ensure that economic and political power are shared equally by them. Yet struggle over language takes place there as well. In Yugoslavia, constitutional rights dating back 30 years are being rapidly withdrawn. In Australia, labour policies continue to pressure immigrants into limited occupational categories, despite the commitment to pluralism. ᵛˢ homogeneity

Despite differences between these cases, all show that lan-guage policy is inseparable from the relationships of power that divide societies. Policies are made by, and reflect the interests of, those who dominate the state policy-making apparatus. Thus individuals confronting language problems without having access to policy-making organs must try to take effective action within social systems in which they have few options. The individual cases show that language policies often offer opportunity to some while denying it for many. The cases also reveal the human dimension of language policy.

MEDIA EXAMPLE 8.1

In 1988, Amnesty International organized a worldwide tour of musical performers to draw attention to human rights and to increase participation in the work of the organization. The tour consisted of Bruce Springsteen, Sting, Peter Gabriel, Tracy Chapman, and Youssou N'Dour, as well as local performers from each city in which the tour played. The final concert of the tour was broadcast live on commercial radio from Argentina to North and South America, Europe, Asia, and Africa. The main announcer for that broadcast, an American, could not pronounce the names of performers and crew from Latin America, nor the name of Youssou N'Dour of Senegal, one of the stars of the tour. A second announcer from England occasionally corrected the American's pronunciation. To those who heard the broadcast, it was clear that the American, who was broadcasting to an audience of tens of millions of listeners, simply was not prepared to read names from Latin America and Senegal.

Questions

1. What would have been the impact if the announcer had consistently mispronounced the names of Bruce Springsteen, Peter Gabriel, Sting, and Tracy Chapman?
2. What was the implicit message in the fact that only non-English names were mispronounced?

LANGUAGE POLICY RESEARCH

Most language policy research fails to capture the human experience of individuals facing the consequences of state language policy. In part, this is due to the dominance of neoclassical theory, which provides a rationale for state power over the individual. As Chapter 2 stated, neoclassical theory defines individuals as rational agents weighing alternatives, and dominant languages ('languages of wider communication') as depoliticized 'national languages' that serve the interests of entire populations (see Williams 1986). Conflict is seen as resulting from linguistic diversity rather than economic and political inequality, and so any resistance to linguistic uniformity is seen as irrational, destructive, and not in the 'national interest'.

But the failure of most research to capture the human experience of language policy is due not only to neoclassical principles; it is due also to the restrictive standards of social science research, which forbids personal description of the lives of the people in whom researchers claim to be interested. No one investigates, for example, the relationship between Philippine language education policy and the condition of the children of Tondo, who are chronically malnourished. Indeed, a graphic description of Hector and Maja Adolpho's home and family would be dismissed as 'unscientific', 'subjective', and 'emotional' and therefore excluded altogether from the professional conversation which claims to be concerned with 'implementation' of language policies.

But it is not only the standards of social scientific investigation that blind investigators to the experiences of the people who are affected by state policies. It is the language of research itself that dehumanizes and depersonalizes; indeed, scientific language deliberately suppresses any direct expression of human experience. Thus research investigates the impact of 'plans' which are 'formulated' and 'implemented' upon 'subjects' and 'populations' by means of 'empirical' research involving 'studies', 'data', and 'generalizations'. Researchers report, for example, that 'of 157 subjects investigated, 57 per cent were found to support second language classes after normal school hours'. Attention to the impact of policies upon real people is stated as 'planners must consider the costs involved in any implementation plans'. In the impersonal language of research, people do not exist as living, breathing, feeling human beings. When real people are discussed at all, it is only in categories of characteristics, such as 'minority', 'Hispanic', 'immigrant', 'Spanish speaker', or 'Asian'.

Yet such terms are not characteristics of people at all: they are fictions that limit, restrict, determine, and disempower. Even terms such as 'power', 'ideology', 'class', and 'language' are fictive constructs; they are useful, but their use entails the risk that researchers lose sight of the real people whose lives are located within these fictive structures.

The issue is not simply that researchers should have greater compassion for their 'subjects', but rather that the language of research is a vocabulary of action that constrains social-scientific thinking and renders social scientists (as well as policymakers) immune from challenge by those for whom they claim to be concerned. The people who know best the impact of language policies are merely 'minorities' without language 'skills', and so are incompetent by definition. In this way, social research denies Xuma Aula, Binh Nguyen, the Adolphos and others the voice that they deserve.

If the terminology of social science is understood as fiction, then its terms can be seen not simply as words, but rather ideologies. This does not mean that this vocabulary should be abandoned, but it must be recognized as metaphorical and laden with value. From this perspective, the implicit ideology is clear in neoclassical categories such as modern/traditional, European/non-European, Great Tradition/Little Tradition, developed/undeveloped, and modernized/unmodernized. Underlying these categories is an assumed evolutionary development of language from traditional to modern, with differences among languages being due to their different position along a metaphorical evolutionary chronology. But in fact, all contemporary languages exist in the same historical time and are the result of differing relationships of power and dominance. Speakers of some languages are disadvantaged not because their languages are 'unmodernized'; rather, the fact that languages are viewed as unmodernized is a reflection of the relationships of power among speakers of different languages.

LANGUAGE AND WORK

Perhaps nowhere is the failure to capture individual experience more evident than in regard to policies that require individuals to use a second language at work. Work is what most human beings do every day; they get up in the morning and go to work. Work is so universal that some psychologists believe there is a work instinct, much like there is an instinct to eat or to procreate (Hilman 1983).

A work instinct differs from a work ethic. A work ethic is

associated with efficiency aimed at maximizing income from investment and with cost–benefit analysis. The principle of 'efficiency' is used to justify policies requiring dominant languages in the workplace. In contrast, the concept of a work instinct acknowledges the dynamic relationship between one's work and one's self. What we do is what we feel we are. Therefore when individuals are not permitted to use their own languages at work, they are alienated not only from their work and the workplace, but from themselves. From this perspective, language policies that deny individuals the use of their own languages at work are unnatural, antihuman, and anticultural.

The policy of having a single 'common' (i.e., dominant) language at work must be understood within the context of power and domination. Indeed, it is part of a broader set of beliefs about language and citizenship that provide the basis for the exercise of state disciplinary power in the workplace.

Language policy as state disciplinary power

A central component of the neoclassical view of language is the assumption that the natural tendency in the world is to gradually expand citizenship rights to broader portions of the population. Denial of education, economic resources, and political power are seen as unfortunate remnants of the past rather than the result of structural inequality and deliberate planning. In the neoclassical view, the role of language planning is to facilitate the 'natural' progression towards expanded citizenship rights; one of the most effective means for doing so, in this view, is to assist linguistic minorities to acquire dominant languages.

But Giddens (1987) has pointed out that citizenship rights reflect power relationships. By granting, withholding, or otherwise manipulating citizenship rights, the state can manage its population, particularly in its role as labour. When wage labour is legally free to change employers and to migrate, the state must find ways to control it. The capacity of the state to control wage labour is called 'disciplinary power'.

Language policy is a form of disciplinary power. Its success depends in part upon the ability of the state to structure into the institutions of society the differentiation of individuals into 'insiders' and 'outsiders' (see Giddens 1982a). To a large degree, this occurs through the close association between language and nationalism. By making language a mechanism for the expression of nationalism, the state can manipulate feelings of security and belonging. In European states, whose borders partially conform with linguistic boundaries, this means that language policy controls access to employment by minorities who have migrated into the state. In Africa and Asia, language policies are part of an effort to manage individuals and groups having little or no loyalty to the state. In both cases, the state uses language policy to discipline and control its workers by establishing language-based limitations on education, employment, and political participation. This is one sense in which language policy is inherently ideological.

The ideology of language policy is most apparent in the workplace, for it is there that explicit state policy has been completely transformed into 'common sense' notions of 'natural' language practices. Indeed, the policy of requiring a dominant language at work is not seen as a 'policy' at all, but rather a 'natural' practice unrelated to the state. In much of the world, but particularly in capitalist countries, the workplace is defined as an economic rather than political domain and thus outside politics and policy making. In neoclassical terms, the language of the workplace is determined by the market, and so dominance and inequality are not perceived to exist, and there is no reason to debate language practice as, for instance, in regards to voting rights. Yet the ideological use of language at work is a major basis for controlling access to work, and therefore to economic resources and political power.

Language policy at work is perhaps the most important means for establishing state hegemony. Excluding the workplace from debates over language rights means that minority groups cannot legitimize the use of their languages at work, except at 'minority businesses' that cater largely to minority populations. As a result, dominant linguistic groups exercise an unquestioned, 'natural' (i.e., ideological) monopoly over the language of work, and therefore over the workplace itself. By agreeing that the workplace is outside the realm of politics or of citizenship rights, including language rights, the citizenry cooperates in its own disempowerment. In this way, language policy is an effective means for pacifying and disciplining labour (cf. Giddens 1987).

The issue here is more complex than workers' power and rights *vis-à-vis* managers'. Even the workers' self-management system of Yugoslavia, which is intended to politicize and democratize the workplace, has not led to legitimation of minority languages within workplaces dominated by members of majority groups.

LANGUAGE POLICY AND DEMOCRACY

Why do human societies continue to adopt policies that contribute to hegemony? One reason is that people who are required by policies to learn a new language for education and work are usually excluded from the decision-making system. Because they lack access to political institutions, they are unable to affect the policies adopted by those institutions. In other words, one of the major reasons for the continued use of language to promote the inequality inevitably associated with hegemony is the predominance of *undemocratic structures*, that is, structures in which those who adopt policies are not accountable to those who are affected by them. The pervasiveness of undemocratic state structures is the fundamental reason for the close connection between language policy, power, and domination.

Language-teaching professionals seek pedagogical solutions to hegemony and inequality. That is, they assume that pedagogy can separate language from power and domination. To this end, they propose improved teacher training, new teaching methods, better testing and evaluation, smaller classes, and new learning theories. While these may affect the 'quality of education', they do not confront the historical and structural forces that impose policies of inequality and that ensure that non-pedagogical factors will overwhelm even the most well-motivated learners: problems with child care and transportation, the need to work two jobs to support family members, hostility from speakers of the dominant language, and, most importantly, exclusion from decision-making institutions.

English language professionals can be more effective in the struggle for equality if they understand that the forces affecting their professional lives, including inadequate funding for ESL programmes, low salaries and benefits, job insecurity, and heavy staff turnover, are also those that disempower their students. This is because language programmes reflect the priorities of the country. In the Philippines, teaching English in elite schools is relatively well paid: teachers' circumstances of employment reflect the privileged position of their students. In the United States and England, the increased flow of refugees and immigrants during the 1970s and 1980s was associated with an explosion of ESL programmes, but also with growing use of part-time staff, separation of ESL from public funding, and adoption of curricula in which language is reduced to a set of skills to be practised for employment. Language education professionals must reject the notion that learning a language is an ideologically neutral act intended simply to develop an employment skill. That some people must learn English to get a job is a *result* of unequal relationships of power – not a *solution* to them.

Human institutions may not yet be able to provide a social structure in which everyone can live their lives using their own language(s), but we should not deceive ourselves into thinking that second language acquisition guarantees equal economic opportunity, political participation, and justice. Each time a society requires some people to learn another language in order to carry out human activities necessary for survival, an act of injustice has occurred that places those people at a disadvantage. Moreover, it defines those individuals as outsiders who will suffer socially and economically. This is because the forces that lead a society to impose such policies have nothing to do with the 'common sense' or 'practical' value of having a common language to communicate. If that were the aim, then: (1) dominant groups would acquire minority languages and change their linguistic repertoire to accommodate other groups; and (2) accents and other variable features would not be stigmatized. In much of the world, second language learning is not a solution to exclusivity, privilege, and domination, but rather a mechanism for them.

VALUES AND STRUGGLE

One of the goals of this book has been to show that language professionals have a responsibility to explore the ideological foundations of their theories and practices. This means they must acknowledge that value judgements are fundamental to their work. The goal should not be to try to eliminate values; that will merely drive them underground, where they will still operate. Instead, values must be made explicit.

What are the values behind this book? One is the belief that respect for diversity is important, but ultimately inadequate as a solution to linguistic inequality. This is because it tends to locate the problems of minorities within their personalities, families, and cultures rather than within social structure. In addition to respect for diversity, a commitment to *structural equality* is necessary (cf. Skutnabb-Kangas and Cummins 1988). Structural equality differs from equality of opportunity, which is a mechanism for sustaining inequality by placing the responsibility for minorities' problems on their lack of motivation or effort (see Chapter 2). Instead, structural equality refers to a system for making decisions in which individuals who are affected by policies have a major role in making policies. That is, structural equality is inseparable from democracy.

A commitment to democracy means that the use of the mother tongue at work and in school is a fundamental human right. This perspective differs from the use of the mother tongue as an expression of ethnicity, which separates language from questions of power and domination. Instead, this perspective views language as parallel to race, gender, and other factors as deserving of legal protection, and it measures social justice by the extent to which societies ensure that individuals may use their mother tongues for education and employment. The major conclusion to be derived from this analysis of language policy in various countries around the world is that a commitment to democracy requires a commitment to the struggle for language rights.

FOR DISCUSSION

1. This chapter defines 'democracy' in structural terms: democracy means that people who make decisions are accountable to those who are affected by the decisions. How do you define 'democracy'? Is there a way to ensure that language policies are just and equitable without democratic decision making?

2. What would be the consequences of permitting individuals to use their native languages at work and in school? Consider this question with regard to 'traditional' public markets, where individuals speaking many languages come together to buy and

sell (see Chapter 1). How does communication take place in such settings? Are there any implications for 'modern' workplaces?

FOR ACTION

1. Interview an employment counsellor, placement officer, state employment security official, or another individual directly involved in placing people in jobs. What kinds of jobs are available for people who do not speak the dominant language? Who determines what language fluency is required for particular jobs? Is there a written policy about language proficiency required for employment?

2. Interview people working at unskilled jobs. Ask the same questions as listed in the first question. In addition, ask them what languages they speak at work. Are there other speakers of minority languages at their workplace? Why are workplaces with many low-paid workers often multilingual environments?

FURTHER READING

For a discussion of minorities' struggle for power in education, see Skutnabb-Kangas and Cummins (1988). For a critical analysis of language at work, see Rossi-Landi (1983).

References

Abu–Lughod J 1975 Comments: the end of the age of innocence. In DuToit B and Safa H (eds) *Migration and urbanization*. Mouton, The Hague, pp. 201–08.

Allen J S 1985 *The radical left on the eve of war: A political memoir*. Foundation for Nationalist Studies, Quezon City.

Amir Y 1969 Contact hypothesis in ethnic relations. *Psychological bulletin* 71(5):319–42.

Amir Y 1972 Contact hypothesis in ethnic relations. In Brigham J C and Weissbach T A (eds) *Racial attitudes in America: analyses and findings of social psychology*. Harper and Row, New York.

Amir Y 1976 The role of intergroup contact in change of prejudice and ethnic relations. In Katz P A (ed) *Towards the elimination of racism*. Pergamon, New York.

Arjomand S A 1988 *The turban for the crown: The Islamic revolution in Iran*. Oxford University Press, New York.

Arter J, Hadley W, and Reder S 1984 *A study of English language training for refugees in the United States – phase three: the influence of language training and employment on adult refugees' acquisition of English*. Report prepared for the Office of Refugee Resettlement by the Northwest Regional Educational Laboratory, Portland, Oregon.

Asher J 1977 *Learning another language through actions: the complete teacher's guidebook*. Sky Oaks, Los Gatos, California.

Ashraf A 1989 There is a feeling that the regime owes something to the people. *Middle East Report* 19(1):13–18.

Associated Press 1988 Amnesty classes packed. *Seattle Post-Intelligencer*, 7 November.

Auerbach E A 1986 Competency-based ESL: One step forward or two steps back? *TESOL Quarterly* 20(3):411–30.

Auerbach E A and Burgess D 1985 The hidden curriculum of survival ESL. *TESOL Quarterly* 19(3):475–95.

Auerbach E A and Wallerstein N 1987 *ESL for action: problem posing at work*. Addison–Wesley, Reading, Massachusetts.

Australian Advisory Council on Languages and Multicultural Education 1988 National policy on languages. *Vox* 1:4–8.

Bach R L 1984 *Labor force participation and employment of Southeast Asian refugees in the United States*. Report prepared for the US Department of Health and Human Services, Office of Refugee Resettlement,

213

under a grant to the Institute for Research on Poverty, University of Wisconsin.

Bach R L and Schraml L A 1982 Migration, crisis and theoretical conflict. *International Migration Review* **16**(2):320–41.

Bagadion B 1986 People power in the Philippines. *Philippine sociological review* **34**:5–15.

Bakhash S 1984 *The reign of the ayatollahs: Iran and the Islamic revolution.* Basic Books, New York.

Barnes D 1983 The implementation of language planning in China. In Cobarrubias J, Fishman J A (eds) *Language planning: International perspectives.* Mouton, Berlin, pp. 291–308.

Beebe L 1988 Five sociolinguistic approaches to second language acquisition. In Beebe L (ed) *Issues in second language acquisition: multiple perspectives.* Newbury House, New York, pp. 41–78.

Beebe L, Zuengler J 1983 Accommodation theory: An explanation for style shifting in second language dialects. In Wolfson N and Judd E (eds) *Sociolinguistics and language acquisition.* Newbury House, New York, pp. 195–213.

Beeman W O 1983 Images of the great satan: representations of the United States in the Iranian revolution. In Keddie N R (ed) *Religion and politics in Iran.* Yale University Press, New Haven, pp. 191–217.

Beeman W O 1986 *Language, status and power in Iran.* Indiana University Press, Bloomington.

Bikales G 1985 Testimony before the Subcommittee on the Constitution of the Committee on the Judiciary, US Senate. In *The English Language Amendment*, US Government Printing Office, Washington, pp. 103–12.

Bikales G 1986 Comment: the other side. *International journal of the sociology of language* **60**:77–85.

Blaustein A P and Flanz G H 1988 *Constitutions of the countries of the world: Philippines supplement.* Oceana, Dobbs Ferry, New York.

Bochner S 1982 *Cultures in contact.* Pergamon, London.

Bourhis R Y and Giles H 1977 The language of intergroup distinctiveness. In Giles H (ed) *Language, ethnicity and intergroup relations.* Academic Press, London, pp. 119–35.

Bowen J D 1977 Notes on bilingualism and language engineering. In Sibayan B P and Gonzalez A B (eds) *Language planning and the building of a national language.* Linguistic Society of the Philippines and Philippine Normal College, Manila, pp. 3–11.

Brende J O and Parson E R 1985 *Vietnam veterans: the road to recovery.* New American Library, New York.

Bullivant B M 1982 Pluralist debate and educational policy – Australian style. *Journal of multilingual and multicultural development* **3**(2):129–47.

Bullivant B M 1987 *The ethnic encounter in the secondary schools: ethnocultural reproduction and resistance; theory and case studies.* The Falmer Press, London.

Bullock A 1975 *A language for life: Report of the Committee of Inquiry.* HMSO, London.

Burchell B 1984 West Indian parents and schools. In *Race, education and research: Rampton, Swann, and after.* Centre for Multicultural Education and the Thomas Coram Research Unit, University of London Institute of Education. London. pp. 1–11.

Byram M 1986 Schools in ethnolinguistic minorities. *Journal of multilingual and multicultural development* 7(2–3):97–106.

Cameron D and Bourne J 1989 No common ground: Kingman, grammar, and the nation. *Language and education* 2(3):147–60.

Carby H V 1982 Schooling in Babylon. In *The empire strikes back: Race and racism in 70s Britain.* Centre for Contemporary Cultural Studies, London, pp. 183–211.

Carver D 1986 Strains and conflicts in planning for teacher education for English language teaching in the Namibian context. *Language in education in Africa.* University of Edinburgh Centre of African Studies, Edinburgh.

Cheng C-C 1982 Chinese varieties of English. In Kachru B B (ed) *The other tongue: English across cultures.* Pergamon, Oxford, pp. 125–40.

Children of Change (documentary film) 1983 University of Washington, Seattle.

Church World Service 1983 *Making it on their own: from refugee sponsorship to self-sufficiency.* New York.

Civil Liberties Union 1984 *Technology as an instrument of domination.* Foundation for Nationalist Studies, Quezon City.

Clarke M A 1982 On bandwagons, tyranny, and common sense. *TESOL Quarterly* 16(3):437–48.

Clarke M A 1984 On the nature of technique: What do we owe the gurus? *TESOL Quarterly* 18(4):577–94.

Clarke M A and Silberstein S 1988 Problems, prescriptions, and paradoxes in second language teaching. *TESOL Quarterly* 22(4):685–700.

Clyne M G (ed) 1976 *Australia talks: essays on the sociology of Australian immigrant and aboriginal languages.* Australian National University, Canberra (Pacific Linguistics Series).

Clyne M G 1982 *Multilingual Australia.* River Seine Publications, Melbourne.

Clyne M G (ed) 1985 *Australia, meeting place of languages.* Australian National University, Canberra (Pacific Linguistics Series).

Clyne M G 1988 Language planning in multilingual Australia. *New language planning newsletter* 2(4):1–5.

Cohon J D, Lucey M, Paul M, and Penning J L 1986 *Preventive mental health in the ESL classroom: a handbook for teachers.* American Council for Nationalities Service, Washington.

Combs M C 1989 Official English in 1989: post electoral fallout. *EPIC Events* 2(1):1–4.

Concepcion J S 1986 Private sector approval of the Ministry of Trade and Industry. In *The 1985–86 Fookien times yearbook.* Fookien Times, Manila, pp. 52, 312.

Constantino L R 1982 *World Bank textbooks: scenario for deception.* Foundation for Nationalist Studies, Quezon City.

Constantino L R 1984a Education, handmaiden of economic policy. In

Constantino L R (ed) *Issues without tears: A laymen's manual of current issues.* Teacher assistance program, Quezon City, pp. 39–50.

Constantino L R 1984b English or Pilipino. In Constantino L R (ed) *Issues without tears: A laymen's manual of current issues.* Teacher assistance program, Quezon City, pp. 23–31.

Constantino R 1974 Identity and consciousness: The Philippine experience. Eighth World Congress of Sociology, Toronto.

Constantino R 1976 Global enterprises and the transfer of technology. First Congress of Third World Economists, Algiers.

Constantino R 1982 *The miseducation of the Filipino.* Foundation for Nationalist Studies, Quezon City.

Constantino R 1984 *The nationalist alternative* revised edn. Foundation for Nationalist Studies, Quezon City, Philippines.

Constitution of the Socialist Federal Republic of Yugoslavia 1974. Dopisna delavska univerza, Ljubljana.

Coro A 1988 OBEMLA sets research agenda. *National Clearinghouse for Bilingual Education Forum* **9**(2):2–3.

Coupland N, Coupland J, Giles H, and Henwood K 1988 Accommodating the elderly: Invoking and extending a theory. *Language in society* **17**:1–41.

Cowan J R, Light R L, Mathews B E, and Tucker G R 1979 English teaching in China: A recent survey. *TESOL Quarterly* **13**(4):465–82.

Cox D 1983 Refugee resettlement in Australia: review of an era. *International migration* **21**(3):332–44.

Cummins J and Swain M 1986 *Bilingualism in education.* Longman, London.

Curran C A 1976 *Counseling–learning in second languages.* Apple River Press, Apple River, Illinois.

Dale C 1983 Legal analysis of H.J. Res. 169 proposing an amendment to the US Constitution to make English the official language of the United States. *The English language amendment* (hearing before the Subcommittee on the Constitution of the Committee on the Judiciary, US Senate). US Government Printing Office, Washington.

Das Gupta J 1970 *Language conflict and national development.* University of California Press, Berkeley.

De Leon H S and Lugue E E 1984 *Textbook on the New Philippine constitution.* Rex, Manila.

Department of Education and Science 1989 *English from 5–16.* National Curriculum Council, London.

Department of State 1984 *Pre-employment training resource manual,* vol. I. Center for Applied Linguistics and Refugee Service Center of the Bureau for Refugee Programs, Manila.

Der-min G 1988 The reform of English teaching in China. *TESOL Newsletter* **22**(4):17–21.

Deutsch K A 1975 The political significance of linguistic conflicts. In Savard J-G and Vigneault R (eds) *Les états multilingues.* Leval, Quebec.

Devall S 1987 Affirmative action and positive discrimination. In Haydon G (ed) *Education for a pluralist society: Philosophical perspectives* on the Swann Report. University of London Institute of Education London, pp. 85–94 (Bedford Way Papers).

Devetak S 1988 The equality of nations and nationalities in Yugoslavia. Wilhelm Braumuller, Vienna.

Donahue T S 1985 US English: its life and works. International Journal of the Sociology of Language 56:99–112.

Doronila A 1985 The media. In May R J and Nemenzo F (eds) The Philippines after Marcos. St. Martin's, New York, pp. 194–206.

Douglas H E 1983 Proposed refugee admissions for FY 1984. Testimony before the Senate Judiciary Committee, September 25. Department of State bulletin 1983:64. Department of State, Washington.

Douglas H E 1986 Prepared statement for the House Judiciary Committee in Hearings on the Refugee admissions program, FY 1986, 19 September. US Government Printing Office, Washington, p. 15.

Druckman D and Green J 1986 Political stability in the Philippines. University of Denver, Denver (Monograph Series in World Affairs).

Duggal N K (ed) 1981 Toward a language policy for Namibia: English as the official language: perspectives and strategies. United Nations Institute for Namibia, Lusaka, Zambia.

Eastman C M 1983 Language planning: an introduction. Chandler and Sharp, San Francisco.

Eggleston J 1986 Education for some: The educational and vocational experiences of 15–18 year-old members of minority ethnic groups. Trentham Books, Stoke–on–Trent.

Enriquez V G and Marcelino E P 1984 Neo-colonial politics and language struggle in the Philippines: national consciousness and language in Philippine psychology 1971–1983. Akademya ng Sikolohiyang Pilipino, Quezon City.

Ervin-Tripp S M 1971 Sociolinguistics. In Fishman J A (ed) Advances in the sociology of language vol. I. Mouton, The Hague, pp. 15–91.

European Communities 1977 Council directive on the education of children of migrant workers (77/486). DES, London.

Fairclough N 1989 Language and power. Longman, London.

Federal Register 1987 52 (102), 19 October.

Federal Register 1988 53(152), 8 August.

Finnan C R 1981 Occupational assimilation of refugees. International migration review 15(1):292–309.

Fishman J A 1968 Language problems and types of political and sociocultural integration: a conceptual postscript. In Fishman J A, Ferguson C A, Das Gupta J (eds) Language problems of developing nations. John Wiley, New York, pp. 491–98.

Fishman J A 1972a National languages and languages of wider communication in the developing nations. In Dil A S (ed) Language in sociocultural change: Essays by Joshua A. Fishman. Stanford University Press, Stanford, pp. 191–223.

Fishman J A 1972b The relationship between micro- and macro-sociolinguistics in the study of who speaks what languages to whom. In Dil A S (ed) Language in sociocultural change: essays by Joshua A. Fishman. Stanford University Press, Stanford, pp. 244–67.

Fitch D 1984 Sweetening the bitter pill and catching crabs at the seaside. *Multicultural teaching to combat racism in school and community* 2(3):19–26.

Forester J 1985 Critical theory and planning practice. In Forester J (ed) *Critical theory and public life*. MIT Press, Cambridge, pp. 202–27.

Foucault M 1970 *The order of things: an archeology of the human sciences*. Vintage Books, New York.

Foucault M 1972 *The archaeology of knowledge*. Pantheon, New York.

Foucault M 1979 *Discipline and punish*. Penguin, Harmondsworth.

Galbally F 1978 *Migrant services and programmes: report of the review of post–arrival programmes and services for migrants*. Australian Government Publishing Service, Canberra.

Garcia G N 1985 Learning English through bilingual instruction: a new report. *National Clearinghouse for Bilingual Education Forum* 8(5):2–3.

Gardner R C and Lambert W E 1972 *Attitudes and motivation in second language learning*. Newbury House, Rowley, Massachusetts.

Gattegno C 1972 *Teaching foreign languages in schools: the silent way*. Educational Solutions, New York.

Giddens A 1971 *Capitalism and modern social theory: an analysis of the writings of Marx, Durkheim and Max Weber*. Cambridge University Press, Cambridge.

Giddens A 1982a *Profiles and critiques in social theory*. University of California, Berkeley.

Giddens A 1982b *Sociology: a brief but critical introduction*. Harcourt Brace Jovanovich, New York.

Giddens A 1984 *The constitution of society: outline of the theory of structuration*. University of California, Berkeley.

Giddens A 1985 *The nation-state and violence*. Polity Press, Cambridge.

Giddens A 1987 *Social theory and modern sociology*. Stanford University Press, Stanford.

Giesbers H 1985 Sociolinguistics and ideology. *Sociolinguistics* 15(2):1–11.

Giles H 1989 Intergenerational communication: Language, culture, and power. University of Washington Seminar on Ethnicity and Nationality, March.

Giles H and Byrne J L 1982 An intergroup approach to second language acquisition. *Journal of multilingual and multicultural development* 3(1):17–40.

Giles H and Hewstone M 1982 Cognitive structures, speech, and social situations: Two integrative models. *Language sciences* 4(2):187–219.

Giles H, Hewstone M, and Ball P 1983 Language attitudes in multilingual settings: Prologue with priorities. *Journal of multilingual and multicultural development* 4(2):81–100.

Giles H, Rosenthal D, and Young L 1985 Perceived ethnolinguistic vitality: The Anglo- and Greek-Australian setting. *Journal of multilingual and multicultural development* 6(3–4):253–69.

Giles H and Saint-Jacques B (eds) 1979 *Language and ethnic relations*. Pergamon Press, Oxford.

Giroux H 1983 *Theory and resistance in education*. Bergin and Garvey, Granby, Massachusetts.

Gitlin T 1989 Postmodernism: roots and politics. *Dissent*, winter, pp. 100–8.

Gonzalez, A B 1980 *Language and nationalism: the Philippine experience thus far*. Ateneo de Manila University, Manila.

Gonzalez A B 1984 Evaluating the Philippine bilingual education policy. In Gonzalez A B (ed) *Language planning, implementation, and evaluation*. Linguistic Society of the Philippines, Manila, pp. 46–65.

Gonzalez A B 1988a Philippine language policy today. *New language planning newsletter* 2(3):1–3.

Gonzalez A B 1988b The 1987 policy on bilingual education. *New language planning newsletter* 2(3):3–5.

Gorlach M 1986 Comment. *International journal of the sociology of language* 60:97–103.

Gordon R J 1977 *Mines, masters and migrants: life in a Namibian mine compound*. Ravan Press, Johannesburg.

Grabe W and Kaplan R B 1986 Science, technology, language, and information: implications for language and language-in-education planning. *International journal of the sociology of language* 59:47–71.

Grabe W and Mahon D 1981 Comments on methodology-oriented teacher training programmes in China. *TESOL Quarterly* 15(2):207–9.

Green J J 1987 The new constitution: A new deal for Filipinos or politics as usual *Pilipinas* 9:11–26.

Guiora A, Paluszny M, Beit-Hallahmi G, Catford J, Cooley R, and Dull C 1975 Language and person: studies in language behaviour. *Language Learning* 25:43–61.

Gutstein S P 1988 The Immigration Reform and Control Act: information for educators. *NCBE Forum* 11(6):1–5.

Habermas J 1973 *Theory and practice*. Beacon Press, Boston.

Habermas J 1979 *Communication and the evolution of society*. Heinemann, London.

Habermas J 1983 *Philosophical-political profiles*. MIT Press, Cambridge.

Habermas J 1985 *The theory of communicative action*, vol. I. Polity, London.

Habermas J 1987 *The theory of communicative action*, vol. II. Beacon Press, Boston.

Habermas J 1988 *On the logic of the social sciences*. MIT Press, Cambridge.

Hall R A 1944 Chinese pidgin English grammar and texts. *Journal of the American Oriental Society* 64(3):95–113.

Halliday F 1989 The revolution's first decade. *Middle East Report* 19(1):19–21.

Harman L D 1988 *The modern stranger: on language and membership*. Mouton, The Hague.

Haugen E 1966 *Language conflict and language planning: the case of modern Norwegian*. Harvard University Press, Cambridge.

Heath S B and Krasner L 1986 Comment. *International journal of the sociology of language* 60:157–62.

Herman E S and Chomsky N 1988 *Manufacturing consent: the political economy of the mass media*. Pantheon Books, New York.

Hewitt R 1986 *White talk black talk: Inter-racial friendship and communication among adolescents*. Cambridge University Press, Cambridge.

Hilman J 1983 *Inter views*. Harper and Row, New York.
Hoogland E 1989 The Islamic Republic at war and peace. *Middle East Report* 19(1):4–12.
Hooley R 1987 Report on the discussion: the Philippine economy, its problems, and some suggested policy approaches. In Lande C H (ed) *Rebuilding a nation: Philippine challenges and American policy.* Washington Institute Press, Washington, pp. 189–201.
Husband C and Khan V S 1982 The viability of ethnolinguistic vitality: Some creative doubts. *Journal of multilingual and multicultural development* 3(3):193–205.
International Catholic Migration Commission 1985 *Cultural orientation curriculum*. Morong, Bataan, Philippines.
Jernudd B H and Das Gupta, J 1971 Towards a theory of language planning. In Rubin J and Jernudd B H (eds.) *Can language be planned?* University Press of Hawaii, Honolulu, pp. 195–216.
Jiobu R M 1988 *Ethnicity and assimilation*. State University of New York Press, Albany.
Johnson P, Giles H 1982 Values, language and inter-cultural differentiation: The Welsh–English context. *Journal of multilingual and multicultural development* 3(2):103–16.
Johnson P, Giles H, and Bourhis R Y 1983 The viability of ethnolinguistic vitality: a reply. *Journal of multilingual and multicultural development* 4(4):255–69.
Jončić K 1974 The constitutional and legal status of nationalities – national minorities in the SFR of Yugoslavia. UN Seminar on the Promotion and Protection of Human Rights of National, Ethnic, and other Minorities, Ohrid, Yugoslavia.
Jones C 1987 Philippine deal with creditors gives Aquino economic breather. *Christian science monitor*, 31 March.
Jones M 1987 Prejudice. In Haydon G (ed) *Education for a pluralist society: Philosophical perspectives on the Swann Report*. University of London Institute of Education, London, pp. 39–56 (Bedford Way Papers).
Jovanović A 1969 *The sociopolitical system of Yugoslavia*. Medjunarodna politika, Belgrade (Studies 31).
Kachru B B 1982 *The other tongue: English across cultures*. Pergamon, Oxford.
Kaplan R B 1987 English in the language policy of the Pacific Rim. *World Englishes* 6(2):137–48.
Keddie N R 1983 *Religion and politics in Iran*. Yale University Press, New Haven.
Kelman H C 1971 Language as an aid and barrier to involvement in the national system. In Rubin J and Jernudd B H (eds) *Can language be planned?* University Press of Hawaii, Honolulu, pp. 21–52.
Kennedy C (ed) 1989 *Language planning and English language teaching*. Prentice Hall, New York.
Kerkvliet B J T 1986 Patterns of Philippine resistance and rebellion, 1970–1986. *Pilipinas* 6:35–52.
Khan V S 1985 *Language education for all?: chapter 7 of the Swann Report*. Centre for Multicultural Education, University of London Institute of

Education, London (Working Papers).

Khomeini A R 1979 *Islamic government*. US Joint Publications Research Service, Translations on Near East and North Africa (no. 1897), US Government Printing Office, Washington.

Khomeini A R 1980 Search and find the east. In Albert D H (ed) *Tell the American people: Perspectives on the Iranian revolution*. Movement for a New Society, Philadelphia, pp. 204–10.

Kingman J 1988 *Report of the Committee of Inquiry into the teaching of English language*. HMSO, London.

Klare M T 1980 Arms and the Shah. In Albert D H (ed) *Tell the American people: Perspectives on the Iranian revolution*. Movement for a New Society, Philadelphia, pp. 15–27.

Kloss H 1968 Notes concerning a language-nation typology. In Fishman J A, Ferguson C A, and Das Gupta J (eds) *Language problems of developing nations*. John Wiley, New York, pp. 69–86.

Kloss H 1977 *The American bilingual tradition*. Newbury House, Rowley, Massachusetts.

Klyhn J 1987 Giving away the power. *TESOL Newsletter* 21(5):1–3.

Komisar L 1987 *Corazon Aquino: The story of a revolution*. George Braziller, New York.

Koppel B M 1987 Agrarian problems and agrarian reform: Opportunity or irony? In Lande C H (ed) *Rebuilding a nation: Philippine challenges and American policy*. Washington Institute Press, Washington, pp. 157–87.

Krashen S D 1978 The monitor model for second language acquisition. In Gringas R C (ed) *Second language acquisition and foreign language learning*. Center for Applied Linguistics, Arlington, Virginia.

Krashen S D 1980 Attitude and aptitude in relation to second language acquisition and learning. In Diller K (ed) *Individual differences in language learning aptitude*. Newbury, Rowley, Massachusetts.

Krashen S D 1981 *Second language acquisition and second language learning*. Prentice-Hall, New York.

Krashen S D and Terrell T D 1983 *The natural approach*. Alemany Press, Hayward, California.

Kristof N D 1989a China pledges to keep close US ties. *New York Times*, 22 February.

Kristof N D 1989b Mass migration of Chinese floods a prosperous Canton. *New York Times*, 17 March.

Kritz M M (ed) 1983 *US immigration and refugee policy*. Lexington Books, Lexington, Massachusetts.

Lachica E 1971 *HUK: Philippine agrarian society in revolt*. Solidaridad, Manila.

Lah A 1972 *The Yugoslav federation – What is it?* Medjunarodna politika, Belgrade (Studies).

Lamm R D and Imhoff G 1985 *The immigration time bomb: the fragmenting of America*. E P Dutton, New York.

Latkiewicz J and Anderson C 1983 Industries' reactions to the Indochinese refugees as employees. *Migration today* 11(2/3):14–20.

Lears T J J 1981 *No place of grace: antimodernism and the transformation of*

American culture, 1880–1920. Pantheon Books, New York.
Lee M 1989 The strange death of Tito's Yugoslavia? *Against the current* **3**(6):19–28.
Lehmann W P (ed) 1975 *Language and linguistics in the People's Republic of China.* University of Texas, Austin.
Lewis N A 1989 Purging 'what-cha' and 'ain't' *New York Times,* 28 February.
Lichauco A 1973 *Imperialism and the national situation.* Monthly Review Press, New York.
Light T 1978 Foreign language teaching in the People's Republic of China. In Blatchford C H and Schachter J (eds) *On TESOL '78: EFL policies, programmes, and practices.* Teachers of English to Speakers of Other Languages, Washington.
Limpanboon P M 1987 On-the-job training: an approach for advanced students in work orientation. *Passage* **3**(1):6–10
Lin E H-B 1984 *An exploration of somatization among Southeast Asian refugees and immigrants in primary care.* Master's thesis, University of Washington School of Public Health and Community Medicine, Seattle.
Lindsey C W 1987 The nationalist view of the Philippine economy: Criticisms and proposals. In Lande C H (ed) *Rebuilding a nation: Philippine challenges and American policy.* Washington Institute Press, Washington, pp. 123–39.
Linguistic Minorities Project 1983 *Linguistic minorities in England.* University of London Institute of Education, London.
Linguistic Minorities Project 1984 *The mother tongue teaching directory survey.* University of London Institute of Education, London (Linguistic Minorities Project Working Paper).
Linguistic Minorities Project 1985 *The other languages of England.* Routledge and Kegan Paul, London.
Liu A P L 1971 *Communications and national integration in Communist China.* University of California Press, Berkeley.
Llamzon T A 1977 A requiem for Pilipino. In Sibayan B P and Gonzalez A B (eds) *Language planning and the building of a national language.* Linguistic Society of the Philippines and Philippine Normal College, Manila, pp. 291–303.
Llamzon T A 1984 The status of English in Metro Manila today. In Gonzalez A B (ed) *Language planning, implementation, and evaluation.* Linguistic Society of the Philippines, Manila, pp. 106–21.
Lo Bianco J 1987 *National policy on languages.* Australian Government Publishing Service, Canberra.
Loescher G and Scanlan J A 1986 *Calculated kindness: refugees and America's half-open door, 1945–present.* Free Press, New York.
McArthur T 1986 Comment: worried about something else. *International journal of the sociology of language* **60**:87–91.
Magaš B 1989 Yugoslavia: the spectre of Balkanization. *New left review* **174**:3–31.
Manila Bulletin 5 November 1987.
Manley J 1983 Neopluralism: a class analysis of pluralism I and

pluralism II. *American political science review* **77**(2):368–89.

Marshall D F 1986 The question of an official language: language rights and the English Language Amendment, and rebuttal essay. *International journal of the sociology of language* **60**:7–75, 201–211.

Martin-Jones M 1984 *The sociolinguistic status of minority languages in England.* University of London Institute of Education, London (Linguistic Minorities Project Working Paper).

Mastnak T 1989 The night of the long knives: military justice vs. a mobilized society in the northern republic of Slovenia. *Across Frontiers* **4**(4):4–6ff.

Mazrui A A and Tidy M 1984 *Nationalism and new states in Africa: from about 1935 to the present.* Heinemann, London.

Menard-Warwick J 1987 Addressing the resettlement needs of S.E. Asians: three Seattle programs. University of Washington Department of English, Seattle, unpublished.

Milan W G 1986 Comment: undressing the English Language Amendment. *International journal of the sociology of language* **60**:93–96.

Miller J R 1981 The politics of Philippine national language policy. *Language problems and language planning* **5**(2):137–52.

Monkman C S 1989 Westin Hotel has no room at the inn for illiteracy. *Seattle Post-Intelligencer*, 20 January.

Monshi-Tousi M, Hosseine-Fatemi A, and Oller J W 1980 English proficiency and factors in its attainment: A case study of Iranians in the United States. *TESOL Quarterly* **14**(3):365–72.

Movement for the Advancement of Nationalism 1969 *M.A.N.'s goal: The democratic Filipino society.* Malaya, Manila.

Muego B N 1987 The view from the youth sector. In Lande C H (ed) *Rebuilding a nation: Philippine challenges and American policy.* Washington Institute Press, Washington, pp. 247–59.

Mullard C 1984 The three Rs: Rampton, racism, and research. In *Race, education, and research: Rampton, Swann, and after.* Centre for Multicultural Education and the Thomas Coram Research Unit, University of London Institute of Education, London, pp. 12–25.

Muller T and Espenshade T J 1985 *The fourth wave: California's newest immigrants.* Urban Institute Press, Washington.

Nafziger E W 1988 *Inequality in Africa: political elites, proletariat, peasants and the poor.* Cambridge University Press, Cambridge.

National Census and Statistics Office 1986 *Monthly bulletin of statistics* (March), Manila.

National Council for Mother Tongue Teaching 1985 The Swann Report: Education for all? *Journal of multilingual and multicultural development* **6**(6):497–508.

Nations and Nationalities of Yugoslavia 1974. Medjunarodna politika, Belgrade.

New York Times 18 September 1989.

New York Times 8 April 1989.

New voices: immigrant students in US public schools. 1988. National Coalition of Advocates for Students, Boston.

Newsweek 1985 The Philippines: Another Iran? 4 November.

O'Callaghan M 1977 *Namibia: the effects of apartheid on culture and education.* UNESCO, Paris.

Office of Refugee Resettlement 1984 Statement of program goals, priorities, and standards for state administered refugee resettlement programmes, fiscal year 1984. Kansas City, Missouri.

Orzechowska E 1984 *What it means to be a bilingual child in Britain today.* Centre for Multicultural Education, University of London Institute of Education, London (Working Paper).

Overholt W H 1987 Pressures and policies: Prospects for Aquino's Philippines. In Lande C H (ed) *Rebuilding a nation: Philippine challenges and American policy.* Washington Institute Press, Washington, pp. 89–110.

Ozolins U 1988 Government language policy initiatives and the future of ethnic languages in Australia. *International journal of the sociology of language* **72**:113–29.

Pahlavi M R no date *The white revolution.* Kayhan Press, Tehran.

Pascasio E M 1977 Language and communication for national development. In Sibayan B P and Gonzalez A B (eds) *Language planning and the building of a national language.* Linguistic Society of the Philippines and Philippine Normal College, Manila, pp. 322–40.

Pascasio E M 1984 Philippine bilingualism and code-switching. In Gonzalez A B (ed) *Language planning, implementation, and evaluation.* Linguistic Society of the Philippines, Manila, pp. 122–34.

Pattanayak D P 1987 *Multilingualism and multiculturalism: Britain and India.* Centre for Multicultural Education, University of London Institute of Education, London (Occasional Papers).

Perez A Q 1983 Vocabulary development of Pilipino. Seventh conference of ANANAL, Kuala Lumpur.

Pinches M 1985 The 'urban poor'. In May R J and Nemenzo F (eds) *The Philippines after Marcos.* St Martin's, New York, pp. 152–63.

Piñeda-Ofreneo R 1985 *Issues in the Philippine electronics industry: A global perspective.* International Studies Institute of the Philippines, Quezon City (research report).

Pipa A and Repishti S 1989 Reflections on the Kosovo crisis. *Across Frontiers* **4**(4):7ff.

Price S, Fluck M, and Giles H 1983 The effects of language of testing on bilingual pre-adolescents' attitudes towards Welsh and varieties of English. *Journal of multilingual and multicultural development* **4**(2–3):149–61.

Pride J B and Ru-Shan L 1988 Some aspects of the spread of English in China since 1949. *International Journal of the Sociology of Language* **74**:41–70.

Purcell J N 1985 Refugee Assistance: overseas and domestic. Address before the Subcommittee on Immigration, Refugees, and International Law of the House Judiciary Committee. In *Current policy* 693, Department of State, Washington.

Rajaretnam M (ed) 1986 *The Aquino alternative.* Institute of Southeast Asian Studies, Singapore.

Ramos E T 1987 Labor conflict and recent trends in Philippine industrial relations. *Philippine quarterly of culture and society* 15(3):173–97.

Rampton A 1981 *West Indian children in our schools.* Interim report of the Committee of Inquiry into the education of children from ethnic minority groups. HMSO, London.

Refugee Reports 1987 8(11):7–8 American Council for Nationalities Service, Washington.

Reimers D M 1985 *Still the golden door: the third world comes to America.* Columbia University Press, New York.

Richter L K 1987 Public bureaucracy in post–Marcos Philippines. *Southeast Asian journal of social science* 15(2):57–76.

Rossi-Landi F 1983 *Language as work and trade: a semiotic homology for linguistics and economics.* Bergin and Garvey, South Hadley, Massachusetts.

Rounds P L, 1987 Characterizing successful classroom discourse for NNS teaching assistant training. *TESOL Quarterly* 21(4):643–71.

Rubin J 1975 What the good language learner can teach us. *TESOL Quarterly* 9(1):41–51.

Rubin J and Jernudd B H 1971 Introduction: Language planning as an element in modernization. In Rubin J and Jernudd B H (eds.) *Can language be planned?* University Press of Hawaii, Honolulu, pp. xiii–xxiv.

Ryan E B and Giles H (eds) 1982 *Attitudes towards language variation: Social and applied contexts.* Edward Arnold, London.

Saint-Blancat C 1985 The effect of minority group vitality upon its sociopsychological behaviour and strategies. *Journal of multilingual and multicultural development* 6(1):31–44.

San Juan E 1986 *Crisis in the Philippines: The making of a revolution.* Bergin and Garvey, South Hadley, Massachusetts.

Saulo A B 1969 *Communism in the Philippines: An Introduction.* Ateneo de Manila University, Manila.

Schell O 1984 *To get rich is glorious: China in the 1980s.* New American Library, New York.

Schell O 1988 *Discos and democracy: China in the throes of reform.* Pantheon, New York.

Schumacher C undated Work orientation. *Passage* (special Galang issue) p. 30.

Schumann J 1977 Second language acquisition: the pidginization hypothesis. *Language learning* 26:391–408.

Schumann J 1978 *The pidginization process.* Newbury House, Rowley, Massachusetts.

Seattle Post-Intelligencer 15 August 1988.

Senate Standing Committee on Education and the Arts 1984 *A national language policy.* Australian Government Publishing Service, Canberra.

Shalom S R 1985 *The United States and the Philippines: 'Sentimental' imperialism or standard imperialism?* Third World Studies Center, Quezon City (The Philippines in the Third World Papers).

Shannon P 1989 *Broken promises: reading instruction in twentieth-century America.* Bergin and Garvey, Granby, Massachusetts.

Shoup P 1968 *Communism and the Yugoslav national question*. Columbia University Press, New York.
Sibayan B P 1985 Reflections, assertions and speculations on the growth of Pilipino. *Southeast Asian journal of social science* 13(1):40–51.
Simpson J 1988 *Inside Iran: Life under Khomeini's regime*. St. Martin's, New York.
Sison J M 1986 Current questions concerning the Communist Party of the Philippines. In Rajaretnam M (ed) *The Aquino Alternative*. Singapore, Institute of Southeast Asian Studies, pp. 54–66.
Skutnabb-Kangas T and Cummins J (eds) 1988 *Minority education: from shame to struggle*. Multilingual Matters, Clevedon.
Smolicz J J 1984 National language policy in the Philippines: A comparative study of the education status of 'colonial' and indigenous languages with special reference to minority tongues. *Southeast Asian journal of social science* 12(2):51–67.
Sonntag S K and Pool J 1987 Linguistic denial and linguistic self-denial: American ideologies of language. *Language problems and language planning* 11(1):46–65.
Southeast Asian refugee self-sufficiency study: final report 1985 Institute for Social Research, University of Michigan, Ann Arbor.
Spolsky B 1972 (ed) *The language education of minority children*. Newbury House, Rowley, Massachusetts.
Spolsky B 1978 *Educational linguistics*. Newbury House, Rowley, Massachusetts.
Statistični koledar Jugoslavije 1976. 1976. Zvezni zavod za statistiko, Belgrade.
Statistični koledar Jugoslavije 1988. 1988 Zvezni zavod za statistiko, Belgrade.
Strand P J 1984 Employment predictors among Indochinese refugees. *International migration review* 18(1):50–64.
Swann M 1985 *Education for all: The report of the Committee of Inquiry into the education of children from ethnic minority groups*. HMSO, London.
Tait D and Gibson K 1987 Economic and ethnic restructuring: an analysis of migrant labour in Sydney. *Journal of intercultural studies* 8(1):1–26.
Tan A S 1984 *The ideology of Pedro Abad Santos' Socialist Party*. Asian Center of the University of the Philippines, Manila (Occasional Papers).
Tannenbaum E 1985 Review of *The effects of pre-entry training on the resettlement of Indochinese refugees. Passage: a journal of refugee education* 1:81. Department of State, Washington.
Tauli V 1968 *Introduction to a theory of language planning*. Acta Universitatis Upsaliensis, Almquist and Wiksell, Uppsala (Studia Philologiae Scandinavicae Upsaliensia).
Taylor M J 1981 *Caught between: A review of research into the education of pupils of West Indian origin*. NFER-Nelson, Windsor.
Taylor M J 1985 *The best of both worlds. . . ?: A review of research into the education of pupils of South Asian origin*. NFER-Nelson, Windsor.
Taylor M J 1987a *Britain's other ethnic minority pupils: A review of research into their education*. NFER-Nelson, Windsor.
Taylor M J 1987b *Chinese pupils in Britain: A review of research into the*

education of pupils of Chinese origin. NFER-Nelson, Windsor.

Taylor R and Nathan D 1980 Resettlement casework: the role of the professional. Paper presented at the annual meeting of the Conference of Jewish Community Service, Denver.

Tepper E L (ed) 1980 *Southeast Asian exodus: from tradition to resettlement*. Canadian Asian Studies Association, Ottawa.

Time 1988 Only English spoken here. 5 December.

The Times (London), 29 June 1989.

Times Journal 26 November 1985.

Tollefson J W 1981a Centralized and decentralized language planning. *Language Problems and Language Planning* 5(2):175–88.

Tollefson J W 1981b *The language situation and language policy in Slovenia*. University Press of America, Washington D C.

Tollefson J W 1986a Functional competencies in the US refugee program: theoretical and practical problems. *TESOL Quarterly* 20(4):649–64.

Tollefson J W 1986b Language policy and the radical left in the Philippines: the New People's Army and its antecedents. *Language Problems and Language Planning* 10(2):177–89.

Tollefson J W 1989 *Alien winds: the reeducation of America's Indochinese refugees*. Praeger, New York.

Trudgill P 1981 Linguistic accommodation: sociolinguistic observations on a sociopsychological theory. In *Papers from the parasession on language and behaviour*, University of Chicago Press, Chicago.

Trudgill P (ed) 1984 *Language in the British Isles*. Cambridge University Press, Cambridge.

US Committee for Refugees 1986 *Refugees from Laos: in harm's way*. American Council for Nationalities Service, Washington.

Vakil F 1977 Iran's basic macroeconomic problems: A twenty-year horizon. *Economic development and cultural change* 25:713–30.

Valdepeñas V B 1977 Cost–benefit analysis of bilingual education. In Pascasio E M (ed) *Studies in Philippine bilingualism and bilingual education*. Ateneo de Manila University, Quezon City, pp. 45–8.

Villa R L 1985a English weakening noted: Strengthening of language urged. *Bulletin today*, 4 November.

Villa R L 1985b Laya analyzes English decline. *Bulletin today*, 5 November.

Villa R L 1985c Upgrading of English urged. *Bulletin today*, 14 November.

Waggoner L 1984 Interview in *Hope for the future* (videotape). International Catholic Migration Commission, Morong, Bataan, Philippines.

Walsh R E 1984 *Basic adult survival English with orientation to American life, parts I and II*. Prentice Hall, Englewood Cliffs, New Jersey.

Williams C L and Westermeyer J (eds) 1986 *Refugee mental health in resettlement countries*. Hemisphere Publishing, Washington.

Williams G 1986 Review article: language planning or language expropriation? *Journal of Multilingual and Multicultural Development* 7(6):509–18.

Wood C H 1982 Equilibrium and historical-structural perspectives on migration. *International migration review* 16(2):298–319.

Wright G 1986 Let's teach English. *San Francisco Examiner*, 23 November.
Yabes L Y 1972 Shortcomings of the national language movement. *Solidarity* 7(2):42–7.
Yin M 1985 *Questions and answers about China's minority nationalities*. New World Press, Beijing.
Youngblood R 1988 Review of *The Aquino Alternative*. *Philippine studies* **36**:120–21.

Index